Good Practice in Counselling People Who Have Been Abused

Good Practice Series
Editor: Jacki Pritchard

Good Practice in Child Protection:
A Manual for Professionals
Edited by Hilary Owen and Jacki Pritchard
ISBN 1 85302 205 5
Good Practice Series 1

Good Practice in Supervision:
Statutory and Voluntary Organisations
Edited by Jacki Pritchard
ISBN 1 85302 279 9
Good Practice Series 2

Good Practice in Risk Assessment
and Risk Management 1
Edited by Hazel Kemshall and Jacki Pritchard
ISBN 1 85302 338 8
Good Practice Series 3

Good Practice in Risk Assessment
and Risk Management 2
Edited by Hazel Kemshall and Jacki Pritchard
ISBN 1 85302 441 4
Good Practice Series 5

Good Practice in Risk Assessment
and Risk Management 1 and 2
ISBN 1 85302 552 6

Good Practice in Counselling People Who Have Been Abused

Edited by Zetta Bear

Good Practice Series 4

Jessica Kingsley Publishers
London and Bristol, Pennsylvania

First published in the United Kingdom in 1998 by
Jessica Kingsley Publishers Ltd
116 Pentonville Road
London N1 9JB, England
and
1900 Frost Road, Suite 101
Bristol, PA 19007, U S A

Library of Congress Cataloguing in Publication Data
A CIP catalogue record for this book is available from the Library of Congress

British Library Cataloguing in Publication Data
A CIP catalogue record for this book is available from the British Library

ISBN 1 85302 424 4

Printed and Bound in Great Britain by
Athenaeum Press, Gateshead, Tyne and Wear

CONTENTS

LIST OF FIGURES

LIST OF TABLES

This book is dedicated
to my partner, Sally, and to our son, Rafael.

Foreword

There are many books available about working with people who have been abused. This one is different in that it explicitly combines the voices of people who have been abused with those of professionals working in the field. For once the experiences of people who have been abused and their views about what constitutes good and useful practice have been accorded the same status as those of professionals.

Some of the contributors to this book write exclusively as survivors. Others combine the perspective of survivor with their role as a professional practitioner. Others write purely as professionals.

I hope this combination of perspectives will enhance the reader's understanding of how people who continue to live with abuse and its effects can best be supported. The compassion and resourcefulness of the survivors writing in this book, and the professionals who strive to provide appropriate and accessible services for them, are an indication of the enormous commitment and good will which is available today.

Care in the community, which is, after all, supposed to be focused upon needs, continues to be implemented. The groups of people represented in this book are in need of, and should be entitled to, resources. Currently, this is rarely the case. Needs are often understood to be physical rather than emotional or psychological and when resources are limited, physical needs are usually prioritised. This means that the legitimate and urgent need for counselling is regularly ignored.

Sadly, no amount of legislation can eliminate abuse. The Children Act 1989 was designed to ensure that children and young people are protected from abuse. As a result, practice has improved, yet, inevitably, we are still encountering young people who have been abused and are in need of counselling in adulthood. Professionals and policy makers must face the fact that this problem will not disappear and allocate resources accordingly. Unfortunately, like many people, professionals and policy makers are capable of denial. This both hampers resource allocation and increases the vulnerability of children, especially those in care. The numerous cases of abuse of children in local authority care testify to the urgent requirement that we all face and deal with widespread abuse. The repercussions of the abuse scandal in Cleveland suggest that professionals may need to extend themselves and suspend their prejudices in order to see clearly the evidence before them. Until this happens, children will continue to live in abusive environments without help.

This book is, in part, an attempt address the counselling services which should be available to people who have been abused. I hope it bears testimony to the extraordinary pain caused by abuse and the resourcefulness of those who learn to live creatively with its effects. I hope also that it serves as a marker for the responsible and ethical allocation of resources in the future.

Zetta Bear

Introduction

In 1992, when the 'Memory Wars' began, the brainwashing therapist became the 1990s version of the brainwashing social worker of the 1980s. Both were blamed for an inexplicable fascination with non-existent abuse. 'False Memory Syndrome', a quasi-legal defence term for those accused of child molestation, became another weapon in the armoury of denial.

What the professionals know is the truth about abuse, sexual and physical, is not the truth that society knows. Professionals walk the same eerie, isolated road as the abused children in a family do, shamed by what is known, outcasts in the wider society. They are outcasts, even more shockingly, within the professional arena as colleagues who should be providing peer support back away, unable to handle the grim content of the material.

A recent Accuracy about Abuse questionnaire for adult survivors of abuse elicited the hard-to-believe statistic that most did not disclose at all in childhood and, of those who did, only ONE found a positive response. Swedish Save the Children, Radda Barnen, interviewing 10 children who had been identified because of their involvement in pornography, found none had disclosed spontaneously, although the abuse had gone on for an aggregate of 42 years. Children rarely speak up voluntarily and adult survivors only do so with great difficulty and reluctance.

Abused children are often threatened with death or violence by their perpetrators if they talk. Only recently have they found adult carers to whom they could unburden themselves. Now, these professionals find themselves under attack. The message all too clearly is that talking about sexual abuse is dangerous – for the child the risk can be physical whilst for the adult survivor a campaign of devastating harassment often pushes them back into silence or prevents disclosure.

For the adult therapist or social worker the risk of talking about abuse or giving support is of losing a career, as social worker Alison Taylor, the whistleblower in the North Wales Children's Homes, found when she was fired for complaining to the authorities on behalf of the children.

The abuser typically distorts reality in an attempt to avoid facing responsibility for their actions – 'it wasn't my idea, they wanted it, it wasn't really sexual, it's love not abuse, it didn't do any damage'. In the wider context these distortions of reality also occur in the bitter science arguments around sexual abuse. In the context of the 'False Memory 'debate we are told that recovered 'pseudo'-memories of sexual abuse are a product of malpractising therapists, usually hypnotherapists. Yet many of the adult children of 'False Memory'

Society parents say they either never forgot or they recovered memories away from therapy or within a mainstream setting.

The studies for amnesia of sexual abuse now number well over 30. Every one finds that a substantial minority of abuse survivors partially or totally forget their experiences for a varying length of time. Alan Scheflin and Daniel Brown's paper in *Psychiatry & Law* calls it a 'robust finding'. It is substantiated by Dr Bernice Andrews' BPS studies. The HMSO 1994 Report on Working Together indicates that 40 per cent of women in the mental health system have a sexual abuse background. Staff in the secure units which house violent patients say that the incidence of childhood abuse there is much higher even than that. Studies on drug and alcohol users point to childhood abuse as a contributory factor. Multiple symptoms, including depression and suicidal behaviour, were found in 2000 abused women studied by Johns Hopkins University researchers for a *Journal of the American Medical Association* paper (May 1997).

Yet these scientific studies from reputable clinicians and researchers have to face potentially annihilating attacks from those who seek to airbrush out the problem. Roland Summit talks of solidly proven abuse cases which just 'seal over' after a while as communities forget, deny or bury the unpleasant experience. The danger in the scientific and clinical arena is that sexual abuse could be driven back into the woodwork again, as it was in Freud's time. In America the damage inflicted by the 'False Memory' argument – malicious professional complaints, threatened litigation and ongoing personal harass-ment – has driven therapists away from working with victims of family violence. The problem is less acute in the UK but the risk is still there unless the mainstream organisations urgently start to improve training and give backing to their reputable members working in this area who come under malicious attack.

Bad practice undoubtedly does exist, partly because trainings have been lax, biased away from sexual abuse and trauma and under-resourced; a good deal of it underplays the problem of sexual abuse. The slant of bad practice which tends to exaggerate abuse is, in my experience, smaller than the media, and certainly the 'false memory' movement, would have us believe. But improving good practice is precisely what will solve the argument. The kind of intrusive, invasive therapy which might create 'False Memories' in non-abused patients (though there is little solid evidence to date of this being possible) is exactly the kind of therapy which is damaging for patients with a genuine abuse background. Once the mainstream starts to take its respon-sibility seriously, the fringes will be pushed, or legislated, out of business.

These are relatively early days in what is (unbelievably) an almost new area of study. The corpus of knowledge is expanding and the focus of understanding shifting, almost month by month. What is needed is a capacity for a discriminating open-mindedness and a tolerance of complexity and uncertainty. Holding to that subtle position in the bitterly polarised atmos-phere of recent arguments is not easy.

Accuracy about Abuse (AAA) was set up in 1994 initially to keep 'False Memory Syndrome' in a balanced context, pointing out the pitfalls and dangers. The underlying concern always was to protect abused children in the legal arena. Recent research stimulated by the memory argument is proving invaluable in this respect, though the findings need to be more widely distributed. The research and information sheets sent out by AAA are designed to promote informed discussion and better understanding amongst doctors, psychoanalysts, psychotherapists, psychologists and counsellors of all persuasions who work with abuse and trauma survivors. Improving the care and proper treatment of sexual abuse survivors in the mental health system and in therapy is its primary concern.

The 'inner track' of professionals who know about sexual abuse and trauma is now growing, getting better informed and less frightened. As the centre develops a solid basis of good practice and knowledge, so will it become possible to expand outwards. Then the 'outer track' – society, the media, the legal arena – will begin to take the problem on board with serious respect rather than dismissive contempt. The experience of other countries is that psychotherapy cannot take on board a problem until society is ready to cope with it as well. We now appear, with some difficulty, to have reached that point.

Marjorie Orr

CHAPTER 1

Becoming Real
The Story of a Long Journey Through Psychiatry, Counselling and Psychotherapy

Runa Wolf

I have written this contribution from the client's perspective, as a survivor of childhood sexual abuse. I was abused by my father in early childhood and this abuse was not recognised by my family. I grew up believing the myth that we were a happy family and that I was lucky to be well cared for. Through my childhood and adolescence I was unable to name or communicate my feelings of unhappiness, abandonment and badness. In late adolescence I became suicidal for no apparent reason and was admitted to a mental hospital.

The account that follows is the story of my journey through psychiatric treatment and various forms of counselling and therapy. It was not until my mid-thirties that I was able to recognise that I had been abused. I believe my experiences in mental hospitals, and then in psychoanalytic therapy, helped to keep me from this realisation; they compounded the fracture that already existed between my lived experience and my beliefs about myself. I experienced this as an ongoing problem with my sense of reality. For this reason, I describe my various experiences of counselling, in the pages which follow, in terms of these themes: respect for client autonomy, definitions, goals and values; quality of counsellor's presence; how boundaries are handled; physical contact and non-verbal expression.

I have allowed myself to draw few general conclusions as this is a highly personal story. My account of my past is inevitably informed by my current understanding of my therapeutic process and will reflect what seems most interesting to me now. Within these constraints of hindsight I have attempted to capture, as far as possible, what I was experiencing at the time and to distinguish this from the current meanings I have made of a particular event or relationship. Constructing my account in this way illuminates the process by which we all continually re-make our pasts and the way in which I, in particular, have done this through the medium of psychotherapy. Furthermore, personal narrative and anecdote, by virtue of their subjectivity, leave open for the reader the possibility of interpretations which differ from my own.

I was admitted to a mental hospital at the age of nineteen after one outpatient appointment with a consultant psychiatrist. I was diagnosed as suffering from a depressive illness. At that time I did not perceive myself as someone who had been sexually abused. I *did* know that I was very angry with both my parents for failing to love and nurture me properly and that I hated my father and wanted to get as far away from him as possible but felt trapped at home by feelings of dependency, need and fear. I was furious, desperately unhappy, lonely and terrified. I had almost stopped speaking because I had lost hope that anyone would see through the mess to the real me and be able to help me. I needed someone to trust, a witness who would listen to my version of reality and help me to express my feelings safely. Instead, I was given an official label by a strange man who had known me for half an hour.

The medical treatments I was subjected to over the next decade were, I realise now, grossly abusive and unnecessary. Though they involved no counselling in the usual sense, they are a crucial part of my story. Many of these abusive practices still exist and other survivors in counselling may have had similar experiences. I believe that counsellors working within a medical setting need to be aware of the dangers of the medical model compounding survivors' earlier abuses and to be clear about their own relationship to that framework.

The diagnosis itself was enormously damaging to me at that crucial stage in my life of struggling to separate from abusive parents. I do not deny that I needed professional help but the mentally ill label invalidated the very feelings which gave me any sense of independent self. I felt I was being told that my feelings were not real. Having been abused as a child in a way that made me feel as if my life was in danger, and then having the reality of that abuse denied within my family, had already undermined my sense of what was real. As a teenager I was already in conflict with the *status quo* because of the anger and disgust I felt towards a father who had a god-like status at home and a highly respectable image outside. The diagnosing of *me* as mentally ill meant that the *status quo* had won. The tragedy was not so much that other people would be less likely to believe my experience of family life but that I stopped believing it myself.

That initial hospital admission reinforced the diagnosis with a sudden shift into a spartan institutional environment. The whole experience of the ward regime – the dormitories, communal washrooms, unappetising food, occupational therapy (we really did weave baskets!), the lack of choice, control, dignity – gave me the message that I was being punished. Whatever had gone wrong in my family was clearly my fault, there must be something nasty and bad about me. I described myself at that time as a 'minus' or 'negative' person. I felt that, in terms of stature, I occupied a space somewhere beneath the level of the floor.

The boundaries in that environment were very much about them (the staff/normal people) and us (the loonies). The staff wore uniforms and used separate toilets and cups. Every day at ten *we* were served sweet milky Camp coffee poured from a huge teapot in a continuous stream across a row of thick white cups. I cried into mine the first time – I liked my coffee without sugar and black.

Other boundaries were about controlling unacceptable feelings and behaviour. Because we were all suspected of harbouring destructive impulses, no scissors, razors or long-handled steel combs were allowed, our possessions were searched and lockers could not be locked. Any outbursts of strong emotion were regarded as symptoms to be quelled with medication but anger was seen as particularly sick and bad. Although I did not realise this at the time, I was full of anger. When I was turning it against myself, I exhibited all the classic symptoms of clinical depression – passivity, self-despisal, isolation, weeping, suicidal thoughts. Then, spasmodically, I would erupt with rage and begin to smash the hospital windows. Several male nurses would pin me down and forcibly inject me with a major tranquilliser.

I also damaged my own body, with razors and cigarettes. I felt both shame and victory as a result of these acts of self-harm, which I understand now as attempts to take control and to desensitise myself. Through self-mutilation I maintained a sense of myself as separate from, and superior to, bodily pain and fear. But this earned me two spells on a locked ward. When on the admissions ward, my day-clothes were locked away to stop me visiting the shops to buy dangerous items.

At no time did anyone explore with me what my window smashing and self-harming were about. Although they were seen as symptomatic of my illness, and therefore undesirable, I also had a sense that they were the sort of behaviour expected of me in that environment – I was doing what I thought mental patients were supposed to do. After all, abusing my body seemed to be a general trend. Smashing windows I now believe to have been a much healthier impulse.

Nearly all the touch I experienced from my 'carers' was coercive – rough handling to stop my window smashing, inject me or stitch my self-inflicted wounds. I include in this physical handling the use of Electro-Convulsive Therapy (ECT) and the prescribing of large doses of major tranquillisers. At one time I was receiving seven different drugs, including a barbiturate. The medication blurred my vision and my thought processes and made me fat and unable to tolerate sunshine. The ECT was a symbolic replication of my childhood sexual abuse, a bodily and spiritual assault by carers which I was expected to submit to willingly and which left me with a dislocated sense of reality. I would come round with no memory of who or where I was. I had had my brain electrocuted and everyone acted as if this was quite acceptable!

I cannot overemphasise how much these treatments, especially the ECT, repeated and magnified the messages about myself which I had learnt from being sexually abused. The whole mental illness experience compounded my sense of intrinsic badness and located this badness in my body. Even my depression was considered endogenous – a chemical imbalance in my brain. In effect, I was blamed and punished for my father's abuse of me. I was unable to resist the enormous weight of that version of reality and gave up the shreds of my own. I became extremely cut off from bodily sensation, healthy anger, grief and fear. I became my own abuser. I felt I truly belonged in the bin because I was rubbish. The doctors confirmed this assessment – after many admissions, I became known as a 'permanent patient' and was told that I would spend the rest of my life on medication and going in and out of hospital.

It was, perhaps, because of this prognosis that I became determined to prove the psychiatrists wrong. During a twenty-eight day section, the implications of my situation finally sank in and I rebelled against this future that was predicted for me with such authority. I set out to get rid of the mental illness label for good. This was an enormous challenge because it put me at odds with the system of 'care' upon which I had become dependent. In a sense, without knowing so at the time, I was making another attempt to separate from an unhealthy set of parental dynamics in which I was seen as the problem. This time, the *status quo* included not just my particular family, along with all the cultural myths about family life, but the full weight of the medical profession and all the stigma surrounding mental illness.

I had been supported by a series of social workers in between hospital admissions and, later, after a period in a Richmond Fellowship Hostel (a half-way house), social workers helped me set myself up independently, away from both hospital and my parents' home. The social workers always treated me with respect and with genuine caring. I was so desperate for this sort of positive regard that these relationships became quite central to me. I wanted these non-medical professionals to help me shed my mental patient identity. And yet my sense of being intrinsically wrong was deeply ingrained and I was terrified of leading a normal life, without understanding why. Although the whole issue of my sanity was, on one level, a re-run of my relationship with my family, it also overlaid those earlier abuses, concealing them from me. I did not realise at the time that redefining myself as mentally normal ultimately would lead me to the realisation that my parents were 'sick' and bad and had abused me. At that time in my life I did not have the resources to bear the grief and rage that would accompany that realisation.

So, in my counselling with social workers, and with the staff at the Richmond Fellowship hostel, I had a rather contradictory agenda. I both wanted and resisted an image of myself as fully functioning and normal. On the surface this conflict played itself out in terms of dependency on the medical system versus a growing confidence in my own ability to cope. It was at this level that the social workers pitched their support of me. Neither they nor I had the resources to tackle the underlying issues, which would have needed long-term psychotherapy. We had a mutual interest in limiting the objectives of counselling to my 'rehabilitation'.

I also wanted to express my anger about the treatment I had received in hospital and I was very keen to come off medication. Repeatedly, I tried to enlist my (female) counsellors as allies in opposition to the psychiatrists. Again, I can understand this now in terms of reworking a family dynamic – getting mum to defend me against dad. At the time, I felt the social workers took medical judgements as their ultimate authority – they were not prepared to disagree, or to be seen to disagree, with the doctors. They supported me enormously as a depressive struggling to come to terms with her illness and to manage independently in the community. But they would not help me flout medical diagnosis and treatment.

Looking back, I can appreciate the dilemmas I might have created for these counsellors. At the time, I felt betrayed by people with huge emotional significance to me. I remember sitting in the consulting room of the male general practitioner (GP) at the university where, over a period of nine years, I studied intermittently for a degree. My counsellor had suggested a three-cornered meeting to discuss my wish to have my medication discontinued. I thought she would be there to help me present my case. But the doctor announced, with great authority, that if I stopped taking the tablets I would certainly become suicidal and might kill myself. That was the end of the 'discussion'. Of course, I understand now the reluctance of anyone concerned about me to defy such a categorical pronouncement. But coming up against what seemed to be some ultimate male law left me feeling annihilated and hopeless. It was a replay, again, of family dynamics, with the 'mum' who professed to care about me rendered helpless by the male authority she chose to be loyal to instead of me.

Within the medical constraints of psychiatric social work, these counsellors did establish genuine relationships with me. Their presence as real human beings outweighed any adverse effects on me of the medical boundaries of their work and their goal of rehabilitation. I also had a vested interest in limiting exploration to issues which were surface in terms of earlier abuses but, nevertheless, were about survival in a practical sense. I believe that without this rehabilitation process I could not have become equipped for more intensive psychotherapy at a later date. I remember a social worker, who was about my age, helping me to 'cope' in a flat in York, the first home of my own. She would bring her dog on her visits and some treat of cream cakes or doughnuts and we would sit on my floor and talk about my progress that week. From such relationships I began to learn that I was a worthwhile human being, depressive or not.

During this period, then, between the ages of twenty-three and twenty-nine, my life was still dominated by my struggle with depression. With the help of social workers and university counsellors, I studied for a degree when I was 'well' and managed without going back into hospital when I was 'ill'. I gradually brought myself off the anti-depressant medication which doctors insisted I needed. Then my relationship with a partner of some years began to break up and I became suicidal. After nearly six years outside hospital, the possibility of an admission loomed again.

Secretly, I was terrified of the future and craved the security of hospital more than I dreaded the mental illness trap. I knew that I had changed since my earlier admissions and had greater inner resources as well as supportive friends. For once, I could look on hospital as a temporary asylum rather than a prison and, thankfully, I found a more enlightened regime which was far more respectful and humane. I was given minimal medication for a few days whilst on one-to-one surveillance in an admissions ward instead of being sectioned. As I came away from the suicidal edge, I was allowed to write or listen to music instead of attending occupational therapy. Staff seemed genuinely caring and much less boundary conscious. Patients were even allowed access to the kitchen!

It was from this conventional ward that I was referred to a psychoanalytic therapeutic community run within the grounds of that hospital. Potential residents were assessed by an interview with each of the two head therapists and a test which involved making up stories about the shadowy images in a set of pictures. Applicants then spent a day on the unit and a theoretically democratic decision was taken by the whole community as to whether one could join. The culture was supposedly one of choice and personal/community responsibility, as opposed to medical treatment of sick patients. In practice, the clinical judgements of the head therapists were not open to challenge and held far more authority in the community than any preferences or opinions residents might express.

Although I was excited by the prospect of genuine change from depressive to fully responsible member of society, I felt my choices were severely limited – it was either mental hospital or this therapeutic rite of passage, which everyone described as gruelling. Suicide seemed like a genuine third option to be kept in reserve if therapy did not work out. Many other residents also described their time on the unit as a last-ditch attempt to sort themselves out after the whole gamut of conventional treatment had failed. To compound this drastic atmosphere, the head therapist gave me a warning which was beginning to sound familiar: on the basis of the story-picture test, he told me that doing this therapy would make me want to kill myself and there was a risk that I might succeed. On the other hand, the therapy had the potential to transform people's lives. I had to take full responsibility for the consequences of my choice. I felt like someone whose one chance of survival is an operation which has only a 50 per cent success rate.

Looking back, I feel outraged that this supposed suicide risk was never discussed again and no specific measures of safety or support were drawn up for me. Presumably, the rules and structures of the unit were considered sufficient (violence to self, others or property was meant to result in instant expulsion but, in practice, the therapists sometimes waived this rule). Also, the ethos of personal responsibility was stringently egalitarian – individually-tailored support systems would have been seen as undermining an implicit notion of 'community' in which individuals are completely (and only) responsible for themselves. So, yet again, I lived with a secret, life-threatening reality that was not acknowledged by those around me.

The therapy was conducted through large and small encounter groups, run once or twice daily, together with weekly dream analysis and art therapy sessions. Community affairs, including housework, reviews of progress and people joining and leaving, were discussed in the daily community meeting. Eighteen months to two years (the maximum) was considered a realistic time-span for lasting personal changes to be established. New residents were expected to spend the first six months working out what their issues were. The therapists claimed to have this information already in the form of their initial clinical assessment, but we were not expected to be able to understand this to start with. First, we had to stop seeing ourselves as patients or helpless victims and to start 'taking responsibility'. In effect, this meant replacing a medical model with a psychoanalytic one – we were deemed to have started work when we began to actively engage with our transferences, identifying the early-childhood dynamics we were recreating within the community.

The therapists' role was to be a blank screen for our transferences. Although they were mostly genuinely caring people with some of whom I felt a real sense of friendship, this was not considered relevant to the therapy. We were encouraged to express feelings of dependency on the therapists in order to confront the reality that they were not our parents and could not meet our childish needs. We were allowed, even encouraged, to be angry about this because this would help us come to terms with the harsh fact that what we didn't get then we couldn't have now. I deduced from this that my extreme neediness was unacceptable and I did indeed learn to be more self-sufficient in order to survive. I believe now that I realised it was not safe for me to engage with my deep feelings of neglect and abandonment in this environment – I think that confronting reality as defined by this brand of psychoanalysis would indeed have made me want to kill myself.

I found the therapists' blank stance, in many ways, demeaning of us all as human beings. I remember that one day a therapist who I was fond of (we shared a silly sense of humour and played piano duets together) burst into tears in a group session. Many residents tried to express their quite genuine concern. We were all rebuffed and told to look at our own issues and projections. No one ever told us why she had cried. We were not afforded the dignity of being able to show some caring to someone who had cared for many of us and she was not allowed the opportunity to receive it. By such means, the psychoanalytic theories and practices in the unit infantilised its residents – just as the conventional wards had kept us locked into the role of patient.

I left the therapeutic community after eight months, following a review of my progress in a community meeting where I was told by the head therapist that I was not doing any work. When I protested that I thought I was doing well and had had good feedback from others, I was told that I did not consciously set out to deceive but had a great capacity for self-deception and this drew others into the pretence that I was doing something worthwhile. He claimed that I had found a way to conform outwardly whilst staying comfortable and avoiding any difficult feelings. I felt devastated by this pronouncement but unable to challenge it. In fact, I had been assailed by deeply disturbing feelings throughout my time on the unit, particularly following a guided fantasy session where I seemed to re-experience some kind of rape. Living so closely with men in an environment where there was constant pressure to expose repressed feelings had brought me very close to recognising that I had been sexually abused. If I had failed to share all this with the community, it was because I was not yet ready to make these experiences real by disclosing them.

This review also helped me recognise something very important about the dynamics of the therapy, though I did not understand this fully at the time. I sensed a double-bind in my situation, a feeling that I would never be able to come out of this process as an alright person. It was as if, in order to carry on with the therapy, I would be required to give up something so precious that I would effectively cease to exist anyway. My survival did seem to be at stake, but not in the way the therapist had predicted.

The review was, for me, another example of my most basic sense of reality being rubbished by a powerful man. As a survivor of childhood sexual abuse, I could not psychically survive in therapy without the support of the therapist for my own right to describe and define what was real for me. Fortunately, some instinct for self-preservation told me to run like hell, and I did, even though leaving made me homeless. I believe now that I did absolutely the right thing, but at the time I had a great sense of failure and confusion. I was haunted by the critical voice of that therapist for years. My experience of psychoanalysis had equipped me to undermine my own thoughts and deeds with great effectiveness – I was always able to accuse myself of really meaning and doing something else. And if other people were fooled into thinking well of me, I could console myself with the thought that I hadn't intended to deceive them, it was just that I had got foolishly carried away into thinking well of myself for a while.

I spent the next six years or so making a place for myself in what I still thought of as the normal world. From living on the sick in rented rooms, through government-sponsored work schemes, completion of my degree and professional training, I acquired my first permanent job and my first mortgage. I also began a long-term relationship which promised greater compatibility and commitment than I had previously known. I believed I had put the mental illness episode behind me. I realise now that I had simply cut off the enormous shame I still felt about my medical history. I knew I had emotional problems, and still felt intrinsically bad, but dealt with this by setting out to prove my normality on a daily basis. I worried constantly about other people's opinion of me, monitoring myself all the time in case I made a mistake.

It was from this stressful, but relatively secure, position that I began to realise that I had been sexually abused by my father. Bizarrely, this realisation was triggered by nightmares following acupuncture treatments. I had no clear memory of abuse but, nevertheless, *knew* that I had been sexually violated in some way as a small child and that I had been simultaneously running away from this knowledge and punishing myself for it ever since. Whole unexplained chunks of my life suddenly made sense. It was as if a mist had cleared, giving me a stark and horrific view of my family and my existence which repelled me and yet was rivetingly real. I veered between rejecting the whole idea as ludicrous and wondering why I had failed to see the obvious for so long. I was in a state of shock for several months, barely able to function.

I sought help from a person-centred counsellor.[1] I wanted a counsellor who would believe me, in the sense of not looking constantly for hidden meanings. At the same time, I wanted to examine all my doubts about whether I had been abused, given my apparent lack of memories. I also hoped an expert would be able to tell for certain whether any abuse had really taken place. Tentatively, and still hoping for an outside authority to settle the matter, I was finally tackling the fundamental issue of my relationship with reality, my ownership of my own experience.

---

1   Person-centred counselling was founded by Carl Rogers. It emphasises a non-judgemental acceptance of the client by the counsellor, empathic understanding of the client's reality and a willingness in the counsellor to relate in an authentic manner.

I saw this counsellor for an hour a week over the course of a year. Sessions were almost entirely talk based. I cried a lot and the counsellor often hugged me, but I did not always feel comfortable with this physical contact. Unlike the psychoanalytic therapists, this counsellor was fully present in the relationship. However, this in itself became problematic for me in that I became too aware, through her disclosures, of her needs and circumstances. Even as I write this now I am tempted to excuse her conduct because of the difficulties she was having in her personal life at the time! These were the dynamics of our relationship – I accepted lapses of attention, exchanges that were more about her needs than mine and even the fact that she took my partner on as a client simultaneously because I wanted to look after her.

On one level, my reward for this was to feel special. We colluded in the idea that ours was more rewarding than run-of-the-mill counselling relationships and that afterwards we would become friends. On a deeper level, by making her feelings more important than my own, I disowned important aspects of my experience, thus continuing a pattern of relating which I had learnt from my parents. In this way, although our very personal relationship was seen by us both as central to my therapy, the workings of it remained out of awareness, unexamined and as difficult to challenge as the blank screen approach of the psychoanalytic therapists. In a way, this misuse of the therapeutic relationship was more dangerous because it was more subtle, masquerading as identification, empathy and friendship. The power wielded by the psychoanalysts had been much more obvious.

The other obstacle to my therapeutic progress in this relationship was its almost exclusive reliance on talk. With regards to my memories of sexual abuse, this emphasis restricted my concept of memory to that which can be mentally recalled and verbally described. I searched my awareness for such memories and failed to find any. Many of our sessions, at my direction, focused on the question of whether I had enough indirect evidence of abuse to satisfy myself, even though without clear memories others might remain sceptical. I also agonised over whether my abuse memories might return and whether I wanted them to. Was I protecting myself from something I did not have the emotional resources to deal with? The counsellor did point out that abuse at a pre-verbal stage might not be available to recall and that not all memories are visual. But this seemed rather academic to someone who wanted proof.

Despite its limitations, this counselling experience did give me the space to explore the realisation that I had been abused with someone who was quite prepared to believe me. During this year I confronted my parents by letter and decided not to see them again. I worked through some of the implications of my 'new' knowledge, beginning to incorporate it into my identity and to reconstruct my life history. Repeating another pattern, I left at the first glimmerings of a return of confidence, looking after the counsellor by showing how I could manage alone. After a few months I became deeply distressed as I began to realise that I had only scratched the surface of the work I needed to do on abuse. My reluctance to contact the counsellor again turned into anger as I began to understand how, through her desire to turn me into a friend who could be there for her, she had let me down badly as a client.

I feel quite amazed now that after so much bad practice in counselling, I was prepared to embark on another therapy relationship. I believe that, whilst damaged to some extent by my counselling experiences thus far, I had, nevertheless, acquired a sense of my own process as having a logic and development of its own, quite apart from the work I did in counselling. I felt increasingly that I could rely on this inner trend to take me towards some sort of resolution. It was this sense of direction that allowed me to discriminate between good and bad counselling experiences. Rather than being put off therapy, I wanted *better* therapy. The nitty-gritty seemed to have been missing so far, but I was sure it was there.

As I write, I realise, with some emotion, that what I am describing is my *self*. Partly because of, and partly despite, my counselling so far, I *had* begun to trust my own reality, to *own* my experiences and to incorporate some of the pain of my childhood, previously denied, into my sense of who I was. But I could not have said that at the time. What I knew then was that I wanted to worked with a skilled, well-trained therapist at a greater depth than before.

I found my new therapist through a local advertisement for a women's Gestalt therapy group,[2] to meet weekly. At the initial interview I felt able to express my fears, particularly about group situations. I did not want to be pressurised as I had been in the therapeutic community, neither did I want to be burdened by the therapist's needs. Somewhat reassured, I made a contract to be in the group for a year. I was excited and scared. A whole year seemed a very daunting prospect.

I have worked with this Gestalt therapist for three years now and intend to continue. Gestalt therapy has brought so many benefits to my life that I almost do not know where to begin to describe them. At the same time, I am aware that sceptical readers may be suspicious of unmitigated praise-singing. I want to be clear that the enthusiasm I feel as I write about my experience of Gestalt therapy is of someone who has spent forty years at odds with herself finally coming into her own. I doubt whether Gestalt is the only therapeutic medium I could have worked with. Readers may be able to decide whether any of the aspects of good practice which I identify are peculiar to Gestalt or to my particular therapist. I hope very much that this is not so.

From the start I felt that I had a different status as a client in Gestalt therapy. The therapist treated me as a responsible adult – but this did not mean I was under moral pressure to change, as in the psychoanalytic community. Rather, it was assumed that I had good reasons for the difficulties in my life and that *I* would decide whether, or what, I wished to change. I was surprised and relieved at the first group meeting when the therapist told us that she felt nervous. I remember thinking: 'My God! This therapist has come as a human being!' But, unlike the person-centred counsellor, her needs and problems have never intruded into my therapy. On the contrary, I was amazed how, right from the beginning, the therapist was able to use her own bodily sensations and emotional responses as a sort of barometer for the group process or one-to-one interaction. By clearly owning her own feelings and

---

2 Gestalt Therapy was established by Fritz and Laura Perls in the 1950s as a radical departure from psychoanalysis. Rather than interpreting the client's unconscious motivations, the Gestalt therapist and client use moment-to-moment awareness (phenomenology) to explore together aspects of the client's way of being-in-relationship.

perceptions, they are available for me to make use of if I wish. I am neither browbeaten into accepting another's interpretation nor hoodwinked into pleasing the therapist. Any decision about what is relevant, meaningful or real for me is mine.

I would describe the therapist's stance as one of *presence* combined with an impeccable sense of her own *boundaries* and absolute respect for my *autonomy*. This cluster of qualities allows us to have a therapeutic partnership where the therapist is fully available *in the service of my therapy*. Treated with such clarity and respect, I have been able to work at my own pace and to set my own limits, thus creating some healthy boundaries of my own. I believe that this crucial building of healthy boundaries could only take place in the presence of someone who has a very clear sense of herself, who is able to non-defensively and honestly own her feelings at any moment. This sort of boundary work is inevitably intricate and lengthy for a survivor of childhood sexual abuse and I believe it should only be undertaken by therapists who have done enough personal therapy to have an exceptional degree of self-awareness.

An example may clarify this point. Early on in my therapy I complained at a group session about the stigma of mental illness that made it harder for me to get a job. The therapist made a comment which, I felt, implied that this was an excuse and that I could let go of this perception of myself if I wished. I was devastated. I felt as if I was back in the psychoanalytic unit. I felt so threatened by what I took to be a denial of my reality that I considered leaving the group. Instead, I came to the next session furious and, with the therapist's encouragement, expressed my anger directly to her. To my amazement, she apologised. She explained that she felt angry and sad about my medical history and that out of her desire to see me free of stigma she had missed the reality of my situation.

This was a milestone in my therapy. There were no authoritative pronouncements here that I could not challenge nor any hidden emotional agendas. We had also brought into awareness the key issue of my confusions and fears about reality and were able to use our relationship to explore this further. By welcoming my anger and respecting my definitions of reality, the therapist had already helped me begin to have a boundary of my own. I learnt how it felt to honour my own experience, to be able to reject another's definitions as 'not me' *and for this to be alright!* Through this and other key exchanges I learnt to trust my therapist in a way I had not trusted anyone since I was first abused.

It is within this context of trust, of respect for my boundaries and support for my autonomy, that physical touch has been enormously healing for me. Because all her boundaries are clearly maintained – including those around time and money as well as ownership of feelings – I have been able to believe my therapist when she has told me that she would never sexually abuse me and that she would be able to keep that boundary even if I was afraid I could not. Besides, I have learnt through all my interactions with her that I do not have to engage in any activity unless I want to and that I do not have to please her. Whenever she has held me, I have experienced this as genuine tenderness but have never felt she needed to do this for some reason of her own. I feel we have proved the head psychoanalytic therapist wrong – I have been loved in a parental way, as an adult, and do not need to come to terms with gaping holes of need.

Being safely held has helped me regain a positive sense of belonging in my own body and to learn that intimacy need not be sexual. This has been fundamental for me – I cannot imagine having progressed in my therapy without this physical aspect to the relationship. But I feel I could not stress too strongly that this has only been possible because of the quality of the whole relationship and that without trust built up carefully over a period of time physical contact with a therapist could have been a hindrance at best, and possibly, quite invasive, even when the therapist has good intentions. Again, I believe the safeguard here is a high degree of self-awareness in the therapist and an absolute clarity about client autonomy and clients' interests always being the main focus.

Other body aspects of Gestalt therapy have also been crucial for me and I suspect that these experiences could be important for other survivors of early childhood abuse who do not have visual abuse memories. When I was working with the person-centred counsellor I spent a lot of time trawling through my childhood memories for 'evidence'. My search was based on the belief that there is one fixed true version of history and that I should be able to access this through coherent, rational memories which would resemble clips from a video film. I expected my past to be like a story with a logical progression from scene to scene. Although I suspect my counsellor tried to challenge this notion of memory, nevertheless, talk-based discursive counsel-ling allowed no room for irrational, non-verbal experiences to be expressed.

Gestalt therapy, in contrast, with its emphasis on non-verbal expression and tradition of experimentation, opened up for me a whole dimension of memory which I had not been able to recognise before. I discovered that abuse which was incomprehensible to a small child, which had no meaning which could be borne, which did not fit into any story because it was denied by adult caretakers and which, therefore, could not be considered real, was, neverthe-less, in my memory as bodily sensation and intense feeling. The first time I tried to 'speak' to my father in the form of a cushion in the therapy group, his enormous, malignant presence seemed to fill the room. I began to cower, to stutter and shudder and to choke. My head tilted backwards and my throat became blocked. I thought I was going to die for lack of air. The therapist shouted at 'my father' to get out and someone removed the cushion. I felt annihilated, as if I had ceased to exist as a human being. When, with the therapist's help, I regained contact with the people present, I felt excruciating pain. The therapist held me like a baby and I howled. I had spoken no words. I could not have 'remembered' or described that scene before I had lived it in the presence of witnesses who could validate its reality through their shocked and concerned responses, helping me to own what seemed unbearable and incomprehensible, enabling me to bring it into my awareness as an adult so that I can understand and express it in words.

I can now say that I was orally abused as a small child and that I experienced this as an attempt to kill me. The fact that nobody recognised that I had suffered this experience left me with no choice but to disown it. I understand now that my sense of what is real has felt fragile ever since. Only by reclaiming full bodily and sensory awareness, and owning the horrors of my childhood, with all the pain and grief and rage that has entailed, have I been able to repair my trust in my own perceptions and to experience my self as consistently real.

The embracing by Gestalt therapy of a whole range of non-verbal forms of expression has enabled me to recover the spontaneity, playfulness and emotional fluency I sacrificed in my childhood. As well as speaking to cushions, I have thrashed them with baseball bats, throttled them, cuddled them and bitten them. I have shouted, screamed, howled, sung and laughed. I have drawn pictures, ripped up paper, modelled with clay and spoken my own poetry. I have danced, played with teddy bears, socks and marbles and made frequent appearances as the Queen of Sheba! Such experiences may not traditionally be seen as counselling but, for me, they have been essential to my rediscovering the joy of being alive, of being fully human and full of potential. As a survivor of abuse, I have needed as much support to enjoy myself as I have to deal with painful experiences. If my therapy could not encompass *all* that it means to be human, if it was only there to deal with distress, then it would, for me, have left the task of reclaiming my reality only half done.

This is where my story ends, for now, with a future wide open with possibilities. I offer this account of my past in the hope that it will be read as one individual's experiences. As such, it may in some ways be typical, in others quite idiosyncratic. I am sure, however, that not all person-centred counsellors do their job badly and that not all psychoanalysts are as aggressive as those in the therapeutic community. Equally, there may well be incompetent practitioners of Gestalt. I do believe that the imposition of clinical interpretations on their clients by psychoanalysts can be considered abusive. However, I am sure there are highly compassionate psychoanalysts whose respect for their clients supersedes their theoretical framework, just as a humanistic, client-empowering approach can be ruined in practice by someone who has a problem with their own boundaries.

A personal account like mine cannot claim to be representative. Rather, I believe its value lies precisely in its uniqueness. If there are to emerge among counsellors any codes of good practice for work with people who have been abused, then it is the clients' stories, *in their particularities*, that most need to be heard. Instead of assessing general outcomes from a position of expert authority, counsellors need to be in constant dialogue with their clients about 'how it is for us'. We are the end-results of counselling relationships and it is surely only through reference to our experiences that good practice can be defined.

FURTHER READING

Clarkson, P. (1989) *Gestalt Counselling in Action*. London: Sage.

Perls, F.S., Heferline, R.F. and Goodman, P. (1969) *Gestalt Therapy: Excitement and Growth in the Human Personality*. New York: Julian Press.

Rogers, C.R. (1961) *On Becoming a Person*. Boston: Houghton Mifflin.

CHAPTER 2

Patrick and the Tumble Drier
Counselling Troubled Children

Madge Bray

Your name is Patrick, you used to be six but now you are seven. It was your birthday last week. Your dad works on the rigs, he comes home every three weeks and spends a few days at home and then he goes away again.

When he's home, you and your sister lie awake and wait for dad to come home from the pub. Sometimes he comes home in a bad mood and then the noises start and you hear your mum crying and screaming: 'Gerroff Jim you bastard'. Sometimes you think she is going to die when your dad smacks her head with his fists. One day in the summer she was choking when he had a belt round her neck.

On a Sunday, when he wakes up and has had his dinner, he takes you out to the park to practice football, you have to practice shooting for goal. Sometimes you miss and your dad shouts at you and says you are bloody useless. He wants you to play for Newcastle United when are you are older. He grabs your arm and twists it behind your back when you are doing your press-ups. And you have to do circuits with him until you fall over because your legs won't work anymore.

When your dad is not there, your mum takes pills. Sometimes she takes other pills from the pretend bean tin in the cupboard, then she sleeps all day and does not get up at all. You have to get your own tea and Marissa's and cook burgers in the microwave.

Your mum works in a card shop and you hear her crying herself to sleep at nights.

Sometimes Tommy comes round, he and your mum are friends. Not even nanny knows about Tommy. When your mum is putting your sister to bed, Tommy and you play at wanking. Tommy says your mum would go spare if she knew, so you keep your mouth shut. Wanking is what you do when you play with Tommy's dick and then you get secret money for sweets or football stickers.

When you did wanking with Marissa in the bedroom and showed her 'lick dick', she kicked you on the leg and said she was going to tell dad on you. He calls Marissa 'his little princess' and he doesn't smack her around the head or punch her in the stomach like he does to you. Sometimes you think you are going to stop breathing when he does that.

You wet the bed and you wet your pants. You try to not wet and then you wet. Everybody knows; kids call you 'wet wet wet'. You don't listen very much at school, you keep thinking about what is going to happen next Saturday when dad comes home and finds out.

You have been to the doctor about your peeing problem and he sent you to another doctor.

Every time it happens at school you have to go and get changed, and you sometimes see the school nurse. You won't let her help you to change your clothes. She might find out about wanking so you put your hands down and cover your dick.

You have been stealing from the other children's lunch boxes at school. Your mum has been up to school about that, but she does not tell your dad. She says she is going to have a breakdown if you carry on like this and sometimes she feels like topping herself because of you. She took too many pills once and you did not know if she was going to come home from the hospital or not, but she did. Nobody knows how she got the burn on her back with the iron or got her two fingers broken, except you and Marissa.

Every time you get a school report it says you could try harder and do better. Your mum does not show it to your dad. When you are scrapping with Marissa she says if you do not behave yourself she will tell your dad about your school report.

So you have been asked to counsel Patrick. Why?

It is unlikely to be because Patrick has asked for counselling. Even if Patrick knew what the word meant, children are seldom offered these choices. Thus any counselling relationship would, by definition, be different from an adult counselling relationship, which works on the basis that the adult seeks help for a problem.

So what does counselling mean? What does the dictionary say the definition of counselling is?

> to give advice or guidance to:, to recommend or urge. (Collins English Paperback Dictionary, 1995, Major New Edition)

Why would you be asked to become a counsellor in Patrick's life? There are many possible ways in which you may become involved:

- Because his sister has made allegations outside the family about Patrick's wanking games with her.
- Because Tommy's sexual activities with other children have been exposed.
- Because Patrick's explanation to the casualty doctor about the bruising to his head was incompatible with the injuries.
- Because his peeing problem has been deemed to be emotionally based.
- Because his mother and father are separating and his wishes and feelings need to be ascertained.

None of these reasons are likely to be because Patrick chooses counselling. As a child, Patrick is unlikely to have the opportunity to make such a choice because we live in an adult world where we, as adults, make decisions in relation to children.

The question is more likely to focus on what will we do with Patrick, what will we do about Patrick's problems, rather than how will we initiate a process of interaction with Patrick in which he is able to express his difficulties and be enabled to find some resolution.

Thus children like Patrick are more commonly 'done unto' by a range of services. These are often based on what we perceive as our adult responsibilities in relation to children and are dominated by society's expectations as to the prescribed confines of our respective jobs.

Often, we see ourselves as having to find out about what Patrick can tell us in order to do something about it. This may be a necessary prescription of our role. Our job may be to investigate child abuse or make a diagnosis about his problem, rather than engaging with him in a process of healing.

So, how might we go about offering him an opportunity where he is offered the capacity to share some of his dilemmas and offer a context in which he can take steps to make sense of his confusing, bewildering and violent world?

It would be easy for us to make assumptions about what Patrick's problems might be, based on what we as adults see as the most difficult problem and prioritise it from one to five.

Some adults may see the violence in the house as the most compelling difficulty. Other adults may have a role which focuses on his bed-wetting problem. Yet other adults may be more interested in his potential sexual exploitation. Seldom does the outside world understand what is happening in a child's life unless the child has an opportunity to raise, and thus prioritise, his or her own dilemmas in a way which is not directed by the adult.

Like many abused children, Patrick's world is characterised by fear, lack of safety and the unpredictability of his external adult dominated world. There are many issues common to children who populate that world. Often, they are afraid, consumed by guilt, having had an unwieldy mantle of responsibility placed upon their small shoulders by adults unable to face up to their own responsibilities to care for and protect. Commonly too, children like Patrick often carry a sense of inner outrage, sometimes too dangerous to express. They are mistrustful of adults, and often of themselves, and may believe that they are worth little.

Adult roles and responsibilities are vested upon them when cognitively and developmentally they are unable to shoulder such a burden, potentially resulting in the development of a precocious pseudomaturity.

Children like Patrick often do not respond well to adult questions or probing, partly because they live their lives in defence mode and self-protection becomes a necessary skill.

So they defend themselves against adult intrusion, against adult attempts to probe, find out, ask questions. Invariably, the Patrick's of this world do not respond well to interviews where they are required to sit on a chair and answer direct questions.

Inside, however, the turmoil of unresolved pain, grief, sadness, anger, loss, outrage and guilt rumbles on, like a tumble drier tumbling washed out clothes on an endless cycle.

One of the additional dangers too is that in the 'counselling relationship' the adult will wish to advise him, control him or direct him because most of the time that is the familiar role adults often adopt in relation to children. That, in itself, has the potential to 'close down' interaction with a child rather than open up to its possibilities.

What seems necessary for Patrick now is the antithesis of this closing down process, the provision of a safe context in which he is free to explore, within the safety of clear boundaries, some of the complex dilemmas which threaten to overwhelm his young life. To slow down the drum, to gently and slowly unravel some of its tangled complexity, to look at it, make sense of it and, having gained mastery over it, put it away for storage in its proper place.

Arguably, what Patrick needs most of all is a context where he can feel safe enough and strong enough to still the canister and look at the contents in his own way at his own pace.

What, in my experience, may often be offered him under the guise of 'counselling' is an adult-dominated agenda, inherent within which may be an invitation to examine the 'sock' tangle, when, in fact, the most pressing issue for Patrick may be the jeans or the anorak tangles. According to the interviewer/counsellor and his or her perceived role parameters, what may be pressing for Patrick may not constitute a subject for discussion: 'I can't talk about sexual abuse. I'm only a nursery nurse – that's not my role!' or 'You've told me you are angry with daddy, now can we go on to talk about Tommy?' or 'Now tell me Patrick, what happens when your bladder gets full and you feel you need to empty it?'

How can the process of truly listening to Patrick best be achieved? The following are simple suggestions for practice which, in our experience as an organisation committed to offering a loving, child-focused service, need to be present in any child/adult interaction which can claim to offer true opportunities for healing:

1. Move to the child's level, physically. Kneel on the floor rather than sit behind a desk.

2. Introduce yourself and your function in words the child can understand. 'My name is Mr Bayliss and I've come to talk to you about any difficulties you're having at home' may be less effective as an introduction than:

INTERVIEWER: I bet you're wondering what I'm doing here?

(*Child nods and looks up directly.*)

INTERVIEWER: Well, my name's Dimitri and I spend a lot of time with children who have muddles... You know about muddles?

(*Child distracts by picking up a toy...looks down.*)

INTERVIEWER: You know, the kind of big worries that make your head go round and round and round – like this little girl? (*Gestures using a toy with a winding mechanism whose head revolves to music.*)

(*Child nods tentatively.*)

INTERVIEWER: Well, sometimes I spend time with children who've got muddles like that to see if we can help to sort them out a bit…and that's why Mr Hussein asked me to spend some time with you – he thought you might need a bit of help.

(*Child may pretend to be absorbed in the toy, but listens carefully nonetheless. The message is received and understood.*)

3.   Provide a child focused context. Children cannot communicate effectively in a formal adult/child-language-based interview context, yet, as adults, we often expect them to express deeply painful material in such a forum. The child's primary language is the language of play. The context, therefore, needs to be child focused with toys, drawing books and stories which can act as vehicles for communication and bridges to the child's experience.

4.   Provide a range of tools useful to the child. Our play materials are many and varied and many reflect the kind of issues common to children like Patrick. Among the toys in the toybox or playroom are monster and victim figures, scared little rabbits who shake in the palm of the hand, muddle dolls whose heads go round and round, dolls who, deep inside, have another little person who is sad inside, mistrustful bears who hide inside a shell and are scared to emerge, puppets with different skin colours, play people, babies who cry a lot, strong action men, pretend medical kits – a whole range of potential for exploration.

5.   Ensure clear boundaries to the interaction: 'This can be some time for you. You can do anything you want to with the toys. I'll make sure that you don't hurt yourself or damage anything, or do anything else that isn't OK, and I will just be with you'. Ensure too that the child understands what the parameters of confidentiality will be and what would happen, for example, if the child talked about something or imparted information that the adult may not be free to keep confidential. An example of this would be information about abuse or victimisation by an adult.

6.   Offer reflective feedback and total attention. It is the *quality* of interaction which makes a very special difference. Special time is when the adult totally attends to the child from a position of 'just being' – switching off the adults own agenda, and on to the child. The adult is then fully able to 'be with' the child.

Feeding back cues, rather than demanding information or asking questions, is what allows for the evolution of the child's own healing process and enables the child to use the context as a vehicle for regaining some kind of equilibrium.

The adult follows the child in such a way as the child believes he is being heard and understood. Often the words 'be with' – 'I will just *be with* you' –

take on a very special meaning as the child is able to dictate the tone and pace of the interaction and can truly explore some of the fears and dilemmas which characterise his precarious world. This process is well outlined in the following piece of text:

> When I work with a child in this way I see myself as providing the child with a board game – it has four clear edges within which it is safe to be. I say to the child, here is a board game – go ahead and play. The playroom is the square and the toys are the pieces.
>
> I give him the opportunity to create his own moves and sequences on the board.
>
> It is agonising to watch because I want to lead him and show him where to go and caution him when he makes a wrong move. Because I am an adult and I think I know the rules.
>
> As he moves and glides with the unfolding of his fantasy he checks on many occasions to make sure the board is still there and the edges are still in the same place. He needs to know that the board is steady enough to take the strain of his discoveries, and sometimes he tests it severely. When he learns that it will endure, he is for a short time in control of this part of his world and feels safe enough to travel on a journey into his fantasies, his sadnesses, anxieties and confusions.
>
> He plays out his life experience and having encountered the strength and power of his own uniqueness, he can take this strength out of the playroom and into other parts of his life where he feels powerless. (Bray 1984)

A typical piece of interaction with Patrick may go as follows:

DIMITRI: You're picking up that big action man and you're twisting his arm up his back.

PATRICK: Waaw, ow ow!

DIMITRI: And he is making 'ow' noises.

              (*Patrick feigns crying*).

PATRICK: Ow, ow, stoppit, ow!

DIMITRI: You're twisting his arm up his back again and he is shouting 'ow', stoppit.

PATRICK: Yeah, 'cos it's sore.

DIMITRI: It's sore when you twist his arm up his back?

PATRICK: Yeah, he's crap, useless.

DIMITRI: You're telling me he's useless?

PATRICK: Yeah, 'cos he keeps missing the goal!

DIMITRI: Keeps missing the goal?

PATRICK: Yeah.

DIMITRI: Oh I see, he's crap, useless, 'cos he keeps missing the goal.

PATRICK: Yeah, he's no good. Stupid he is.

DIMITRI: You're saying he's stupid?

PATRICK: My dad used to play in the league…

DIMITRI: Oh, your dad used to play football?

PATRICK: Yeah, he's better than me.

DIMITRI: Better than you…

                (*Patrick turns to punch the action man in the stomach*).

PATRICK: Useless bastard!

DIMITRI: You say he's a useless bastard?

PATRICK: Yeah…you're a useless bastard you are (*gesturing to the action man doll*) and you're gonna get a good hiding.

During the interaction above, the adult, having taken responsibility for boundaries, has enabled the child to express some of the most pressing information. The adult is beginning to gain a picture of some of the fears and preoccupations in the child's world.

The adult, in an interaction like this, is very often faced with information that seems incomprehensible at the time. But, provided that interpretations are kept to an absolute minimum, the child is often able to reveal aspects of inner distress which can then be externalised and examined in the safety of a two-way adult/child communication:

PATRICK (*holding a teddy, pressing small playdoh lumps into his mouth*): He's stuffing them in!

DIMITRI: You're filling his mouth with those little lumpy things.

PATRICK: Them's pills. Cor, he's gonna choke soon (*throws himself backwards, hands round the teddy's neck*) aarch, gurgle, gurgle… (*making choking sounds*).

DIMITRI: Teddy's choking on all those pills.

PATRICK: How many will he have to take to die?

DIMITRI: You want to know how many pills he would have to take to die?

PATRICK: Yeah, pretend he was a person, how many would he
                  have to take before he was dead?

In this situation the foundation has been laid for a safe two-way conversation
which imparts much needed information and which has the potential to
explore a myriad of confusions from adult suicide attempts to fear of loss and
abandonment.

The adult may or may not understand some of the reasons behind the
child's search for answers. This understanding is often not present, but if
conditions are right, the child's making-sense process can take place provided
the child-focused context outlined above is in existence.

As trust develops it is often the case that more and more painful material
emerges and, provided that a safe child-centred context which offers opportunities for safety and containment and a sense of belonging can be established, an opportunity for real growth and healing can be afforded the child.

Patrick's most pressing issue at this moment may be the dilemmas which
his father's physical abuse of him raises. Am I a bad boy? Am I useless? Why
do some grown-ups tell children off for hurting people? Why do daddies hurt
children? Does daddy love me? Do all men hurt children? Are all good
footballers good people? Another pressing confusion may also be his mother's
suicide attempts.

Such confusions, it would seem, currently preoccupy Patrick's life and he
may be able to use his developing relationship with Dimitri to explore and
make sense of them.

Within that communication, too, there is often a window to the child's
world, which, with careful and sensitive negotiation, can often provide a basis
for understanding what the child is trying to convey.

An adult like Dimitri, therefore, can very often be a vital bridge from the
child's experience to the rest of the world and can be a vehicle for enabling
the child to have a true voice in the events surrounding his or her life.

There can be little doubt that to be heard and understood, to be cared for
and protected, are basic human needs and fundamental to a child's existence.
These needs can only be met if adults are willing and prepared to operate in
a genuinely child-focused way, thereby committing themselves to the provision of a context where true exploration, sharing, understanding and healing
can occur.

In terms of days, hours and months in the total context of Patrick's life, his
time with Dimitri may have formed only a tiny part. But the contribution that
this tiny amount of time has the potential to make to the child's emotional,
physical and spiritual health may be enormous and, at times, life changing.

AFTERWORD

Together with her colleague Mary Walsh, Madge Bray runs an organisation
called SACCS (Sexual Abuse Child Consultancy Service) in Shrewsbury,
Shropshire, which offers skills training to professionals in therapeutic help to
abused children. Its sister organisation, Leaps & Bounds, offers an integrated
service of residential care and therapy for a number of small severely abused

children who cannot live in their own families. Also attached to the agency is a home-finding service for abused children.

Further details can be obtained from:

S.A.C.C.S.
Mytton Mill
Montford Bridge
Shropshire SY4 1HA
Tel: 01743 850015
Fax: 01743 851060

REFERENCES

Bray, M. (1984) In N. Evans (ed) *Taking the Lid Off*. Out of print.

FURTHER READING

Axline, Virginia (1971) *Dibs: In Search of Self*. Harmondsworth: Pelican Books UK.

Axline, Virginia (1989) *Play Therapy*. Edinburgh: Churchill Livingstone.

Bray, Madge (1989) 'Communicating with Children, Communicating with the Court.' In A. Levy (ed) *Focus on Child Abuse*. Hawkesmere.

Bray, Madge (1989) *Susie and the Wise Hedgehog Go to Court*. Hawkesmere.

Bray, Madge (1994) 'Communicating with Children, Communicating with the Court.' In A. Levy (ed) *Refocus on Child Abuse*. Hawkesmere.

Bray, Madge (1997) *Sexual Abuse: The Child's Voice. Poppies on the Rubbish Heap*. London: Jessica Kingsley.

Cavanagh-Johnson, Toni (1993) *Sexualised Children – New Insights and Creative Interventions*. Lexington.

James, Beverly (1989) *Treating Traumatised Children – New Insights and Creative Interventions*. Lexington.

James, Beverly (1994) *Handbook for Treatment of Attachment – Trauma Problems in Children*. Lexington.

Saphira, Miriam (1993) *Look Back, Stride Forward*. Papers Inc.

CHAPTER 3

Drug Users Who Were Sexually Abused as Children

Ronno Griffiths

This chapter draws on material and discussions from training I have co-developed on drug users and past sexual abuse, my own work with drug users dating back to 1978 and from my supervisory role in a number of generic and specialist settings.[1] It explores the connections and parallels between childhood sexual abuse and later substance use, a practical assessment model and some issues for workers.

Original ideas which arose from practical experience have been shaped and informed by the numerous participants who have undertaken this often painful experiential training with great honesty and integrity and who have shared their personal and professional experiences willingly. But the most profound impact and understanding surely comes from our clients, to whom this chapter is dedicated with great respect for their suffering, courage and wisdom and their generosity and humour.

THE RELATIONSHIP BETWEEN SUBSTANCE USE AND PAST SEXUAL ABUSE

The research evidence

As with many aspects of sexual abuse, the relationship between past sexual abuse and subsequent substance use remains under-researched. However, Finkelhor (1986) has summarised the research evidence on the association between child sexual abuse and later substance use:

> Peters (1984), in a carefully controlled community study, found that 17% of the victimized women had symptoms of alcohol abuse (versus 4% of nonvictimized women), and 27% abused at least one type of drug (compared to 12% of nonvictimized women). Herman (1981) noted that 35% of the women with incestuous fathers in her clinical sample abused drugs and alcohol (versus 5% of the women with seductive fathers).

---

1   In 1990, Margot Williams, an experienced social worker with the Coventry Community Drug Team, approached me with a view to developing training on working with drug users who were sexually abused as children. Since then we have developed materials and facilitated training on a regular basis and I would like to acknowledge her contributions in laying down the foundations of good practice in this area. Further insights have been provided by Brian Pearson and Zetta Bear, who have also acted as co-facilitators.

Similarly, Briere (1984), in his walk-in sample to a community health center, found that 27% of the childhood sexual abuse victims had a history of alcoholism (compared with 11% of non victims), and 21% a history of drug addiction (versus 2% of the nonvictims). (p.162)

The evidence from practice

Finkelhor proposes a conceptual framework for understanding the effects of past abuse which suggests that there are four traumagenic factors that make the trauma of childhood sexual abuse unique: traumatic sexualisation, stigmatisation, powerlessness and betrayal. Substances may be employed to deal with the effects of any of these factors but of particular significance to this discussion is the notion of stigmatisation. Stigmatisation can ensue because the abuser blames and denigrates their victim – explicit and implicit messages of shame and guilt are communicated to the child along with pressure for secrecy – or it may occur as a direct result of shocked and horrified reactions to disclosure and attempts to seek help. The psychological impact can include guilt, shame, lowered self-esteem and a sense of being different from others. Finkelhor suggests that there is a potential for people to be attracted to other stigmatised groups and activities, including drug use.

Liz Hall and Siobhan Lloyd (1989) make a number of references to the links between past sexual abuse and substance use. They suggest that: 'Many incest survivors have never learned appropriate ways of dealing with their anger, and frequently turn it in on themselves. This leads to self mutilation, alcohol and drug abuse and suicidal attempts.' (p.50). They also comment that anger and hostility can be used as a protective shield to stop others from getting too close. This certainly resonates with my own experience of working with drug users where chaotic substance use functions to keep others at bay through aggressive or 'unattractive' behaviour. They refer also to the use of substances, particularly alcohol, as a means of blocking out memories.

The experience of specialist drugs services suggests that more drug users are disclosing past sexual abuse. This is logical: if the overall number of people disclosing is increasing, this will be reflected in areas of specialist provision. As drug workers become more confident in responding to – in listening to – such disclosures, so more clients pick up signals that it might be safe to speak out.This is not confined, of course, to specialist drugs workers. Other service providers, also more alert to indicators of abuse and more familiar with substance-related issues, may create an atmosphere more conducive to disclosure. And substance users are not immune to contemporary debates which heighten their awareness, triggering suppressed memories which bubble to the surface as defences are lowered through intoxication, withdrawal or abstinence.

The evidence from the training courses

A significant part of the training aims to explore the relationship between past sexual abuse and drug use. This is often complex and has pitfalls for client and counsellor. Participants are divided into groups and asked to consider a series of questions. These are outlined in Tables 3.1–3.4 below, along with the characteristic responses.

Table 3.1: What are the connections, parallels and commonalities between the experiences and effects of childhood sexual abuse and those of problematic substance use?

Outcomes of question should indicate the commonalities and how many of the effects of sexual abuse are replicated in the experiences of problem substance users. Many of the methods of dealing with the effects of problem substance use are mirrored in mechanisms for dealing with the effects of the abuse.

Effects of abuse
Effects of problem drug use

- poor self-esteem
- adopt role of victim
- role of victim is enforced
- powerlessness
- guilt
- helplessness/hopelessness
- alienation from society
- labelled as sad, mad, bad
- label as 'master status'
- believed to be bad parents
- stigmatised
- depressed
- isolated
- angry
- unable to express anger
- discriminated against
- fall between services
- no services locally
- homeless
- poverty
- pushed into associated crime
- mental health diagnosis
- pathologising of the problem
- relationship problems
- problems with boundaries
- dependent on others – including workers
- want to please and protect
- want to die

Ways of coping with the effects of abuse
Ways of coping with the effects of use

- TAKE MORE DRUGS
- testing-out behaviours
- try to take control of anything or everything
- aggressive to others
- anger turned in on self
- substance use
- how far can they push people
- risk-taking behaviours
- self-harm
- suicide
- self-medication
- compulsive behaviours
- medical treatment
- sleeping disorders
- eating disorders
- sub-cultural affiliation
- prostitution
- set self up to fail
- act as if everything is okay
- fear of relationships
- unrealistic goals
- denial
- ambivalence
- dissociation

Table 3.2: Why might people who have been sexually abused turn to drug use?

- escape
- pain-killer
- suppress memories
- self-harm
- suicide and parasuicide
- gain confidence
- attraction to risk
- identity
- sub-cultural affiliation

Table 3.3: Why might drug users be vulnerable to further sexual abuse?

- a woman (or young man) drinking is seen as 'asking for it'
- if intoxicated – definitely 'fair game'
- male and female users involved in prostitution to raise money for drugs – not seen as having sexual rights so susceptible to rape
- prostitution/sexual relations may occur to gain affection/ accommodation/drugs
- prostitution can reinforce traumatised sexuality
- poor judgements about people exacerbated by intoxication and desperation
- pressure to allow home to be used for dealing or drug use – more strangers in the home
- if stoned or unconscious you cannot stop the assault
- aggressive and abusive pimps

Table 3.4: What are the implications of this complex relationship for workers?

- Assessment: it is difficult to assess whether the 'symptom' or the way of dealing with it arises from the abuse or the substance use.

- Drugs work or sexual abuse work: clients disclose sexual abuse to drugs workers because they feel safe – not all drugs workers feel confident in undertaking abuse work and even where they do, they may not be able to respond because of organisational constraints. Non-drug specialists may find themselves in the counter position whereby a client reveals the extent of their substance problems because they have been able to disclose their sexual abuse.

- Delayed development: Finkhelhor has suggested that the configuration of the four traumagenic dynamics in sexual abuse can effect the cognitive and emotional development of the child into adulthood. It is an old adage in the substance field that 'a 20-year-old user is going on 14'. The obstacles to maturity are often hidden behind a projected image of being 'street wise'. The process is also effected by the potential for regression which can be facilitated by the clients intoxication or withdrawal.

- Dissociation can be facilitated by substance use.

- Mental Health: the effects of abuse such as depression, anxiety, compulsive behaviours, self-harm are sometimes diagnosed as mental health problems. Similarly, behaviours and states arising from drug use (paranoia, depression, amphetamine psychosis) may result in mental health interventions. There is a danger that neither the abuse nor the drug use feature in the assessment. Ironically, some people acquire a set of totally inappropriate interventions whilst others are seen solely as 'survivors' or 'drug users' and do not receive the mental health interventions that they do require. The problems of dual diagnosis are immense. Whilst we do not want to impose yet more labels on clients, neither do we want a situation whereby their distress is increased for want of appropriate treatment. Trying to untangle the abuse from the use is hard, trying to untangle them from mental health problems is another complexity.

(continued)

Table 3.4: What are the implications of this complex relationship for workers? (continued)

- Sex and sexuality: The potential for traumatised sexuality is well documented by Finkhelhor. The following points are pertinent here:

  i.   People who have been abused may be attracted to prostitution because of the confusion over the role of sex in giving and receiving attention, affection and other rewards, because of affiliation with marginalised groups and or activities or because of homelessness or poverty brought on by being excluded from or leaving the family home or care. Men and women involved in prostitution, and people who are homeless, are vulnerable to substance use.

  ii. Substance users may resort to prostitution to raise money for drugs for themselves or their partner or to generate income for the partner or dealer.

  iii. Discussions about HIV and safer sex can be threatening – especially if sexuality is an uncomfortable issue. They can trigger memories and alarm about abusive experiences as well as feelings of shame and guilt.

  iv. Some people are forced into sexual acts that they find unacceptable, or which make them negate the associated risk, because of the need to generate income. This can put them at risk physically, psychologically, emotionally and spiritually.

  v.   Abusive experiences and others' reactions to them ('she must be promiscuous'; 'he's got to be a pervert'; 'she's damaged goods'; 'he must have enjoyed it – its every young man's dream') can leave people confused about their sexuality. They may use drugs to cope with the distress and the injustice.

  vi. There is an influential view that monogamous, heterosexual relations are the norm and that anything else is seen as unhealthy, abnormal and wrong. If a gay man or lesbian is also a drug taker, the very fact of the drug use is seen as further proof of their deviance.

WORKING WITH DRUG USERS WHO HAVE BEEN SEXUALLY ABUSED

Problem drug use

For many years the terms 'addict' or 'abuser' were used to describe people dependent (or believed to be dependent) on drugs. They are rarely helpful to either client or worker as they function as a 'master status' which legitimates the application of a litany of stereotypical characteristics (Griffiths and Pearson 1988). Regardless of the degree of active commitment to anti-discriminatory practice, these negative labels and their associations can influence the therapeutic relationship and be very restrictive to working creatively or seeing where change can occur. This is especially so when clients have internalised the label and believe themselves to be worthless, bad, deviant, dirty and so on. Although they are often interwoven, it is useful to view dependence from two perspectives: physical and psychological.

Physical dependence tends to receive most attention as it is most readily understood. For physical dependence to occur, the drug has to be taken on a regular basis. Contrary to popular myth, there is no substance that results in immediate addiction. Tolerance to the drug develops and the body adjusts to its presence so as to maintain relatively normal functioning. The drug-induced state becomes the 'normal' physiological state. If the individual ceases drug use, a withdrawal syndrome, which can be unpleasant and distressing, occurs as the body readjusts. The severity of withdrawal may be influenced by the person's motivation to be drug free, prior experience of withdrawing, severity of use, physical and mental health, degree of support and material resources.

Faced with the pain of physical withdrawal, the obvious step is to recommence drug use. Some drug users (particularly heroin dependents) undergo a medically supervised detoxification which can last from a few weeks to many months. Others may be prescribed a maintenance dose – sometimes over several years – to stabilise both drug use and associated lifestyle. Such prescribing might be appropriate for a client engaged in sexual abuse counselling. Abstinence could leave them vulnerable to relapse and without access to coping mechanisms as pain is restimulated. A prescription may give the client more opportunities to engage, undistracted by anxieties of how and where to acquire drugs.

Many heroin users withdraw without medical assistance through choice, but some enter withdrawal because they cannot obtain the drug or have acquired drugs of a lower purity than they are used to. This can mean that a client who has hitherto engaged in counselling sessions may become unable to take part to the same extent. It is not unknown for people who are physically dependent to stop use abruptly because they want to prove themselves to their counsellor or because they feel that they have made a significant breakthrough and mistakenly believe that they no longer need the drug.

Many of the services and treatment options available are primarily concerned with physical dependence. While valuable, these interventions are unlikely to be fully successful unless psychological dependence is also attended to.

Psychological dependence is more important in understanding why people continue to use drugs and have difficulty in achieving and maintaining a drug-free state. It is possible to become psychologically dependent on any substance. The dependence stems not just from the physical properties of the drug but from the role that the drug plays in users' lives.

The drug is used to achieve a desired state – maybe to feel relaxed, for excitement, to belong or to be able to cope with stress. Most people have a variety of means of achieving these outcomes, but for the drug user there is the potential for drug use to become the habitual route to desired states, with other means of achieving them effectively absent or blocked. Thus drug use becomes the only means to a valued state, to being able to cope and, ultimately, to feeling normal. No matter how much insight the client may have into their destructive behaviour, they also believe that their lives would be even worse without the substance. This knowledge and conflict can be very distressing and in itself lead to further use as a way of dealing with the stress of this insight – an awareness which may very well arise from counselling. If they cease drug use, they are likely to feel depressed, unable to cope, vulnerable and abnormal. This, along with external pressures, leads to a desire or craving to use again.

THE NEED FOR THE DRUG EXPERIENCE

Stereotypical images of drug users often lead to them being dismissed as people who do not deserve services as 'they brought it on themselves' or 'they have no intention of changing'. Organisations may not afford them any degree of priority in a climate of budgetary constraints and over-stretched resources or criteria for intervention that effectively exclude substance users. Professionals and informal carers may not be immune from negative attitudes, whether because of the impact of organisational policies, broader societal prejudices or the evidence of an individual's apparent disregard for those who are trying to help or their resistance to change. Such resistance is often seen as a sign of obduracy and selfishness rather than a fear of the implications of becoming drug free. Many problem drug users are ambivalent about their substance use and its consequent problems and accompanying lifestyle but are enmeshed in a relationship that they cannot move on from. For some, the relationship with their drug requires in-depth, long-term work similar to bereavement counselling.

There is a tendency among some counsellors to adopt a basic ground rule that they will only work with substance users when they are drug free. A commitment to abstinence is seen as a commitment to therapy. This is appropriate in some settings (such as a drug-free rehabilitation programme) and it is common sense to postpone or take a break from sessions if the client is slipping in and out of consciousness or too chaotic to make use of what is on offer. However, I would argue strongly against a blanket approach in all settings. To wait until the client is drug free rather misses the point – they may need the security or the challenges of the relationship and the opportunities to explore personal material to achieve abstinence or stability. They may not be able to make changes in their drug use without developing a deeper understanding of their behaviour or other coping mechanisms. Furthermore, the very process of counselling may be difficult, possibly reactivating memories and feelings, thus leaving the individual vulnerable to substance use as a form of self-medication. A client may attempt to withdraw in order to fulfill a counselling contract, thus rendering themselves unable to engage in it.

Contrary to some anxious observers, harm reduction neither precludes abstinence as an optimum outcome nor colludes with illicit or otherwise harmful activities. Rather, it ensures that drug users have the necessary factual, practical and personal resources to reduce or minimise harm (both for themselves and others) and to improve physical, psychological and emotional health until such time as the drug user is able or ready to make greater changes. The goal of complete abstinence may be so unrealistic, threatening and irrelevant as to dissuade an individual from making use of services or addressing any difficulties that they might have. A harm reduction approach, at its most basic level, might save lives. It can certainly benefit the relationship with the service provider who is perceived as accepting, non-judgemental and trustworthy – often leading to more committed work. And it can enhance the client's self-esteem as they achieve change and take control over aspects of their life.

THE ADDICTION AND SELF-REGARD CYCLE

It is helpful here to draw on the work of Peele (1981), who employs two feedback mechanisms to describe how substance users can become disempowered.

Those immersed in the Addiction Cycle will routinely use drugs as a way of dealing with problems. Intoxication provides momentary escape from the problem but results in reduced ability to attend to or deal with it. When the effect of the drug wears off, the problem may well have worsened because of failure to deal with it or have been exacerbated by the drug use. This triggers the need to take the drug again. Drug use provides immediate solutions but is dysfunctional in the longer term. The individual may be aware of this process but not know how to break the cycle. It is the counsellor's job to facilitate other means of problem solving.

The individual's ability to take control, and/or believe that they can affect change, will be further weakened if they are trapped in the Self-Regard Cycle. If their self-esteem is poor, they may take drugs to block out the accompanying distress (which is likely to be heightened for people who have been abused). In using, they may exacerbate their low self-regard as they feel guilty, stupid or weak or meet with disapproval from others. The cycle is set for more substance use.

The sense of helplessness and hopelessness that arises for individuals as a result of these traps projects onto the counsellor, who experiences a similar sense of powerlessness which is reinforced by, and mirrored in, their own uncertainty about how to proceed. This can lead to over-identification with the client or to becoming cynical and vulnerable to societal prejudices which have been reinforced by experiences of working with the client and apparently achieving nothing. Both responses are understandable but neither are satisfactory for client or counsellor. The transferences and counter-transferences, the complexity of whose needs and whose powerlessness is driving the agenda, all become an urgent matter for supervision.

One way of attempting to steer a path through this minefield, and to maximise the opportunities for effective interventions, is to apply a model of assessment which helps to make sense of a situation and to see where the problem may actually lie. One such model that can be particularly helpful in counselling people who have been abused is that of Drug, Set and Setting.

DRUG, SET AND SETTING – AN ASSESSMENT TOOL FOR UNDERSTANDING THE NEED FOR THE DRUG EXPERIENCE AND PLANNING EFFECTIVE RESPONSES

This model suggests that an individual's attraction to, and experience of, substance use is made up of three factors: the drug, the set (i.e. the make up of the individual user) and the setting (i.e. the circumstances of use). The configuration of these factors will differ from person to person and over time. In exploring them, counsellor and client can reach a clearer understanding of the need for the experience, the function of the substance, where risks may lie, the relationship to sexual abuse and other traumatic experiences and, ultimately, indicate how to tailor interventions to meet the actual – rather than assumed – need of the person.

The drug

At first sight it might appear rather obvious to cite the effect of the drug as a reason an abused person might use it. However, an understanding of an individual's preferred drug and the way that it is administered and used can reveal a great deal about the function of drug use in the life of the drug user.

Heroin and other opiates, for instance, can act as an emotional anaesthetic, wrapping the user in cotton wool, distancing them from the pain of the past, protecting them from the daily triggers of childhood memories. Heroin is very effective in suppressing memories and in providing a security blanket – a place and object of safety. It also helps to maintain the secret:

> When I think it's going to come out I push it down with more gear. I can't handle it…if I tell you…if I tell anyone it'll do my head in.

One person may prefer heroin to suppress the trauma. Another might find that the confidence-boosting properties of amphetamines are attractive as they help them deal with poor efficacy or difficulties in socialising – two of the possible effects of childhood abuse.

SAM: On speed I could be anybody…do anything. I wasn't a scaredy cat Daddy's girl anymore. Until I came down. Then I'd just stay in my room not sleeping…just thinking about what he did and how she let him and just laughed at me.

Over the years I have worked with a number of young women who enjoy amphetamines because they are effective appetite suppressants. This can have a range of desired outcomes, for example as an aid to delaying or denying sexuality, of taking control over their bodies, of shrinking so as not to attract attention and of amenorrhea. At the suggestion of her counsellor, Megan started to keep a diary so as to gain some insight into her drug use. In it she very clearly laid out the fact that if she stopped taking amphetamine she would probably start eating and ultimately gain weight and lose the bodily attributes of the little girl that her father loved. For Megan, the drug's function

was two-fold: to remain attractive to her father (who had stopped the inces-
tuous relationship when she was 14) and a means of escaping from her
ambivalent and unsettling feelings for her father, who she recognised as
abusive.

There are also those who simply want to be 'stoned' and who are attracted
to chaotic, excessive and high-risk drug use, using any drug that comes to
hand with little discrimination. For some people it is withdrawal from drugs
that prompts the crisis. Withdrawal can be both physically and psychologically distressing, as body and mind react to the shift from a 'normal' (drug-
induced) state to an 'abnormal' one, with reminders of physical and emotional
distress arising directly from past sexual abuse. Such reminders may not be
fully understood. Into this frightening experience come suppressed memories, fears or generalised anxieties that the person has not yet attached to the
abuse experience. People who have been abused can face monsters at every
turn – sometimes explicit, sometimes as ill-defined shadows – which hide in
everyday objects and activities, such as eating certain foods or the opening
bars to a song. People may recognise the connections instantly, come to
understand them in time or simply be aware of a generalised anxiety or
unattached paralysing fear. For problem drug takers this learning process my
be hindered because of intoxication or because in withdrawal or abstinence
they may have to contend with many unexplained fears that make a resump-
tion of substance use – the return to safety – compelling.

In one group session a member said:

> As soon as I heard the theme tune for the Archers I'd
> hit the bottle. Have you any idea how often its on? I'd
> just be getting straight from the lunch time session and
> I'd have to start again! Saturday was my dry day for a
> while – no country chatter, no drink. But I'd make up
> for it on Sundays with the omnibus edition. Then
> somebody pointed out that I always turned the damn
> thing on and that made me sit up pretty sharpish.

Jules told the story as an amusing anecdote but there was a serious content.
Her story is a good example of how memories can be triggered: in Jules' case
the radio programme usually heralded an abusive episode perpetrated by her
father. In later sessions she described how she would make herself listen to
the programme so as to take away the fear, to detract from other triggers and
to provide an excuse for drinking.

In the same group, Paula described how:

> I'll be 'clean' for weeks. But then I suddenly get this
> rising tide of panic. It is terrible...really scary. I can
> hardly breathe. It's like I'm going to choke. I honestly
> don't know what sets it off but the only thing I can do is
> get the pills.

It is interesting to note the experience of some women who withdraw from
substances when they find they are pregnant. The absence of their means of

coping with past abuse, current trauma, and the triggers arising from pregnancy and accompanying gynaecological examinations can be very distressing.

MARY: I had to use again. I'm so sorry. I couldn't handle knowing what had happened to me knowing it might happen to my baby. I feel terrible – wicked – about using. I don't want to hurt my baby. Please God don't let the junk get through. But as God is my judge I'd have got rid of it if I hadn't used.

Mary and her key worker had to attend to a number of issues, not least a medically supervised treatment and detoxification alongside an exploration of the implications of being drug free, which provided the context for discussing the abuse and the pregnancy. Some women in Mary's position have been refused a service because they are perceived as manipulative and time-wasting. Fortunately, such attitudes are waning in the face of increased awareness of both sexual abuse and drug use but they still persist to too great an extent. Jason's story has some parallels with Mary's:

I went into shock when I found out about the baby. Part of me was excited, proud even – I loved the fantasy of the three of us being a normal family laughing and crying and growing together. Doing normal things. But part of me couldn't. This little boy inside me was screaming NO, NO, NO. It was a nightmare. I got off my head for three weeks. I can't believe she took me back after I sodded off like that. I can't remember much about it. I just had to get out of it. Well out of it.

The above extracts from case histories are in the context of a harm reduction approach. Using the model of drug set and setting the worker or counsellor can explore questions such as:
- Does the client prefer a particular drug or method of use? What effect are they looking for and why?
- Is the client discriminating in their patterns of use? Are they compulsive or chaotic? Why?
- Is the client in any physical danger from the way that they are using or what they are using?
- Are they aware of the actual or potential dangers to themselves and others?
- Is the worker in a position to give harm reduction advice or refer on to somebody with more specialist knowledge?

The set

This aspect of the drug experience considers the way that the person views themselves (their self-image) their perception of whether they can bring about changes in their lives or around their drug use, the way that they relate to the world and the people in it and how they believe others see them. A great deal of material can be generated for client and counsellor to explore. Is the client's chaotic or extreme drug use or risk taking a form of self-harm? What is the function of the self-harming – to take control of the pain, self-punishment, a way of staying alive? Is the risk taking (for example high doses and 'cocktails', shared injecting equipment) associated with a flirtation with death, a way of proving that they have risen above it all, maybe that they have superhuman qualities? Is it because they have been taught that they are cheap and, therefore, that their life is cheap? Is it that they can acquire 'street cred' and gain importance? One client, John, came to a point in his counselling when he was able to clarify that his 'on the edge' existence was a means of having an identity, of being really good at something. It also gave him the courage to act out some of his anger and rage against a world and abusers who had let him down badly.

The setting

Are there any particular circumstances that lead to substance use? What is it about the environment or situation that prompts a client to use or use to excess? Is it simply that they cannot say 'no' when friends are using? For someone who has been abused, does this resonate with occasions when they have been unable to say 'no' to abusive sexual advances? Is an increase in drug use related to a life event such as birthday, birth, death, the anniversary of when the abuse began, ended, was disclosed or disbelieved? Does the fact that they live alone increase their sense of isolation and alienation and, therefore, their need to use? Conversely, do they live in a multi-occupied house or hostel depriving them of necessary privacy and controlled access to the bathroom? Perhaps a fellow resident or room-mate masturbates, has sexual partners or pornographic material. Maybe they live with other substance users and so their sense of being different from mainstream society is reinforced. The individual may consequently use drugs to affirm their sub-cultural affiliation or to counteract the effects of stigmatisation and alienation.

The above merely gives some examples of how this model can be used and the broad areas that can be covered. Obviously, the experiences of each drug user who has been sexually abused are unique to them and the counsellor must use professional judgement as to what angle to pursue. In working together the counsellor and client can start to untangle the potential relationship between past abuse and current substance use. Where a worker is in a purely counselling role, they may need to refer the client for practical help with, for instance, an accommodation problem or other feature in 'the setting' or for specialist drug or alcohol intervention, such as a heroin, alcohol or minor tranquilliser detoxification/prescription, or harm reduction advice around their drug use, injecting practices and disposal of injecting equipment. An assessment may indicate that the drugs and the sexual abuse should be separated out and dealt with by specific services. However, many generic and drugs specialists will be able to cover the range of issues.

SUMMARY

There are many associations and commonalities between sexual abuse and substance use. Work with drug users and work with people who have been sexually abused can be both challenging, frightening, exciting and rewarding in their own right. Together, the problems can appear to be overwhelming. It is essential then to return to basics. Be accepting. Don't judge. Don't assume. Above all, don't underestimate the strength of the client or the value of listening to their story. We are privileged to be told it. At the very least we can hear it. For too long, people who have been abused have been silenced. People who use drugs have no voice. We have a responsibility to bear witness. If we can do this, we can give our clients a little of what they deserve.

REFERENCES

Briere, J. (April 1984) 'The long-term effects of childhood sexual abuse: defining a post-sexual abuse syndrome.' Paper presented at the Third National Conference on Sexual Victimization of Children, Washington, D.C.

Finkelhor, D. (ed) (1986) *A Source Book on Child Sexual Abuse*. Newbury Park: Sage Publications.

Griffiths, R. and Pearson, B. (1988) *Working With Drug Users*. Aldershot: Wildwood House.

Hall, L. and Lloyd, S. (1989) *Surviving Child Sexual Abuse*. Basingstoke: The Falmer Press.

Herman, J. (1981) *Father–Daughter Incest*. Cambridge, MA: Harvard University Press.

Peele, S. (1981) *How Much Is Too Much: Healthy Habits or Destructive Addictions*. Englewood Cliffs, NJ: Prentice Hall.

Peters, S.D. (1984) 'The relationship between childhood sexual victimization and adult depression among Afro-American and white women.' Unpublished doctoral dissertation, University of Los Angeles (University Microfilms No.84-28, 555).

FURTHER READING

ACMD (Advisory Council on the Misuse of Drugs) (1982) *Treatment and Rehabilitation: Report of the ACMD*. London: HMSO.

ISDD (Institute for the Study of Drug Dependence) *Drug Abuse Briefing*. London: ISDD.

CHAPTER 4

'What Happens Now?'
Issues for Good Practice in Working with Domestic Abuse

Siobhan Lloyd

ALEX

Alex is thirty-eight years old, living with a partner of fifteen years. They have two young children. Alex comes to your agency in a distressed state. Slowly, with much tearfulness, it emerges that Alex's partner is abusive. The abuse has escalated in frequency, complexity and severity since before the children were born and Alex, who works in a senior local authority administrative post, has got to the point of wondering if it is any longer possible to stay in the relationship. It seems incredible that things have turned out this way, when they started with such high hopes for a future together. Alex wonders who or what is to blame. Both partners are in full-time work and sometimes the pressures of managing home, children, family, friends and work feel too much. There have been money worries in the past but this is not a current concern. Their friends have no idea of the situation. They think that Alex has a good relationship – and to the outside world that is what it looks like – mutually concerned, spending most of their social time together. In reality, that 'closeness' is synonymous with possessiveness. Alex is allowed little freedom in the relationship and even less space to pursue personal interests and friendships. Jealousy is all-pervasive. Alex's mother, who visits regularly, has long suspected that all is not well with the relationship and has started to question Alex closely about aspects of home life. Alex is frightened that it will all come out and things will get worse as a result. The children need a roof over their head and what would happen to them if their parents' relationship ended? Maybe it would be better to stay, to grit teeth and bear it, until the kids leave home. Alex is worn out, confused and feels hopeless when thinking about what the future holds.

This scenario is not untypical of an abusive relationship – abuse which is long established, escalating over time, well hidden from public gaze, with confusion about the reasons for it, a considerable amount of self-blame and a desire to protect children from what is going on. Consider your response to the following questions:

- What assumptions did you make about Alex's gender, sexual orientation and cultural background?
- Did these have any influence on the way in which you reacted to Alex's story?
- Would your reaction have been different if Alex was male, female, straight, gay or bisexual?
- What significance, if any, did you attach to the presence of children in the relationship? Did this affect your reaction to the situation or to Alex?
- What knowledge do you have about local resources which might be available to Alex if a decision is made to leave the relationship, or to stay?
- Did any of the details of this case 'ring bells' for you, from your own work or personal experience? If so, what might be the significance of this in your work with Alex?

These are just some of the questions which might be asked of anyone who is in a helping role with survivors of domestic abuse and this chapter explores some of the issues which arise from them for any helper, irrespective of their agency context.

NAMING THE ABUSE

Taking time at the outset to define terms is essential in domestic abuse work. It is only in the last twenty years that the nature, extent and social implications of the abuse of adults, especially women, in intimate relationships has emerged as an issue of public concern. Finding the most accurate descriptor of the violence which is inflicted on one partner by another entails considering the variables involved in the acts of violence. The couple may be heterosexual, bisexual or gay, so 'battered woman' may not always apply. 'Domestic dispute' is unsatisfactory because it can minimise the degree of violence or ignore the full extent of the abuse which is perpetrated. The term 'domestic violence' itself implies that the abuse takes place inside the home and this is not always the case – it can occur outside it, in the home to which one party has been rehoused or it can happen before they have set up home together. The word 'domestic' can also be said to trivialise the abuse, to keep it in the private sphere and, by implication, to imply that it is not a matter for public concern. The term 'domestic abuse' is used here in preference to the more commonly used 'domestic violence' because it includes not only physical violence but emotional, sexual and economic abuse of one individual by another. Mackay and Macgregor (1994) define the abuse in relation to the way in which women experience it in this way: 'The physical, emotional or sexual abuse of an adult woman by a male with whom she has or has had an intimate relationship, whether or not the couple are living together' (p.4).

Finally, the word 'victim' to describe the person on whom the abuse had been perpetrated is not always accurate or helpful. It may be temporarily exact but is not a label which any person should carry into their subsequent life if they disclose what has happened to them. It implies passivity and an inability to change their situation and it takes no account of the many pressures which can be felt to stay in the abusive situation.

Domestic abuse is widespread, it is not confined to particular social classes, ethnic groups or geographical locations. It is experienced by young people and older couples, able-bodied people and people with disabilities. We know that the majority of people who are abused by their partners are women and there has been some debate about women who are violent to men in hetero-sexual couples (Smith 1989). In one of the few studies which looked at this issue (Straus, Gelles and Steinmetz 1980) it was initially concluded that women were only slightly less likely than men to abuse their partners. However, when the data was reworked to look at severe attacks it concluded that violence by women was defensive rather than offensive and that women resorted to violence when they had been subjected to severe and prolonged attacks over a considerable period (Straus 1983). Kelly (1996) has raised the issue of violence in lesbian couples and she notes that an understanding of this violence 'requires taking account of the context in which lesbian relation-ships exist ...one of marginalisation at best and secrecy and fear at worst' (p.39).

Although there are features common to all violent behaviour within intimate adult relationships, this chapter will focus on the experience of women who have experienced violence from their male partners. Even here there are a whole range of experiences and consequences. Black and minority ethnic women, lesbian and older women, women living in rural areas and women with disabilities face particular difficulties and have specific needs. Mama (1989), for example, argues that the treatment of black women 'epito-mises grudging reluctance and even refusal of British society to meet their basic needs' (p.6). Black women also face the additional pressure of racism from within their own communities. Coerced loyalty and silence about violent partners is one consequence. Another is the fear of adding to racist stereotypes if the abuse is reported to a predominantly white police force. There may also be cultural pressure to stay in the relationship for fear of deportation. Older women too have specific needs. They may have spent years in a violent relationship and might not know where to turn to for help. Shame and fear of change are also factors to be taken into account and there may be additional pressures if a woman is the main carer for a violent partner (NALGO 1991; Hughes and Mtezaka 1992). For lesbian women, their sexuality may have been used by a male partner to 'justify' the abuse and they can have added difficulties in relation to custody if they leave the relationship (Lobel 1986; Cosis Brown 1992).

Whilst it is impossible to make statements which will be universally applicable to all women who experience domestic abuse, what follows is an attempt to alert the reader to some of the issues which may arise at different stages of disclosure of abuse, starting at the point when she acknowledges it and the process of trying to decide what to do next.

The way in which domestic violence is understood is critical in the re-sponse made to it both by agencies and individual helpers. One of the achievements of the women's movement has been the defining of domestic violence as a social problem rather than a phenomena of particular violent individuals or relationships. This has ensured that women who are abused in this way have been supported by organisations such as Women's Aid, Shakti and Southall Black Sisters in having their voices heard. These feminist organisations have provided refuge for women from their violent partners, ongoing support for women and their children and much of the political impetus for changes in the response of police, social work and healthcare agencies to domestic abuse. They have also provided vital research material on which to base their arguments for change.

Smith (1989), in a sobering review of literature relating to agency responses to domestic abuse, suggests that: 'many agencies, including social services departments, branches of the medical profession, local authority housing departments…all point in the same direction – domestic violence is condoned to a certain point…only when violence exceeds the limits (*sic*) does the condemnation become overt' (p.102).

HOW CAN AN ABUSED WOMAN BE IDENTIFIED?

Women who are abused by their partners have many reasons to hide the source of their difficulties. Going public about such a private experience can be harrowing and it may take years for a woman to pluck up the courage to tell someone. Research indicates that the violence may have started soon after the couple started living together and that it has continued for at least four years before a woman decides to tell someone about it. The persons most frequently told about the abuse are members of her family, followed by family doctor and social workers (Pahl 1985; 1995).

There are women who come for help speaking of feeling depressed, of not being able to cope, of having a partner who drinks too much or who is short tempered with herself or her children. Most women who experience domestic abuse feel a very strong sense of shame at what is happening to them. They may play down the abuse or shrug it off in a manner that suggests they are not unduly affected by it. They may present it in this way to gauge the reaction of the helper, to check out his or her views of the situation. Being alert to the possibility of domestic abuse is clearly crucial here and it can be helpful to be aware of some of the signs which may indicate abuse. These can relate to the woman and her description of her partner or her children. They are listed in Table 4.1.

Alongside these indicators is the very real reluctance of a woman to admit to the abuse she is experiencing from her partner. She may blame herself for it and, as a consequence, may experience a sense of hopelessness and low self-confidence. The degree to which a helper can understand and work to alleviate these common responses can have a considerable influence over any decisions which a woman subsequently makes to change her life.

GOOD PRACTICE AT THE POINT OF DISCLOSURE

Recognising signs which indicate that a woman is experiencing abuse from her partner is one thing, responding to them in a way which is valuing of the woman and non-judgementally accepting of her reality is another. It may

Table 4.1: Possible indications of domestic abuse

In a woman

- self-directed abuse
- violent nightmares
- depression
- insomnia
- anxiety
- alcohol or drug abuse
- describes jealous, possessive partner
- defends partner's abusive behaviour
- hit, slapped, punched or kicked by partner
- frightened of partner's behaviour
- minimises injuries received from partner

In a man

- explosive temper
- over-protective
- constantly criticising or denigrating
- jealous
- controlling of partner
- suspicious
- breaks or throws objects when angry
- has hit, slapped or punched partner
- makes all decisions about family matters
- defensive about partner's injuries

In children

- school difficulties
- unexplained injuries
- poor attention span
- somatic or emotional difficulties
- withdrawn
- behavioural problems
- increased fears
- sleep problems
- violent behaviour, especially in boys

seem like an obvious statement to say that the first significant aspect in working with domestic abuse is to believe what a woman is saying. Unless she experiences a sense of acceptance from a helper, she will be unable to talk about the often contradictory emotions she may be feeling and her confusion in relation to them. A helper's response may be determined by his or her own value system and perceptions of women's roles within families. Helpers in all settings are also open to the contradictory messages relating to the privacy of home and family life for adults and the challenging of that privacy when there are questions raised about the protection of children. The consequence for women in violent relationships is that they may experience a greater readiness to be given help and assistance once the break has been made from the family. Only then does there appear to be a greater willingness to define the woman's needs in her own right and to recategorise her as 'deserving'. The situation is neatly summed up by Borowski, Merch and Walker (1983): 'The irony is that privacy contributes to and reinforces the intimacy and sense of solidarity in family life that society values, whilst it also nurtures and protects "the conditions" in which conflicts and violence develop' (p.72).

Clearly, the range of helping agencies and contexts will have different foci for working with women in abusive relationships. Social workers, for example, can provide information on practical matters – legal redress, alternative housing and benefits – yet Smith (1989) summarises the social work response to domestic violence into two main categories: a concern with keeping families together and putting the needs of children first. This was confirmed by Dobash and Dobash (1979) who noted that social workers gave practical assistance on housing and legal issues only when children were perceived to be in physical danger. In this situation women can be caught in a double bind, feeling threatened with the potential loss of their children into care because they do not have adequate or secure accommodation. This threat can, in turn, be enough to make them return to the family home with the possibility of further violence perpetrated on themselves and their children.

It may also be difficult for a helper to see a woman as a person in her own right, separate from her children, if she has them, or from her partner. A further consequence of this is that a woman may not feel she has been believed by the helper or she can experience disapproval or dismissal of her reality. The task here for the helper is to engage in a dialogue of challenge – challenging personal assumptions and values so that there is no possibility of 'accepting some part of the client and not others' (Thorne 1992, p.38). Being aware of personal prejudice is never a 'once-and-for-all' event and none of us are value free. What feels most important, however, in working on issues concerning domestic abuse, is that the helper is constantly checking out the limits of her acceptance. It is put very clearly by Walker (1993) who says: 'I have no desire to turn myself into a politically and therapeutically blank screen. I have to own and acknowledge my own values…however I still have a professional responsibility to ensure that I work with whatever is presented to me' (p.78).

An additional part of acceptance is expressing warmth and this can be conveyed in a host of ways: from the privacy afforded to a woman when she comes for help, rooms which are comfortable and calm in aspect, a place for children to be kept occupied, clarity about what can be offered in terms of time and resources and the limits and code of ethics on issues such as confidentiality. Table 4.2 outlines some basic areas of practice which can contribute to a woman's sense of acceptance at the early stages of talking about what has happened to her.

Table 4.2: Good practice following disclosure of domestic abuse

- Validate a woman's experience by recording violent incidents in casenotes.
- Value a woman's strengths in surviving in the relationship and for protecting her children as best she can.
- Be clear about confidentiality, especially when the work includes child-protection issues.
- Be realistic about the support which can be offered to a woman immediately and in the longer term.
- Do not rush the woman to make any decisions which could have an effect on her immediate safety and that of her children.
- Check out how safe she feels if she is returning to the family home.

PRACTICAL OR EMOTIONAL SUPPORT?

Helpers can respond in a variety of ways to a disclosure of domestic violence but many appear to have no clear idea about the sort of assistance they might give. Maynard (1985), in a study of social work response, for example, reported that little was immediately done to help the woman. A common response was to 'talk about the problem' rather than to give practical assistance or to outline the available options for a woman and her children, irrespective of whether she chose to leave or to remain in the relationship (Lloyd 1995). Maynard also found a significant number of cases where women were blamed for a man's violent behaviour. Her perceived 'failings' were expressed in terms of poor housekeeping and not meeting her partner's sexual demands. These were regarded as 'understandable' reasons for the domestic abuse. Indeed, one casenote quoted in Maynard's study noted: 'it seems her nagging is a trigger for domestic violence' (p.34).

Agencies such as Women's Aid, on the other hand, can provide a range of practical and emotional support and do this from a woman-centred perspective, taking the needs of the woman and her children into account. More general counselling agencies are also more likely to concentrate on emotional support, yet here too there is room for practical information to be held by, and available to, the woman if she seeks it. Whilst it may not be helpful to be prescriptive or to state guidelines for 'good practice' on this issue, there appear to be a number of areas in which all helpers can reflect on the help they give and the context in which it is given. It is important for them to understand the difficult and tentative way in which women begin to come to terms with the fact that they are in an abusive relationship. They often feel an enormous sense of personal failure, they can have fears about 'going public' on a matter of such private personal concern and they can have justifiable fears about their own safety and that of their children. They may also be concerned about the reaction of helpers to a disclosure of domestic abuse. The way in which a woman is interviewed plays an important part here. If she feels that she is believed and responded to in a supportive way, this can facilitate her recovery from the traumatic events which have led her to seek help. Table 4.3 outlines some suggestions which can be employed by helpers in this respect.

Table 4.3: Helping a woman to disclose domestic abuse

- Try to conduct the interview in a quiet, private place away from the violent partner and the family home.
- If the woman's children are present, try to have them looked after while the interview is taking place.
- Be aware that the woman is checking out how safe you are to tell. She has every right to do this.
- Be aware that you may be the first person, particularly the first professional, to acknowledge problems she has experienced.
- If she discloses domestic violence, validate her experiences and the difficulties she now faces.
- Find out if she has any other sources of support, e.g. family, friends, colleagues, and how she plans to use them.
- Ask what she *wants* to do rather than give a view on what you think she *ought* to do. Remember how difficult it is for a woman to leave her home and that she may have taken many years to get to this point.
- Ensure that up to date information on local sources of help, especially Women's Aid and legal help, are available.
- Be prepared for her to return to a partner who is violent; many women make attempts over a number of years to leave before finally doing so.

It is of vital importance for a helper not to collude, or to appear to collude, in any way with the abuse or to minimise its severity or the danger in which the woman may find herself. If that happens, the woman will be unable to trust that helper. If the woman is self-critical or self-blaming, it will also be important for the helper to support the woman in looking at this since it is likely to be a consequence of messages she has received about herself from her partner. Giving her positive messages about herself and acknowledging her courage in coming for help are straightforward but hugely empowering for a woman in this situation. The result of a sustained period of abuse often results in a woman expressing feelings of worthlessness. Helpers are in a key position to help her to rebuild her self-confidence and this can be facilitated by:

- conveying her worth as an individual, along with acknowledging that her needs are as important as anyone else's
- ensuring that she knows that the abuse is not her fault and that she does not deserve to be treated in this way
- reassuring her that it is normal to feel depressed, confused, lethargic or hopeless in her situation
- refusing to collude with the abuse or to minimise its severity or the danger she is in as a result of it.

STAYING, LEAVING AND RETURNING

There has been vigorous debate over the value of a therapeutic response to domestic abuse. Dobash and Dobash (1992) are highly critical of a 'therapeutic society' which focuses on conceiving the problem in terms of 'faulty individual traits and personalities requiring therapy' (p.213). One theoretical perspective which has informed this approach is the theory of 'learned helplessness' (Walker 1984). This concept concentrates on the woman's early background rather than on the perpetrator of the violence, suggesting that, once planted in childhood, the seeds of victimisation take root in her relationships with men. It is argued that women in abusive relationships reinterpret events as a consequence of their failure as partners, becoming more shamed and humiliated with each abusive incident, with silence as their ultimate response. Walker argues that once women perceive themselves to be helpless they start behaving in ways which reinforce that helplessness, passivity and submissiveness. Inevitably, the view of woman here is of helpless and hopeless, held captive by a combination of their psychology and gender socialisation.

Ferraro and Johnson (1982) present an alternative perspective. They argue that women are only ready to leave an abusive relationship when they are psychologically ready to stop minimising or denying the abuse. Once this happens they are ready to choose an alternative to remaining in the relationship. Catalysts which prompt this to happen include: an increase in the severity or frequency of the abuse, the external definition of the problem by an 'outsider' such as a counsellor, healthcare worker or social worker and a change in the woman's available resources which encourages her if she is in the process of leaving a violent partner. Dobash and Dobash (1992) reiterate this point in a summary of the evidence that the most important factors in a woman's efforts to leave an abusive partner are her economic and employment opportunities. Furthermore, they argue that a theory of learned helplessness renders it impossible to tell 'whether a woman suffering from (learned helplessness) finds it impossible to seek help or whether she begins to pursue help and then stops because she suffers from this psychological ailment' (p.227).

They point to the dangers inherent in this static model, suggesting, instead, a dynamic pattern of help seeking. It is argued that women in violent relationships, far from remaining passive, engage in an active process of seeking help, referred to as 'staying, leaving and returning' (Dobash and Dobash 1979). Here it is argued that theories which rely on a partial understanding of women's psychology are rigid in their categorisation, seeing people as either healthy (acting consistently and deliberately) or unhealthy (suffering from a condition which makes it impossible for them to do so). If the latter is the case, it follows that women 'cannot be hesitant, confused or ambivalent. Women either leave or stay. They, like everyone else, cannot engage in diverse even contradictory action' (Dobash and Dobash 1992, p.233).

This has obvious important consequences for helpers who are working with a woman in an abusive relationship and it has implications for the extent to which a helper identifies a woman as a victim or a client 'in need' of therapy. It also has consequences for whether the focus is on her needs or those of her children and for the extent of the woman's accommodation of the abusive behaviour at the expense of herself. If her needs are ignored or minimised, attention is diverted from the root of the problem – the violent partner and the structures which support that behaviour.

Many women return, in the absence of a viable alternative for themselves and their children, to the violence of their home. Others may approach the homelessness section of their local housing department, where the reaction to their situation depends on the availability of resources and the definition of 'unintentionally homeless' adopted by the housing authority. It will be important, therefore, for a woman not to feel that there are expectations of her to behave in a particular way, for her to feel accepted in the difficult territory of negotiating between wanting to leave and making or not making this decision, whilst exploring the potential consequences of all of this for herself and her children. The simple question 'what do you want to happen here?' can help her to focus on her immediate needs and wishes and to work out, with the help of a supportive person, what is possible in the short, medium and long term. She may have a clear or tentative idea of what she ultimately wants for herself and her children and the exploration of her feelings and emotions, as well as a clear idea of what is possible in a practical sense, can be hugely important in helping her to realise these aspirations.

WHAT ABOUT THE CHILDREN?

There are a number of aspects to this issue. First, it is important for helpers to understand and be aware of the ways in which children can be involved in the abuse. Second, they need to have an understanding of its effects on children. Third, they need to be more aware of ways in which women can be supported to care for children who may exhibit a range of disturbed behaviour and they need to challenge within themselves the view that all children who witness violence will themselves become violent in their adult relationships.

What children know and remember about domestic violence varies and, in contrast to adults who have been sexually abused as children, the long-term effects of their experiences are less well documented (Hall and Lloyd 1993). Sometimes children are directly involved in the violence and they can be hurt in trying to protect their mother. Children may be forced to watch or partici-pate in the abuse, they often hear the violence and they can see its effects on their mother. There is no doubt that living in an atmosphere of fear and tension can be damaging for children and this is heightened if they see their mother being beaten or abused in other ways (Women's Support Project 1991). Dobash and Dobash (1979) found that almost half the violent incidents in their study happened in front of observers, more than 60 per cent of whom were children in the care of the couple.

One review of the literature summarised the effects of domestic violence on children (Jaffe, Wolfe and Kaye Wilson 1990). Sleep disturbance, temper tantrums and an inability to concentrate were common. Some children's behaviour fluctuated between extreme passivity and sudden, unprovoked aggression. Others were acutely anxious or guilty about their inability to prevent the abuse. Many also exhibited the watchful behaviour of an abused child or were exhausted from being kept awake at night. Children can also be used by violent partners to control or manipulate women after they have left a violent partner. O'Hara (1993) cites examples of verbal abuse, threats at access visits and even the abduction of children in an effort to force women to return to the relationship. Additionally, children may themselves be subject to abuse. Bowker, Arbitell and McFerron (1988) found that 70 per cent of men who were violent to their partners were also physically violent towards children living in the same house and Morley and Mullender (1994) give figures of between 28 and 70 per cent.

A woman is likely to be only too well aware of the effects of her partner's abusive behaviour on her children and for the helper there are two main tasks. First, it will be important to help her to verbalise this and not to make any suggestion that she should do something 'for the sake of the children'. The consequence of this might be even more guilt on her part if she fails to do so or she may be precipitated into action before she is ready. It can be important to remember that a woman will widen her help-seeking network once she has made the transition from seeking help in trying to make the relationship work to seeking help in ending or leaving it, however long this takes (Bowker, Arbitell and McFerron 1988).

LISTENING TO WOMEN THEMSELVES

'The starting point for any approach to violence against women and children must be the actual experience of women' (NALGO 1991, p.4). The need to ensure that women's voices are heard is supported by research which consistently finds that the majority of violent crimes against women go unreported, especially when the crimes are of a sexually violent nature and/or have been committed by a man known to the woman (Dobash and Dobash 1992). So, it is doubly important that the voice of women who have experienced these gross abuses of trust and power are listened to. They have much to tell agencies and individual helpers about the nature of their experiences and what can be helpful in supporting them as they decide what they are going to do.

At initial contact with a helper, women themselves stress the importance of someone who will listen to them in a non-judgmental way, someone who will not force them to make decisions which they are not ready to make and who will understand the difficulties of going public on such a private affair (Dobash and Dobash 1992). Later, they emphasise the importance of having up-to-date, accurate information, help with finding accommodation and learning about a refuge. Further on, they use helpers for support in making a new life and coping as a single parent. The most consistently valued support after leaving an abusive partner is advising on available services, having knowledge of relevant legislation and, where appropriate, negotiating with other agencies. Women's Aid is one of the most important agencies at this stage, along with social services and housing departments. Women's Aid recognises, however, that it can only meet a fraction of the needs of abused women and their children. They are also the 'expert voice' in the field of domestic violence, yet are frequently marginalised and ignored by other helping agencies. This is well evidenced by the consistently low, intermittent or irregular level of funding for Women's Aid groups.

GENDER ISSUES IN WORKING WITH DOMESTIC ABUSE

The question of who works with violent men and women who have been subject to their violence remains a topic for debate (Beagley 1987). On one hand, it is argued, only male workers can truly understand men who are violent. The counter-argument demands proof that men can be entrusted with this responsibility. There are also issues relating to the collusion of men with each other, however inadvertently, in domestic violence work. It has, therefore, been suggested that, especially for programmes involving violent men, good practice entails women and men working together to provide a positive role model. This is an obvious area where training can be of great use. A related concern is the funding of programmes for violent men and for the support of women abused by them. There may be a risk that the former will drain resources from the already limited amount of financial assistance for women who have been abused by their partners.

CONCLUSIONS

There is much that helpers can do to support women who are being abused by their partners. Good practice in relation to the issues outlined in this chapter can be summarised under three main headings:

1. *Respecting the woman's account:* a woman may give partial, confused or contradictory accounts of what is happening to her. If she admits to abuse by a partner, she is likely to feel distressed and ashamed. Remember that a woman will be reluctant to admit the cause of her distress or physical injuries unless she is confident that she will be met empathically and with an acceptance of her on the part of the helper.

2. *Knowing relevant information:* if it is not in the remit of the agency to give information, it should at least be available in leaflet form for her to take away or to consult in a safe environment. If it is possible to give this material, legal, financial, housing and practical information will be most helpful.

3. *Time:* working towards an outcome which feels good for a woman and her children may take a long time. It is important that she does not feel rushed into any major decision and that she feels supported in the decisions which she does make, even if these include returning to the relationship with an abusive partner.

It may be that many more women than in the past are now leaving violent relationships simply because of the publicity given to the issue by the media, public awareness campaigns such as Zero Tolerance (Kitzinger and Hunt, 1994) and a greater knowledge of the help available to them. The final word must rest with an acknowledgement that women who have experienced domestic abuse or are still living in an abusive relationship are indeed survivors with undoubted strengths and resourcefulness, some of which have become temporarily diminished by their situation.

REFERENCES

Beagley, J. (1987) 'Does gender illuminate your practice?' *Social Work Today*, 16 February.

Borowski, M., Merch, M. and Walker, V. (1983) *Community Response to Marital Violence*. London: Tavistock.

Bowker, L., Arbitell, M. and McFerron, J. (1988) 'On the relationship between wife beating and child abuse.' In K. Yollo and M. Bogard (eds) *Feminist Perspectives on Wife Abuse*. Beverly Hills: Sage.

Cosis Brown, H. (1992) 'Lesbians, the state and social work practice.' In M. Langan, and L. Day (1992) *Women, Oppression and Social Work*. London: Routledge.

Dobash, R.E. and Dobash, R. (1979) *Violence Against Wives: A Case Against the Patriarchy*. Shepton Mallett: Open Books.

Dobash, R.E. and Dobash, R.P. (1992) *Women, Violence and Social Change*. London: Routledge.

Ferraro, K.J. and Johnson, J.M. (1982) 'How women experience battering: the process of victimisation.' *Social Problems 30*, 3, 325–339.

Hall, L. and Lloyd, S. (1993) *Surviving Child Sexual Abuse*. Basingstoke: The Falmer Press.

Hughes, B. and Mtezaka, M. (1992) 'Social work and older women: where have the older women gone?' In M. Langan and L. Day (eds) *Women, Oppression and Social Work*. London: Routledge.

Jaffe, P., Wolfe, D. and Kaye Wilson, S. (1990) *Children of Battered Women*. New York: Sage.

Kelly, L. (1996) 'Feminist perspectives on violence by women.' In M. Hester, L. Kelly and J. Radford (eds) *Women, Violence and Male Power*. Buckingham: Open University Press.

Kitzinger, J. and Hunt, K. (1994) *Evaluation of Edinburgh District Council's Zero Tolerance Campaign. The Full Report*. Edinburgh: Edinburgh District Council.

Lloyd, S. (1995) 'Social Work and domestic violence.' In P. Kingston and B. Penhale (eds) *Family Violence and the Caring Professions*. London: Macmillan.

Lobel, K. (1986) *Naming the Violence – Speaking Out About Lesbian Battering*. New York: Seal Press.

Mackay, A. and Macgregor, L. (1994) *Hit or Miss. An Exploratory Study of the Provision for Women Subjected to Domestic Violence in Tayside Region*. Dundee: Tayside Regional Council.

Mama, A. (1989) *The Hidden Struggle: Statutory and Voluntary Sector Responses to Violence Against Black Women in the Home*. London: Runnymede Trust.

Maynard, M. (1985) 'The response of social workers to domestic violence.' In J. Pahl (ed) *Private Violence and Public Policy*. London: Routledge and Kegan Paul.

Morley, R. and Mullender, A. (1994) 'Domestic violence and children: what do we know from research?' In R. Morley and A. Mullender (eds) *Children Living with Domestic Violence. Putting Men's Abuse of Women on the Child Care Agenda*. London: Whiting and Birch.

NALGO (1991) *Responding with Authority. Local Authority Initiatives to Counter Violence Against Women*. London: National Association of Local Government Women's Committees.

O'Hara, M. (1993) 'Fistful of power,' *Social Work Today*, 4 February, 8–10.

Pahl, J. (ed) (1985) *Private Violence and Public Policy*. London: Routledge and Kegan Paul.

Pahl, J. (1995) 'Health professionals and violence against women.' In P. Kingston and B. Penhale (eds) *Family Violence and the Caring Professions*. London: Macmillan.

Smith, L. (1989) *Domestic Violence: An Overview of the Literature*. Home Office Research Study 107. London: HMSO.

Straus, M.A. (1983) 'Ordinary violence, child abuse and wife-beating: what do they have in common?' In D. Finkelhor *et al.* (eds) *The Dark Side of Families*. Beverly Hills: Sage.

Straus, M.A., Gelles, R.A. and Steinmetz, S.K. (1980) *Behind Closed Doors: Violence in the American Family*. New York: Anchor Books.

Thorne, B. (1992) *Carl Rogers*. London: Sage.

Walker, L.E. (1984) *The Battered Woman Syndrome*. New York: Springer.

Walker, M. (1993) 'When values clash.' In W. Dryden (ed) *Questions and Answers in Counselling in Action*. London: Sage.

Women's Support Project (1991) *Leaving an Abusive Relationship*. Glasgow: Women's Support Project.

CHAPTER 5

Therapeutic Responses to People with Learning Disabilities Who Have Been Abused

Janet Hughes and Nerys Hughes

INTRODUCTION

In this chapter we aim to give a general overview of good practice in working with people with learning disabilities who have experienced abuse. We will examine issues relevant to frontline staff who are in a supportive or caring role, to those offering formally structured counselling and therapy, and to those involved in overall care planning and the purchasing of services. Much current thinking about the emotional needs of individuals who have experienced abuse will, of course, apply equally to people with learning disabilities. However, this chapter will look at the particular issues faced by people with learning disabilities and how these inform good practice.

WHAT DO WE MEAN BY LEARNING DISABILITY?

People with learning disabilities are individuals with wide-ranging needs and abilities. Formal definition of Learning Disability is usually made by intelligence quotient and the bands of ability commonly recognised in the United Kingdom are: Profound learning disability (I.Q. 0–20), Severe learning disability (1.Q. 20–50) and Mild learning disability (I.Q. 50–70).

However, the way in which a person presents and functions socially can fluctuate over time and will depend not only on their intellectual ability but also on the response of others to their special needs, the opportunities for development which they have received, their own emotional response to their disability and the quality of their relationships.

The capacity of people with learning disabilities to benefit from therapeutic help is often questioned. Yet an ability to show and express feelings and to pick up on the feelings of others is key to the use of therapeutic help and this is not directly related to intellectual ability.

We have been able to offer direct counselling/therapy across the range of mild and severe learning disability, whilst our work with people with profound learning disability has been mainly indirect, through supporting key-workers.

VULNERABILITY TO ABUSE

People with learning disabilities are vulnerable to sexual, physical and emotional abuse, teasing and bullying, deprivation and neglect. There has been some increase in awareness of this in recent years, with a particular focus on sexual abuse. The high incidence of sexual abuse amongst people with learning disabilities has been confirmed by research based on a survey of all new cases and allegations of sexual abuse occurring in the South East Thames Regional Health Authority in 1989/1990 (Turk and Brown 1993). The findings, based only on those cases where there was a high degree of certainty that abuse had taken place, suggests that there will be almost 950 new cases reported each year in the United Kingdom.

It is important to be aware of the factors which may make people with learning disabilities vulnerable to abuse as this can help us to think about preventative and protective measures. These include:

- People with learning disabilities have an extended period of dependence on family and/or carers, which continues well into adulthood and will probably be life-long.
- They may be dependent on others for assistance with intimate physical care – this may lead to confusion about appropriate boundaries of touch and leave them open to sexual exploitation.
- They may be encouraged to be physically close to carers beyond the appropriate stage of development and this can lead to confusion about sexual feelings in adolescence. A tendency to kiss and hug strangers and acquaintances may be indulged and seen as part of a 'loving' nature, whereas this behaviour can put them at risk.
- They may often need to set aside their own needs and preferences in order to fit in with those whose approval is essential for their survival and well-being – in other words, they learn to be compliant.
- Traditionally, this group of people has had relatively little practice in making choices and decisions in their everyday lives. Their relative lack of knowledge of life can make them vulnerable to all sorts of exploitation. In particular, lack of sexual knowledge and understanding of their own sexuality can increase their vulnerability to sexual abuse.
- Through the use of daycare, residential, respite and leisure services they are likely to be involved with large numbers of changing carers, who could potentially exploit them. There may be nobody they can trust enough to tell about any ill-treatment.
- Abuse by a carer can easily remain hidden because of the victim's fear of the repercussions of disclosure and/or communication difficulties.
- Misconceptions about people with learning disabilities can make it more possible to abuse them, for example the belief that they are insensitive to pain and ill-treatment or that nobody would abuse a child or adult with a disability. The media often suggests that it would be better to abort a foetus where there is a possibility of handicap. This assumption devalues people with disabilities. Where

a foetus is diagnosed as having a physical or learning disability, termination of the pregnancy is now legal, right up to the moment of birth.

- The legal system, as it currently operates, does not serve people with learning disabilities well. They are seen as unreliable witnesses and very few cases of abuse against them have ever been brought to the courts.

AN INTEGRATED ECOLOGICAL MODEL OF ABUSE

Sobsey (1984) has developed an integrated ecological model of abuse, showing the context in which abuse against people with disabilities arises. The model provides a framework for considering how environmental and cultural factors impact upon the physical and psychological aspects of the interacting individuals (potential offender and potential victim). It moves away from a model of blaming the victim, in which people with disabilities are seen as causing stress, which produces abuse. The model acknowledges the contribution of external factors, such as attitudes within society towards disability, as well as internal factors, such as an individual's emotional security and vulnerability. It indicates a need for a broad response to the problem of abuse against people with learning disabilities, involving public education, changes in the law and increased educational and developmental opportunities for people with learning disabilities. A further implication of the model is that different modes of therapeutic intervention – such as individual work, family work, group work, work with staff teams and support networks – should be considered. Group work with people with learning disabilities can help to develop an awareness of environmental and societal responses to them as a group. Through meeting other survivors of abuse they can increase their knowledge about the prevalence of abuse and this can enable them to move on from a position of self-blame.

IMMEDIATE RESPONSE TO DISCLOSURE OF ABUSE

All too frequently allegations of abuse against people with learning disabilities are not taken seriously or the response is confused and ineffective. Frontline workers may feel unsupported by their organisation and unsure how to proceed, particularly if the allegation involves a colleague.

It is essential that each locality has well-thought-out policies and procedures which have inter-agency agreement. It is the responsibility of social service departments, as the lead authority for learning disability, to make sure that this happens. It is primarily a managerial responsibility to ensure that procedures are in place locally, that staff are familiar with procedures and that they have the necessary training and support to put them into practice. However, it is good practice for staff to bring any deficiencies in the system to their manager's attention.

The importance of attending to the survivor's emotional needs should be highlighted in any procedural guidelines. Above all, the survivor needs to have his or her experience validated and feelings acknowledged. Even communications which seem odd or bizarre should be carefully considered and consultation sought.

Survivors with learning disabilities have a right to justice through the courts and should be informed of this option and helped to pursue it, if they wish. Care should be taken to preserve any evidence to maximise the possibility of a successful prosecution. Being supported to make a formal statement to the police or recording a statement on tape or on video may be an important act of recognition for some individuals, even when a conviction is not achieved.

To meet the fundamental requirements for recovery, the survivor needs to be in a safe place and to be sure that the abuse has stopped. There are particular difficulties in ensuring that this happens for people with learning disabilities. First, because successful prosecutions are rare, the abuser is more likely to be seen in the community. Further, when the perpetrator is another service user, it will take great commitment to ensure that the victim does not come into contact with the abuser within the service network.

Placement issues require careful consideration. The victim may need to be moved from an abusive environment but, first, consideration should be given to moving the perpetrator if the survivor's needs for safety can be met in this way.

REFERRALS FOR INDIVIDUAL COUNSELLING/THERAPY

It can be difficult to locate a counsellor who feels able to work with people with learning disabilities. There may be a counsellor, or a professional with a counselling role, within local specialist services, such as a social worker or member of a multidisciplinary team, who can provide counselling as part of a co-ordinated response to the client's needs. Sometimes there is nobody available within the statutory services and it may be necessary to refer on to a voluntary agency, independent counsellor or therapist.

It is good practice not to assume that everyone who experiences an abusive incident needs ongoing therapeutic help, particularly if they are properly supported at the time of the incident. Some survivors may value the opportunity to have a private space to share their feelings and reflect on their experiences. This can develop self-esteem and prevent reabuse. Counselling and therapy are particularly indicated where a victim of abuse has become traumatised and is experiencing serious emotional difficulties. This is more likely to occur when hurt has not been recognised or there have been repeated experiences of abuse, separation and loss which have not been acknowledged or addressed.

The main purpose of structured therapeutic work is to provide a boundaried space in which feelings and experiences can be explored. In particular, the containing nature of the therapeutic relationship can help an individual to make sense of feelings previously experienced as intolerable and unbearable. Over time, the painful feelings associated with abusive experiences can become both less predominant and less self-destructive, so that the individual can live with these feelings and make use of the positive and nurturing aspects of relationships available.

There are a number of issues to be considered at the point of referral. It would, perhaps, seem empowering of people with learning disabilities to insist that their counselling sessions are completely private and separate from the rest of their lives. However, it is rare that a person with a learning disability makes a self-referral – their sessions are often funded by a third party and, because of their relatively dependent position, they often need the support of others in their network to engage in counselling. It is vital to pay attention to the context in which the referral arises, to consider whether the client wants to engage in counselling and whether the necessary back-up will be available.

Referrers should provide basic information about the client before counselling starts, so that the appropriateness of the referral can be assessed, the client's needs can be planned for and any materials or resources which might be useful for the first meeting can be organised in advance. It is useful to know:

- what has led to referral at this particular time
- what are the referrer's concerns and what seem to be the client's concerns
- whether the client appears to be experiencing distress and how he or she is showing this
- specific details of any challenging behaviour
- to what extent the client is concerned about his or her emotional state
- what has been said about the referral and the perceived understanding of this.

It is useful to have some sense of a person's history before he or she comes for counselling, particularly relating to significant relationships, past and present, and experiences of abuse, separation and loss. It is more common for clients to have experienced several traumatic events, although a specific event may act as a trigger for referral. It is essential to consider the client's needs in the context of his or her whole life experience, particularly as a traumatic event can evoke feelings associated with past separations and losses. Although there is sometimes pressure to consider clients for short-term counselling, the continuity of a long-term relationship is usually needed for such work. It is important to discuss the possible duration of counselling with funders at the outset as a counselling relationship which is brought to an end too soon or too suddenly can be another experience of loss for the client.

Clear agreements need to be made between counsellors, referrers and funders, particularly in relation to confidentiality and risk. Confidentiality is fundamental to ethical counselling practice and a key ingredient of an effective working alliance with the client. At the same time, because of the relative dependence and vulnerability of the client group, there is a need to liaise with other workers where there is a risk of harm to the client or others. These conflicting needs can be difficult to balance. Having a contract which includes any agreements relating to confidentiality and risk, funding, escorting, timing and duration of counselling, arrangements for cancellations and bringing the counselling to an end, will help prevent the work with the client being jeopardised.

Referrers need to suggest counselling to the client in the context of concern, as something which may help, building on their own experience of the client and his or her needs. For example, if a client is showing distress, counselling can be described as an opportunity to get help with difficult feelings. It is important not to give the impression that the client must talk about what happened to him. The client will need time to build up trust and get a sense of how he or she wants to use the counselling space. It should be emphasised that clients have a choice about coming for counselling and they may need the experience of a few sessions before they can decide. The counsellor may need to be alert to some of the non-verbal signs of engagement described below.

Counselling and therapy can, initially, stir up very strong feelings and this will place demands on carers. It may be helpful for a separate professional – for example a different member of the multidisciplinary team – to offer consultation and support to a carer or keyworker.

Clients who cannot make the journey to their counselling sessions on their own will need a sensitive escort, preferably someone consistent or from their known staff group. It is important that the escort can be supportive without being intrusive and allow the client some space around the session. They should not, for example, suggest topics for discussion or enquire about the session afterwards.

ASSESSMENT AND INITIAL CONTACT

The client may find it helpful to have a trusted keyworker/social worker present for an initial introductory session. This can be a way of ensuring that, as far as possible, referral information is shared between all parties. When a client has limited or no verbal communication, the counsellor will be able to observe how the worker and client communicate with each other and the worker can explain the particular meaning of any words, signs or vocalisations which the client commonly uses. Some clients use Makaton, a signing system which is used both as communication and to support speech development. They may use few signs and use them idiosyncratically, so it really does help at this early stage to have them explained.

The assessment period helps to establish whether counsellor and client are able to engage with each other and this may take several weeks. Some clients are able to establish a working alliance using mainly words. Others will demonstrate non-verbal signs of engagement, such as good eye contact, a readiness to come into the counselling room, an interest in the objects in the room, being able to concentrate for short periods and a sense of relief at feeling understood. Some clients may only be able to stay in the room for a limited time at first.

In making an assessment, counsellors should also use their awareness of the emotional tone of the session(s) and their own feelings about the client, experienced in the countertransference. Counselling supervision to help reflect on the process is vital for ethical and effective counselling practice.

COUNSELLING APPROACHES

Different models of counselling/therapy have been used effectively with people with learning disabilities – see, for example, Valerie Sinason (1992) on psychoanalytic psychotherapy, Joanna Beazley-Richards on transactional analysis (Waitman and Conboy-Hill 1992) and Anna Chesner on dramatherapy (Chesner 1995). It is important that an individual counsellor's approach is consistent with his or her own theoretical understanding and supported by relevant training and supervision. Some of the ideas and approaches which we have found useful are as follows.

The setting and boundaries of the therapeutic space are important in providing a containing structure in which thought can occur. Regular weekly sessions which take place at the same time each week and are of the same duration are recommended for this reason. Some clients who have severe learning disabilities and who are thought not to be able to tell the time have very quickly known when it is time to start and end a session by looking at the shape the hands make on the clock. People with learning disabilities are as likely as any other client in counselling to feel the impact of disturbances and changes to the counselling setting and we would recommend as stable and consistent a setting as possible.

In therapeutic work with people with learning disabilities it is crucial to bear in mind the impact of the external circumstances of their lives on their internal world and emotional well-being. Many clients are referred because of a known or suspected history of sexual abuse. It often emerges in counselling that they are experiencing other forms of abuse and discrimination, that they are aware of being denied opportunities and of being socially and financially at a disadvantage. Having a learning disability and the experience of being different can be central to their distress. Some clients have a sense of being a source of grief and disappointment to those closest to them.

Attachment theory and its implications

Attachment theory can be helpful in thinking about the emotional impact of the conditions in which people live and are cared for. John Bowlby (1988) recognised the central importance for human beings of an emotional 'secure base' which provides care, comfort and security over a period of time. The growing child, adolescent and/or young adult is able to explore at a greater distance from this base, knowing that he or she can return at times of crisis, illness or insecurity for support and care. Bowlby (1979) points out that the presence of primary relationships remains significant throughout life and draws attention to the way in which the pattern and quality of adult relationships can be influenced by early relationships. In the 1960s James and Joyce Robertson (1989), following on from Bowlby, researched the emotional impact on young children of a separation from their parents and made some observational films which have been very influential. They highlight the importance of a sensitive, personal carer who the child can relate to as a parent substitute. Children who are cared for in institutional settings, such as a more impersonal nursery where there are multiple and changing carers, can become increasingly less able to cope with the separation and more prone to feelings of depression and, eventually, despair, with greater risk of long-term difficulties. (Robertson and Robertson 1989)

These ideas have had a great influence on mainstream childcare practices and it came to be generally accepted that substitute family care is preferable to institutional care during a period of separation. Services for children with disabilities, however, have tended to lag behind, with institutional care still being much more usual. There have been some pockets of good practice over the last twenty years and the 1989 Children Act, which, for the first time, includes children with disabilities in mainstream legislation, has given an added impetus to service developments which recognise the emotional needs of children with disabilities. There has been an increase in family-based respite care schemes, which provide a more developmentally appropriate experience of being away from home. However, children and adults with disabilities are still often placed in strange situations without adequate thought or preparation. In our experience this is more likely to happen to children and adults who have profound and multiple disabilities and we have found that the severe distress which can be caused by sudden changes in the environment is not always acknowledged.

Bowlby (1988) applied attachment theory to his clinical practice, seeing the therapist as a 'trusted companion' who provides a 'secure base from which the patient can explore the various painful aspects of his life, past and present.' (p.138). The therapeutic relationship provides an opportunity to explore separation and loss, for example through the counsellor's holiday breaks, but this time with the possibility of acknowledging the pain experienced. Clients may be able to get in touch with the painful reality of the losses in their lives, be it experiencing abuse, having a learning disability or actual separation and bereavement, and this allows them to go through the healing process of mourning.

Bion's ideas about containment

Bion's (1959) idea of the analyst as a 'container' for the intolerable feelings of the patient is helpful in thinking about the process of work with people who have learning disabilities. Just as the mother is able to be in touch with the frightening experiences of the infant and think about them and return them in a more manageable form, so the counsellor can think about the client's unbearable and intolerable feelings, process them and return them in a modulated form. Gradually, the individual becomes more able to think and, eventually, to make sense of feelings and experiences which have previously been felt to be overwhelming. As Sinason (1992) points out, containment is a crucial component of therapy with people with learning disabilities: being able to bear the client's grief and anger and being able to make use of feelings experienced in the countertransference is vital to work with clients who are non-verbal or have limited verbal ability. The process of containment does not require the client to be able to give a verbal account of past or current events and experiences or to be able to make cognitive links between the past and the present.

Secondary Handicap

Valerie Sinason, a psychoanalytic psychotherapist who has worked extensively with people with learning disabilities, has developed the idea of
Secondary Handicap. She sees this as a psychological response to the original
disability and the experience of unfavourable difference, involving an exag-
geration of the disability and a cutting off from the intelligence available. This
can be seen when people with learning disabilities sometimes diminish
themselves in order to keep the approval of those around them. One version
of this is the 'handicapped smile', where the person appears constantly happy,
seemingly unaware of any other feelings. A secondary handicap can also
develop in relation to trauma, where an individual exaggerates his or her
handicap as a way of defending against the painful feelings relating to trauma
and loss.

It is crucial in counselling to be open to the meaning of the clients'
presentation and, above all, to be willing to face with them the pain of their
disability. The concept of Secondary Handicap also reminds counsellors of the
need to be open about the range of a client's abilities, the potential which may
emerge in counselling and the many different ways in which a client can be
contacted. Clients' understanding can fluctuate within sessions according to
their emotional state and it is important in preparing for a session to bear this
range of functioning in mind.

Communication and the process of attunement

Anxiety about understanding a client and being understood can be disabling.
Clearly, information about any special needs must be sought on referral.
However, the demonstration of the desire to understand, through active
listening and attention to non-verbal as well verbal communication, can be as
important as actual understanding. It may be the client's everyday experience
that he or she is not understood and counselling may be the first time this is
openly acknowledged. Through sustained attempts to communicate, clients'
communication will sometimes improve. They may, for example, acquire a
vocabulary for feelings, through the counsellor's naming of their feelings.
Stern (1985) has observed in great detail the interactive nature of communication between infants and their carers, describing a process of non-verbal
attunement which remains part of human communication throughout life.
Stern observes how the mother responds to her infant's non-verbal communications at a feeling level, sometimes non-verbally, more often verbally, not
imitating the infants behaviours exactly but building on or amplifying them,
conveying a sense that feelings are shareable and that reciprocity is possible.
This process of attunement can be significant in any counselling relationship
and will be particularly important when working with non-verbal clients.

It is important to make use of a client's receptive language in counselling
as this may well be more developed than his or her use of spoken language.
Counsellors can use words to show that they are attentive and noticing the
use that the client is making of materials in the room to communicate with
the counsellor. Counsellors can wonder out loud about what the clients are
presenting non-verbally, for example, if they are showing anger through their
facial expression, posture or actions, the counsellor can share that observation

with the client. This can encourage the client's ability to think about his or her experience in the session. It is crucial when working in this way not to be dogmatic or intrusive and to be open to the client's response. Story-telling can also be used to expand and build on what the client brings – for example if the client mentions Cinderella, telling the client the story of Cinderella or parts of it, tuning in to his or her feelings and concerns.

When working with people with fewer verbal skills, it is useful to provide a range of materials for use in the session. These can include drawing materials, plasticine, doll families, soft toys, trucks, cars and mechanical vehicles, hard and soft balls, fabrics and pebbles and a dolls house with small figures and furniture. The materials provided are used very differently by individuals, and, indeed, by the same individuals over time, and can be used to enact an internal or actual experience. Sometimes it is useful to adopt the child-psychotherapy practice of providing a client with his or her own box or drawer of materials which is kept for the sessions.

The client may need to talk about what happened to them, or reveal this in some way in therapy. Sharing a shameful secret, if and when the client is ready, can bring relief and is one way of accessing feelings and re-evaluating experiences. However, the counselling should not be led by the worker's anxiety to 'know what happened'. This anxiety needs to be contained outside the session in supervision. Anne Alvarez (1992), writing about psychotherapeutic work with severely deprived and abused children, makes the point that the thinking about and telling of a narrative needs a great deal of emotional integration. An individual may need to explore different aspects of emotional experience connected with abusive experiences in a variety of ways without an over-eager worker making direct references and connections to the client about abusive experiences.

Clients with limited speech may bring their own material concretely to sessions. This may involve important objects, such as books, dolls, teddies, tapes and photographs. Whilst it can be useful to think about the transferential aspects of bringing this material at that time, as we would with any other material, for example a verbal communication or dream, it is important to respect and think about the particular meaning of this material to the individual. Sometimes, characters in films, television soap operas or stories can be significant in clients' internal emotional world, particularly where they have limited role models and relationship experiences in actual life. They may bring these fictional characters to counselling in the way that another client may bring partners, friends or colleagues and it is important not to dismiss these communications as social chit-chat.

WHAT IS HELPFUL IN THE RESIDENTIAL SETTING

Any person with learning disabilities needs and deserves to be cared for in a sensitive and thoughtful way in an environment where their individuality is respected. This will be particularly important for someone who has been traumatised by abuse. Good basic care provides the foundation for therapeutic work. It may take time before the survivor can start to feel safe. This will

be particularly so where emotional, physical or sexual abuse has been perpetrated in the guise of friendship.

Any kind of abuse involves a breaking of boundaries and staff will best
help the client deal with the resulting confusion by being absolutely clear
about the boundaries of their own role and relationship with the client. Clients
may need to learn, or relearn, that their body is private and it will be important
to demonstrate the need for privacy, for example by knocking before entering
a resident's room and not entering if they are half-dressed.

Residents with profound learning disabilities, or multiple disabilities, may
need a high level of physical care, including intimate care. Careful consideration should be given as to how care can be offered in the least intrusive way,
respecting privacy and choice as much as possible. People with profound
learning disabilities experience the world, to a large extent, through the
quality of the physical care which they receive. Delivering care in a respectful
and nurturing way can enable residents to take in a sense of their own value
and they may begin to recognise that they are in a safe environment.

People with learning disabilities, especially those with limited verbal
communication, may find it difficult to articulate their distress. They may
become withdrawn, seem to lose some of their abilities, self-harm or become
physically violent towards others or the environment, including their own
possessions. Where the experience of abuse has been internalised, a person
can feel self-destructive and, in this state of mind, be unable to make use of
comfort and support and sabotage any help offered. Some survivors who have
been moved from an abusive environment, especially if they have been
abused by a carer, may need time to build up trust and may not be able to
respond immediately to positive experiences.

Where the residents express their distress through extremely challenging
behaviours, it is clearly paramount to seek ways to contain and manage the
behaviour, for the safety of the client, other service users and staff. However,
it is equally important to give careful thought to the meaning of the behaviour.
The worker who is able to think about and comment on the anger and distress
being expressed may offer the resident the first indication that there is some
meaning in the experience, that the feelings are understandable and that they
can be thought about and contained. Gradually, in a sensitive environment,
individuals can grow to recognise feelings for themselves and communicate
these differently.

DEMANDS ON STAFF AND THEIR SUPPORT NEEDS

Working with people who present with profound emotional difficulties and
behavioural challenges is emotionally draining, at times, for those staff members who can bear to know about their client's difficult feelings. Staff may
experience long periods when they feel they are getting no positive response.
It is common for staff working with this degree of trauma to pick up feelings
of despair, vulnerability, powerlessness and uselessness from the client.
Skilled support, supervision and consultation is needed in order to help staff
think about and understand their feelings in relation to the client and to enable
them to continue to function in a professional role with a greater sense of

perspective. Distancing from feelings is sometimes viewed as professional but we consider that staff need to experience and reflect on their feelings in order to be able to help their clients.

Sometimes, therapeutic help is best offered in conjunction with carers. Clients who are very fragile, extremely withdrawn or in a dissociative state may not have sufficient basic trust to engage in structured therapy. We have found that in these circumstances a counsellor can fruitfully work with a client alongside a keyworker, helping them to think about what is going on for the client or, alternatively, offer consultation on a regular basis to a keyworker who is supporting the client.

SUMMARY

The dependent position of people with learning disabilities, the culture of compliance, devaluing attitudes in society towards them and their increased exposure to experiences of unexplained separation and loss compound the trauma of abuse. A broad response to the high incidence of abuse against this client group, which takes account of sociopolitical as well as interpersonal and intrapersonal factors, is vital. Where an individual is traumatised by the experience of abuse, a long-term relational therapy, which can provide containment, is recommended. A range of materials should be available which can facilitate communication between the client and counsellor. However, the process of containment does not depend on the client being able to give an account of events. It is essential that the counsellor is able to bear the client's feelings, however painful these may be, and be open to the possibility that having a learning disability and the experience of unfavourable difference may be central to the client's distress.

REFERENCES

Alvarez, A. (1992) *Live Company, Psychoanalytic Psychotherapy with Autistic, Borderline, Deprived and Abused Children.* London: Routledge.

Chesner, A. (1995) *Dramatherapy for People with Learning Disabilities: A World of Difference.* London: Jessica Kingsley Publishers.

Bion, W. (1959) 'Attacks on linking.' In Bott Spillius, E. (ed) (1988) *Melanie Klein Today, Part 2.* London: Routledge.

Bowlby, J. (1979) *The Making and Breaking of Affectional Bonds.* London: Routledge.

Bowlby, J. (1988) *A Secure Base: Parent–Child Attachment and Healthy Human Development.* New York: Basic Books.

Robertson, J. and Robertson, J. (1989) *Separation and the Very Young.* London: Free Association Books.

Sinason, V. (1992) *Mental Handicap and the Human Condition: New Approaches from the Tavistock.* London: Free Association Books.

Sobsey, D. (1994) *Violence and Abuse in the Lives of People with Disabilities.* Baltimore, MD: Paul H Brookes.

Stern, D. (1985) 'Affect Attunement.' In Coll, Galensan and Tyson (eds) *Frontiers of Infant Psychiatry, Vol.2.* New York: Basic Books.

Turk, V. and Brown, H. (1993) 'The sexual abuse of adults with learning
disabilities: results of a two year incidence survey.' *Mental Handicap Research 6*,
3, 193–216.

Waitman, A. and Conboy-Hill, S. (1992) *Psychotherapy and Mental Handicap*.
London: Sage.

RESOURCES

British Institute of Learning Disabilities (BILD)
Wolverhampton Road,
Kidderminster Road,
Worcestershire,
DY10 3PP
Tel 01562 850251

Multidisciplinary organisation producing quarterly journal. BILD has a library of resources in the form of books, training packages and videos and provides training.

The National Association for the Protection from Sexual Abuse of Adults and Children with Learning Disabilities (NAPSAC)
Department of Learning Disabilities,
Floor E. South Block,
University Hospital,
Nottingham NG7 2UH
Tel 0115 9709987

NAPSAC, and the Association for Residential Care, have produced comprehensive policy and procedural guidelines specifically relating to sexual abuse. NAPSAC provides training and consultancy and is a useful forum for networking with other workers.

RESPOND
3rd Floor,
24–32 Stephenson Way,
London, NW1 2HD
Tel. 0171–383 0700

Provides individual and group therapy for survivors of sexual abuse and sexual offenders who have learning disabilities. Provides training.

Royal Society For Mentally Handicapped Children And Adults (MENCAP)
123 Golden Lane, London, EC1 ORT
Tel 0171–454 0454
Provides information and advice and in some areas local support.

Tavistock Voice
Christiana Horrocks,
P.O. Box 238
Derby DE1 9JN
Tel. 01332 519872

Offers help to adults with learning disabilities who have been abused, their families, friends and advocates. Campaigns for changes in practices and in the law.

Local multidisciplinary teams for people with learning disabilities

These may provide counselling or other relevant services such psychiatry, psychology or social work.

CHAPTER 6

Counselling Survivors of Ritual Abuse

Sara Scott

Survivors of ritual abuse are only just beginning to talk about their experiences. Those who have sought counselling and support over the last few years have done so with trepidation, uncertain whether their experiences would be validated or denied. Most people currently working around the subject of ritual abuse acknowledge that they have learned most of what they know from survivors themselves and that the learning has not always been easy.

Given that the existence of ritual abuse is still widely disputed, it is not surprising that there is no commonly accepted definition of such abuse. In this chapter I am using the term to refer to abuse which is highly organised, involves a group of perpetrators, combines physical, emotional and sexual abuse and is supported by a religious or occult ideology. The abusive practices and ideology find simultaneous expression in abusive rituals. At the simplest level, what sets ritual abuse survivors apart from other survivors of trauma is the sheer extent of the torture and abuse they have endured. This chapter is intended as an exploration of the implications of the 'difference' of ritual abuse for counselling practice.

I am not writing from a lofty height of expertise but rather from personal experience of successes and mistakes – my own and those of other supporters and survivors. It is written in order to share some of the insights that have been gained and to encourage people new to such work to make sense of the difficulties they experience within a broad social context. There is no 'how-to' kit on counselling survivors of ritual abuse (I am generally suspicious of step-by-step programmes for 'fixing' people). However, while I am aware that any discussions of good practice tend to generalise and simplify the complexity of individual counselling encounters, they can also be enormously encouraging and validating.

I have been a Rape Crisis counsellor for the past 13 years. Eight years ago I started working with a young woman in her early teens seeking support to stop her father's sexual abuse. She was adamant that she would not allow any social service or police involvement and was careful to give no information that would facilitate such intervention. Very gradually, as trust developed, she began to disclose the extent of her abuse. She told of her prostitution within a paedophile group, her involvement in child pornography and the ritual abuse she had suffered within what she described as a 'Satanic cult'.

What I remember most vividly from that time is the absolute terror of the young woman and my own anxiety and helplessness. In a frantic search for books and 'experts', I joined RAINS (Ritual Abuse Information and Support)[1] and found support and cautious advice. I also discovered that compared to many members, I was extremely lucky. I was working within a supportive organisation; some people had managers who were sceptical or hostile and colleagues who they did not dare share their work with. Others, including foster carers and counsellors in private practice, endured a level of isolation far worse than the loneliness I experienced. RAINS was set up to combat such isolation, an endeavour which forms the foundation stone of good practice around ritual abuse.

The material used in this chapter is drawn from three main sources: my recent research based on life history interviews with adult survivors of ritual abuse, conversations with counsellors encountering ritual abuse for the first time and my own experience of counselling and supervision. The aim is to explore six themes which I think are key to ensuring that useful work – work which supports survivors in changing their lives – can occur.

WORKING IN A CLIMATE OF DISBELIEF

It is difficult to over-estimate the impact that the current climate of high scepticism about the existence of ritual abuse has on both survivors and supporters. The dominant discourse about ritual abuse in Britain today is a discourse of disbelief. When, in the late 1980s, stories first appeared in the press about people being taken to court for abuses of children which included drugs, dressing up, black candles and killing cats, fascination and denial were closely entwined. Prominent cases, including Rochdale, Epping Forest and the Orkneys, collapsed and the explanation which was widely disseminated went as follows: evangelical Christians from the USA had run training courses for British social workers, who had then gone on a 'witch-hunt' and coached children in making completely imaginary accusations. A few years later, with the setting up of the False Memory Syndrome Foundation in Britain in 1992, a similar story was developed to account for the claims of some adult survivors of sexual and ritual abuse. In this case, therapists were held to be 'implanting' false memories in vulnerable clients. Less frequently, it was suggested that naïve and poorly trained therapists might be duped by imaginative and manipulative clients into a *folie à deux*.

Few counsellors feel comfortable at the prospect of being widely regarded as zealots or dupes. Both careers and friendships can be threatened and one's rationality questioned. Our assumptions about the taken-for-granted social world we inhabit is shaken by what we hear from ritual abuse survivors. A new level of human suffering and cruelty opens up, or at least comes far closer to home. Belief and disbelief are choices made in this context, but they are not once-and-for-all decisions. I am a 'public' believer in the reality of ritual abuse

---

1   RAINS is a network of people involved in supporting survivors of ritual abuse. It has about 140 members who include social workers, foster parents, psychologists and counsellors. The Membership Officer can be contacted on: 01483 898600.

and after three years of research with adult survivors, there are still mornings when I wake up thinking: 'Oh God, what if none of it's true?' After all, who would want to believe such things?

The discourse of disbelief impacts just as powerfully on survivors as on their allies and counsellors. It encourages them to disclose and shape their accounts in particular ways – often testing the water with the most widely acknowledged experiences first, as in the gradual disclosure I referred to earlier. Survivors are aware that the dominant discourse defines them as unreliable witnesses to their own experiences. In addition, denial and avoidance of the awful things they have suffered may be well-developed coping strategies. Often, people feel torn between the need to be believed and the desire not to acknowledge what has happened. This inner conflict often seems to be played out in the counselling relationship so that either way round the two parties are cast in the roles of believer and doubter. The following scenario gives an impression of how such issues can appear in a counselling session:

SURVIVOR: Do you think they really could have killed my baby?

COUNSELLOR: I think they could have.

SURVIVOR: I can't believe people can do such things.

COUNSELLOR: Even when you think of all the other things…

SURVIVOR: What if none of those happened either? What if I made them all up?

COUNSELLOR: Why would you have done that?

SURVIVOR: Because I'm evil. They always said I was evil and that I'd screw up anyone who came near me with my lies and stuff.

It is easy to lose sight of the fact that what we accept as true accounts of real experiences are shaped by the social and historical context we inhabit. Analysing the context that surrounds a particular instance of belief or disbelief takes it out of the realm of individual fear and guilt: 'You don't believe me do you?' Even better, it can become a joint project of working out what might have been the case. The lack of validation which society currently gives to ritual abuse survivors makes 'belief' a crucial plank of the counselling relationship. However, unrealistic expectations of absolute honesty and uncritical belief are an unnecessary strain. A colleague of mine makes the whole subject of belief/disbelief part of what she discusses with survivors in the introductory period. She introduces the subject like this:

> There are a lot of people who don't believe ritual abuse happens – I'm not one of them. I know a bit about the extremes of terror and degradation it can involve. That doesn't mean I am going to swallow uncritically everything you say to me. I'm sure you are just as competent at telling a lie as the next woman and have

had to be good at it at times. And the real story can sometimes feel too hard to face. Also, drugs and starvation and pain can mess up your grip on reality, so memories may sometimes be pretty confused. There are probably things you have doubts about, it's OK not to be sure. I'll always be honest with you if I have doubts about something. Sometimes we may be able to work things out together. Other times we may both have to put up with a bit of uncertainty.

In this counsellor's experience, honesty pays off better than issuing a blank cheque of belief. Acknowledging the impact of the outside world – anger and despair when children appear to be left in the care of abusers when a prosecution fails, or relief and affirmation at the conviction of Rosemary West[2] – is important to survivors and those supporting them.

Good practice around belief is a juggling act. Ritual abuse survivors need their lives validating by those they turn to for help. On the other hand, deception and disinformation has probably been practised on them as an integral part of their abuse. Deception may be practised to protect the cult, discredit the future survivor or increase an abusers control. It can range from a small child's conviction that he was raped by Mickey Mouse to a teenager's belief that she has been groomed as the next High Priestess. Facing up to the deceptions induces considerable shame and anguish at having been so conned. It helps if survivors can uncover deceits for themselves at their own pace.

AVOIDING ISOLATION

Acknowledging the social context within which work with survivors of ritual abuse currently occurs is closely linked to the problem of isolation. Counsellors can find themselves mirroring the distrust and anxiety of survivors about discussing their work with anyone else. The contagious nature of survivors' fear is reflected in some of the difficulties counsellors describe. A counsellor and survivor experiencing themselves as being 'alone against the world' is a counselling relationship heading for the rocks. Counsellors need to model a reasonably open and optimistic relation to the world and the ability to trust their own judgements about others. They also need to demonstrate their commitment to people looking after themselves and sharing their distress and difficulties with others. Survivors can sometimes resist this 'opening up' of the counselling relationship, requesting secrecy around their disclosures, even suggesting other people in the field may be involved in organised abuse. In turn, counsellors can become protective of their colleagues, not wanting to

2 In November 1995 Rosemary West was convicted of the murder of 10 young women, including her own daughter. In the course of the investigation it emerged that she and her husband, Fred, had tortured and sexually abused their children for years. Eventually 12 bodies were discovered in 3 locations, including several exhumed from the cellar in the family home. Fred West committed suicide before being brought to trial. Rosemary West is currently serving 10 life sentences.

burden others with the horrors they are hearing. All these factors pave the slippery slope towards the isolation of becoming 'the only one'.

Survivors may sometimes feel that only an 'expert' in dissociative disorders or ritual abuse can possibly cope with them. Counsellors, in turn, can feel only someone with 'the answers' based on dozens of similar 'cases' is a suitable supervisor. The perception of the special and different nature of ritual abuse can be extremely isolating. In reflecting on the conversations I have had with numerous counsellors seeking advice and support, I can think of none where specific expertise was actually vital to improving the situation. This is not to deny that skills around handling abreactions, or recognising dissociative problems, cannot be learned and improved upon. However, the difficulties counsellors seem to encounter are most commonly in the dynamics of the relationship and the way in which the 'specialness' of the subject matter gets in the way of seeing the wood for the proverbial trees.

Survivors of ritual abuse sometimes ring Rape Crisis seeking counselling and, at the same time, doubting whether there is anyone who could 'hack' working with them. They have an ambiguous relationship to their 'special' status. On the one hand their supposed 'specialness' was used to justify their abuse and on the other, it may be the only status they have ever enjoyed. Counsellors sometimes collude in the idea that 'their' survivor is different somehow and that information and advice from others is, therefore, irrelevant.

Good supervision is always vital to good counselling. When I was first working with a ritual abuse survivor it felt like a life-saver. My supervisors distance from the immediately gruesome contents allowed her to stand in a different relation to whatever the 'problem' was. Through supervision I gradually began to see the similarities between the survivor of ritual abuse and other survivors, other young women, rather than being entirely attuned to the differences. Of course, this shift in perspective fed back into counselling and I realised this young woman was fighting for 'permission' to become ordinary.

Supporters also have to fight at times to be seen as 'ordinary'. One can be cast as saintly or insane for doing this work, but neither position is very comfortable. Contact with others through RAINS helps reduce isolation. In addition, two American subscriptions can keep you in touch with an international therapeutic and scientific field[3], and there are three UK newsletters which feature campaigning, training and survivor perspectives around sexual abuse, false memory and dissociation.[4]

---

3   *Survivorship: A Magazine for Survivors of Ritual Abuse and Other Torture*:
    3181 Mission #139, San Francisco, CA 94110, USA.

    The International Society for the Study of Dissociation Journal and Newsletter:
    4700 W. Lake Avenue, Glenview, IL 60025–1485, USA.

4   *Accuracy About Abuse*:
    PO Box 3125, London NW3 5QB.

    Action Against Child Sexual Abuse:
    PO Box 9502, London N17 7BW.

    Collective Consciousness:
    c/o The Priory Centre, 11 Priory Rd, High Wycombe, Bucks HP13 6SL.

THE WILL TO RESCUE

When counsellors first encounter ritual abuse, the accounts often seem like nothing they have ever heard before. Their first focus is often on how 'fragmented', 'vulnerable' or 'damaged' a survivor is. Their strength, cleverness, adaptability and survival can become eclipsed by the horror of their accounts. In the face of these, even counsellors who have worked with sexual abuse survivors for years can suddenly find themselves crashing through every boundary in the book. For want of an alternative, a number of women have become foster parents to teenage survivors they initially met as counsellors or social workers (I am one of them). However, far more common is the breaking of ordinary counselling boundaries with adult clients. Survivor-guilt is frequently discussed, counsellor-guilt is a variation on the same theme. One counsellor described it to me like this:

> When I first began working with 'Maggie' I was so appalled and overwhelmed by what she'd been through, I couldn't deny her anything. One-hour sessions turned into four hours, I'd let her ring me up at any hour of the day or night, I always had her favourite biscuits in... She was constantly testing me and I felt I had to prove to her how much I cared and how different I was to the people that abused her. What right had I to rest and relaxation when she was living through such hell?

The desire to protect someone and 'make them better' is not wrong in itself, the fact is it doesn't work. Setting up a dependant relationship where the dynamic is that of 'victim' and 'rescuer' disempowers survivors. Not surprisingly, they often fight back by increasing the level of need and crisis they express. I interpret this as a way of trying to find the limits, the edges of this other person they are trying to trust. One survivor described the problem like this:

> She was so easy to push around. I knew all about manipulating people, my abuse taught me that. Of course I wanted her to worry about me, I wanted the cuddles. I'd never had any of that and it was sheer luxury. At the same time I despised her...and I felt terrible about that because she was such a nice person.

Powerlessness, fear and anxiety are dreadful feelings, it is tempting to try and give them to someone else. Outright rejection or absolute rescue can seem like the only alternatives because 'we', the supporters, cannot live with these feelings.

'Rescuing' another person in this way is not possible. Supporters and counsellors can only provide a little company and encouragement to someone engaged in rescuing themselves. Attempting to rescue is part of the emotional process described above, but it also entails a serious misunderstanding of ritual abuse survivors' lives. If I fall into the sea, someone can save my life by fishing me out. But if I was brought up as a mermaid, believing the sea to be my natural habitat, the choice to live on land must be my own. Ritual abuse survivors have usually grown up within, and, therefore, constructed them-selves in relation to, a ritual abuse cult – what they fear and wish to escape is as much within themselves as it is outside.

When a survivor seeks our support we often assume that they are just like us and the 'other' is the cult. It does not feel like that to some survivors:

> I carried on seeing you at Rape Crisis but I also carried on living at home, and I didn't want the police involved or anybody. Which was important really. I think that went on for six, maybe eight months? Seeing you and living with them. I think that's what helped me get out... because I needed the contrast of home living and a life outside...but still going back and not making that direct confrontation with them until I was sure that the outside life was what I wanted. Until I was sure that people outside were safe. I had to stay at home, I could have run away there and then but I would have ended up going back to the group eventually because it would have been such a culture shock if you like. I needed that period at home, contact with the group and contact with Rape Crisis.

It is important to recognise that to the survivor who has known abuse all her life, finding her feet on terra firma is a process not an event. What is to the counsellor unparalleled horror has been everyday life to the survivor.

This is not to suggest that the only way to work with ritual abuse survivors is with boundaries set in concrete. However, changing boundaries to fit the needs of a particular survivor is not the same as abandoning boundaries. Some survivors may only be able to use counselling if their needs for other practical and emotional support can be met at the same time. No one person can provide everything. In order to be useful as a counsellor it may be necessary to help a survivor build a support network, find safe housing and start enjoying everyday life. However, if the safe housing is your back bedroom and the support network your family and friends, the survivor has found herself a good landlady but now needs a new counsellor.

POWER AND CONTROL

I have already touched on the issue of boundary pushing, but I think it can also be seen as one aspect of more pervasive issues around power and control. Survivors who have grown up in extremely abusive families have learned a great deal about power and control, namely that they don't have any and that it is the most valuable thing in the world. In the cult hierarchy, only power brings freedom and security. Control is what anybody else will take given half a chance, the only person that can be relied on is oneself. In addition, survivors describe being taught to despise kindness, openness and equality as weak-ness. People expressing such qualities are seen as 'sheep', their purpose is to be exploited by the strong. This sense of absolute alternatives, complete control or abject helplessness, can get acted out in the support relationship. For example:

> I would feel like I was on a see-saw. All her energy
> seemed to be engaged in bringing me down. Then it
> would be like a tug of war. I eventually worked out that
> this was all she knew. Co-operation, mutual respect,
> power sharing, this was all unknown territory.

Survivors seeking help do not make a once-and-for-all decision: 'OK, now I'm going into counselling to work through my past'. Resistance to facing the past can be very strong and have many dimensions. Sometimes, counsellors describe feeling that they are the ones holding all the hope, optimism and desire for a better life. It can feel like a tug of war. When this happens, only 'dropping the rope' can enable a survivor to pick up that energy to go forward for themselves. Ritual abuse survivors have grown up with the adrenalin of constant conflict, to seek it seems habitual; it also serves to distract from the pain of the past, which it has become a life project to avoid.

However, the issue of power is two-way. Survivors of ritual abuse have been so controlled, so over-powered by their abusers, that their dread of being overwhelmed and destroyed in the counselling relationship can be huge. The counsellor becomes another potential controller who must be fought. A counsellor can help by negotiating options where these exist, what a colleague calls 'Offering clients a menu of control – while being clear what is not on the menu!'.

Five years ago I remember talking to a number of therapists who were uncertain how effectively boundaries could be set with highly dissociative survivors. They wondered whether contracting with one personality for 'no violence' would stand for another personality who decided to ignore it. Could one part of the self be held responsible for what another part did we wondered? Probably as a direct result of this uncertainty, I have encountered therapists who have been bitten, thumped and threatened. The acceptance on the part of the therapist of the involuntary nature of multiplicity, where amnesia and disconnection 'just happen,' removes responsibility for their actions from the survivor (might not any of us be tempted to take advantage of such permission to express our needs and feelings?).

I will expand on this a little in the following section. For the present, the important point is that highly dissociative survivors are quite capable of sticking to a 'no violence contract', finishing sessions on time and abiding by all the usual limits of a counselling relationship. They may not at first believe this to be the case – the important thing is that their counsellor does.

KEEPING OUT OF SURVIVORS' HEADS

This chapter will be of little use to most people supporting ritual abuse survivors if it says nothing about dissociation. On the other hand, there is room to say very little. Dissociation is about disconnection, it involves failing to associate one experience with another, one day with another and one part of the self with another. If 'repression' is a metaphor that suggests the 'pushing down' of undesirable thoughts and feelings into the cellar of the unconscious, dissociation suggests the separation and compartmentalisation of such materials within one dimension. Repression tends to be seen as something done 'after the event', as a defence against uncomfortable feelings, and dissociation as something that occurs during an event, as a defence against the traumatic impact of an experience. It serves to disconnect painful memories from everyday consciousness.

There are many degrees of dissociation, ranging from day-dreaming to dissociative identities – where someone may see themselves as having many separate parts or personalities. Although still contentious, dissociative disorders are beginning to be fairly widely diagnosed by the psychiatric/therapeutic establishment in North America but have barely begun to be considered in the UK. Not all survivors of ritual abuse see themselves as multiple personalities and not everyone who is highly dissociative comes from such a background. What is important is that cutting off through dissociation is cutting off *from* something and the development of a multiple self appears to have it's roots in early childhood experience. The relationship between dissociation and childhood trauma is, therefore, strong. It is thought that the degree of dissociative ability may be inborn but its development as a skill will be dependent on traumatic experiences.

Extremely dissociative people have tremendous imaginative powers, by which counsellors are sometimes awed and absorbed. They have the ability to 'imagine' away painful experiences and to become utterly absorbed in alternative fantasies as a distraction from 'real life'. The two scenarios that follow are typical of many conversations I have had with confused and distressed workers:

(*On telephone.*)

COUNSELLOR: She's here with me now. She's called Jude and she's deaf. I don't know what to do. We've been writing notes to each other all session. She says no one else will come through and take over the body. I've cancelled my next couple of meetings 'cos obviously I can't let her go home on her own – she'd never make it.

COLLEAGUE: Is your client deaf?

COUNSELLOR: No, but Jude is. She says they damaged her ears when she was little – pushing wasps into the ear canal – and she's been deaf ever since.

COLLEAGUE: But there is nothing wrong with your clients hearing? (*pause*) Can you hear what you are saying?

(*In supervision.*)

COUNSELLOR (*in some distress*): I think I've lost her. They said Sheila, that's the core personality, has been kidnapped by what she calls 'the dark ones'. She hasn't been around for the

> last ten days. They're really frantic about it and I don't know what to do.

SUPERVISOR: Where do you think she has gone?

COUNSELLOR: Well, inside. They've got her tied up in a dark room.

SUPERVISOR: Where is that?

COUNSELLOR: Inside…(*pause*) In her mind… This is in Sheila's imagination isn't it?

Two things make it easy to get caught up in a survivor's imagination. The first is a lack of understanding of dissociation and the way in which fantasy is crucial to its effectiveness. The second is the conviction with which some survivors describe the realness of their inner lives, coupled with the embodiment of different roles and emotions in the performances of different personalities. One survivor described it like this:

> It's as real as real is. When I turn off and go inside, things sound and taste and feel just as vivid as this room does now. I suppose it's years of practice and so badly needing some place to escape to… It had to be more real than everything I wanted to pretend wasn't real at all.

This is crucial. We all relate to ourselves through what we imagine ourselves to be. Someone who has dissociated their identity into many parts is no less real to themselves than I am with my multi-faceted, but associated, self-image. The above scenarios are not about 'someone playing games'. On the contrary, both are packed with material pertinent to the work. They can offer ways in to issues in the present and the past. In the first case, Jude's appearance as a deaf personality may indicate that the counsellor is saying things her client doesn't want to hear or she may be bringing a dissociated memory of abuse which it is time to integrate but hard to communicate. Such issues are only likely to be drawn out if the counsellor maintains her own perspective from inside her own head.

There are two books which are essential reading for anyone starting work in this area: Judith Herman (1992) and Colin Ross (1989) (see Further Reading at the end of this chapter). In addition, I offer the following advice which was given me by a friend to whom I expressed my sense of wonder and fascination with the first multiple survivor I worked with:

- Never forget that the 'personalities' you meet are packed full of pain. People with just normally miserable childhoods don't get to be that way.
- No favouritism. These are all aspects of one person – she needs all of them and you need to accept all of them.
- The aim for all personalities is co-operation with each other, not co-operation with you. What matters is they get to know each other, not that you get to know them all.

- Remember, they're all watching and listening all the time. Or, put another way, the walls between parts are awfully thin and full of holes.
- Your client is not multiple to make sessions more interesting for you. She has already spent half her life as entertainment for her abusers.
- Every society in the world has a basic assumption that one body equals one person. It's a handy rule of thumb.
- The relationship between dissociation, imagination and suggestibility is very close. Watch what you are doing to 'inspire' and mould what your client is producing.

THE PROBLEM OF GETTING STARTED

Good practice means knowing what you're doing and why. I think, sometimes, ritual abuse survivors get a raw deal from counselling, largely because otherwise adequate counsellors throw everything they normally do out of the window at the first disclosure. Like anyone else, survivors of ritual abuse need to define what the aims of counselling are for themselves. The contract needs to be regularly reviewed and the aims amended as needed.

A question I've often been asked about ritual abuse counselling is: 'How long does it take?' Hiding under the skirts of this question is often the uncertainty, or outright panic, of the counsellor, who is really asking: 'Can anyone recover from this degree of maltreatment?', 'Can I face another three years like the last three months?' and 'Where do I start?', for the time scale of ritual abuse counselling will depend on the goals set, the application and resources of the individual survivor and the quality of the support relationship. However, one colleague grasped the nettle:

> ...Three years. I'm thinking of a survivor in her twenties. She's still in contact with her family when she comes to you...she's multiple and bulimic... About six months should see her safe and build a working relationship. Keep off doing any memories until she's relatively stable and there's no ongoing abuse. My experience is that working through memories needs to be spread over a couple of years. It needs to be broken up with time off, time to analyse and integrate the past and real positive support for building a better life. The future is something that needs to get started in the present – really, who's going to wade through this shit if they can't see the roses grow along the way?

The first stage of 'safety work' is crucial. Trying to process memories while abuse is ongoing, or major self-harm is happening, is simply re-traumatising. The first few months are also the time for counsellors new to this work to concentrate on their own education and support needs as well as those of the survivor. This first stage of work may well contain the following elements:

- Establishing who is safe and who isn't. Family and childhood contacts all require careful scrutiny.
- Facing up to any current abuse involvement – cult or otherwise. Keeping a journal often helps survivors begin to get a grip on dissociated episodes (often evocatively referred to as 'lost time').
- Analysing current coping strategies for dealing with anxiety, memories, etc and practising less harmful ones if necessary.
- Developing more conscious choice about dissociation and skills for containing flashbacks and panic attacks.
- Learning a little about the effects of child abuse and the healing process. Establishing trust.
- Understanding dissociation and beginning to acknowledge different parts of the self as well as the self as a 'whole person'.
- Building a support network and establishing a reasonable level of routine and self-care.

A friend of mine calls this work 'chaos control' and, mixing her metaphors gleefully, says: 'It frequently feels like wading through treacle when everything is as clear as mud'.

OF SAINTS AND DEMONS

I have already touched on the difficulties that can arise from people transferring their reactions to the experiences of ritual abuse onto survivors, thereby perceiving them as simply the sum of their appalling victimisation. What sometimes seems to arise from this is an inability to face up to a survivors involvement as an abuser, particularly when this is current. Sadly, I have known survivors, previously 'sanctified' by their supporters, suddenly 'demonised' when the realisation of their abusing behaviour has come to the fore.

Organisations such as Rape Crisis Centres, and many individual counsellors, have a policy of not working with abusers. Survivors of ritual abuse have generally been forced to participate in the abuse of others from an early age. Any adult who continues to be involved in a cult will be involved in the abuse of children. 'Safety work', therefore, is about the protection of others as well as of the survivor in counselling (some women have had to face the difficult decision to put their own children into care as they were unable to protect them from abuse). Organisations and individuals need to be clear about the relationship between therapeutic work and child protection issues. They also need to be up front about their policies with clients. If ritual abuse challenges ones thinking about the line that can be drawn between 'victims' and 'perpetrators' of abuse, this challenge needs time and attention.

It is my view that survivors in the process of extracting themselves from organised or ritual abuse may need the kind of breathing space described earlier by a survivor. However, it should be time limited. I have met counsellors who have struggled to support someone who has continued to be involved in abuse over a long period. Situations like this destroy supporters. They may come about because a counsellor doubts that escape is possible, does not feel able to insist on an end to involvement as a pre-condition of support or cannot accept that survivors have a choice – however terrifying – and that some may 'choose' continued involvement as the safest option.

What ritual abuse survivors have survived is extraordinary, but they, like their counsellors, are ordinary mortals. The counselling relationship is often the first, and may be the only place, where these two truths can be held in balance. One survivor I consulted about this chapter had the following to say:

> Tell them not to be afraid of us and not to stick us on a pedestal either... Remind them that we can fuck up but so can they. And tell them just how important it is to be honest... People who've been through what we've been through can smell a lie at a hundred paces[...] Yeah, and say something about God and all that stuff...

Many counsellors confronting ritual abuse for the first time find themselves thinking about ultimate questions about good and evil and the meaning of life. Some find themselves deeply frightened by the occult or supernatural beliefs of survivors. Ritual abuse occurs within the wider cultural context we all inhabit, it draws on religion, superstition and horror fiction. Few of us are such thorough-going materialists that we remain entirely unaffected by this aspect of what we hear. As someone who relies heavily on a social constructionist approach to life, and as an atheist and a feminist, I found the occult elements of ritual abuse initially embarrassing. One friend, an ex-Catholic, found herself buying a rosary in a junk shop, while another threw away the Tarot pack she had treasured for years. What seems important is that space is made for these issues to be examined as part of a supporter's total response to ritual abuse.

A colleague describes her Islamic faith as a resource in her counselling around ritual abuse. She describes it as a source of personal spiritual strength, but also that her religious upbringing has given her insight into some of the possible impacts of ritual abuse. Good practice in counselling is fundamentally based on self-awareness and the ability to guard against imposing one's own path on others – this is as relevant to matters spiritual as to those secular.

There is so much more to be said. I have not begun here to address the content of therapeutic work. There is a burgeoning international literature on dissociation, trauma and torture, and on the international industries of child prostitution and pornography. Ongoing self-education is key to good practice in any field. However, more than anything, I would like to emphasise the importance of learning from survivors themselves. It is an enormous privilege to work with survivors of ritual abuse, to be trusted by people who have had their trust so badly abused. It is new and challenging work that we undertake in a largely hostile environment and we are bound to get things wrong and change our minds. As a friend pointed out:

> We are learning on our feet. It's OK to tell your client you got it wrong, to tell your support network, to tell yourself. You can only do the best that you can. Survivors don't need perfection, they need real people whose imperfections can be tolerated.

FURTHER READING

Sinason, V. (ed) (1995) *Supporting Survivors of Satanist Abuse*. London: Routledge.

Herman, J. (1992) *Trauma and Recovery*. New York: Basic Books.

Ross, C. (1989) *Multiple Personality Disorder: Diagnosis, Clinical Features, and Treatment*. New York: Wiley.

Sakheim, D. and Devine, S. (eds) (1992) *Out of Darkness: Exploring Satanism and Ritual Abuse*. New York: Lexington Books.

Oksana, C. (1994) *Safe Passage to Healing: A Guide for Survivors of Ritual Abuse*. New York: Harper Collins.

Goodwin, J. (1993) *Rediscovering Childhood Trauma*. Washington, DC: American Psychiatric Press.

TRAINING VIDEO

Sara Scott and Harriet Wistrich, *Supporting Survivors of Ritual Abuse*, 1994, (60 minutes).

Copies available from: RA Video, SAFE, PO Box 1557, Salisbury SP1 2TP. Price: £12.50 (UK/Europe) £17 (USA/Overseas).

CHAPTER 7

Counselling and the Male Survivor

Pete Brown and Ron Wiener

INTRODUCTION

This chapter is not intended to be a complete account of all aspects of the sexual abuse of males. There are excellent, comprehensive books which already do this, which are listed at the end of this chapter. What this chapter sets out to do is to put men's experience of counselling into the framework of what the literature reports as being helpful interventions. Part One, written by Pete Brown, looks at counselling issues within the context of the setting up and operation of Leeds Survivors' Collective. Part Two, written by Ron Wiener, is a personal account.

PART ONE: LESSONS FROM LEEDS SURVIVORS' COLLECTIVE

For the past two years I have worked and struggled as a volunteer to develop a service for adult male survivors in the Leeds area. The experience has been both totally frustrating and incredibly rewarding. In this section I shall write about the issues of good practice which have arisen during this process and how they relate to my personal experience. To do this I shall focus on a number of key themes: boundaries, confidentiality and secrecy, memory and doubt, sexuality (briefly) and survivor-led services.

Boundaries

For survivors, boundaries are a crucial issue. When a child is sexually abused, his/her boundaries are destructively violated – physically, sexually and emotionally. Adult survivors often have great difficulty in re-learning how to maintain appropriate boundaries – when it is safe to relax them and when it is very unsafe. We have been taught that we cannot say 'no' or, that if we do, it will not be respected.

Personal boundaries are crucial. In my work at the project I have to be extremely careful. Another survivor engaging in similar work failed to maintain any boundaries between his work and other areas of his life. Consequently, he reached a crisis point and could not cope, choosing to bail out completely.

I work on the basis that my first duty to the survivors I wish to support is to take care of myself. If I am not up to doing the Helpline or meeting a survivor, I don't do it. To do anything else is a betrayal – if I am unable to look after myself, how can I support anyone else? If I am not balanced, centred and grounded myself, I am far more likely to 'spin out' if raw material is touched on unexpectedly.

My first experience of therapy was an extremely negative one. This was when I was first beginning to wonder if it was possible that I had been abused. My therapist failed to maintain any boundaries at all. The sessions were cut short or extended as she saw fit. Fees were often waived. Social visits were encouraged. The therapist was working with both myself and my partner, separately, yet seemed to take 'my side' in disputes. Finally, she related a story to me of how she had entered into a sexual relationship with one of her clients who was of the same age and appearance as myself, etc. She did say that 'of course I had to tell him that was the end of the therapy'! Whilst I was in this, supposedly, therapeutic relationship, I could see none of this. It finished because I moved to a new city, and only then did I realise what had been happening. I had been too scared to speak to my partner about my fears, though when I did, it became painfully clear what had been taking place. At this point I had my first real memories of sexual abuse.

Boundaries, then, are crucial. Their importance cannot be overestimated. Physical, sexual, emotional, time, even financial boundaries must be firmly upheld in counselling. Physical touch, however apparently innocent, however much intended to be comforting, can easily seem a re-betrayal and another violation to a survivor. In our self-help group we have to gain permission before we touch in any way, even if one of us is sobbing uncontrollably. We can offer touch but we never assume.

Sexual boundaries would, I hope, be obvious. Counsellors should never, under any circumstances, become sexually involved with their clients. Powerful feelings of sexual attraction will almost certainly arise at some stage in the process. This is to be expected, and is useful material to work with, but to act on those feelings is to re-abuse the client. 'No sex between members' is another ground rule of our self-help group. The issue has arisen a number of times, as it should and will. If it can be talked about openly in the group, it is extremely useful. I used to believe that when I eventually had clear memories of the abuse I suffered, they would definitely be memories of extreme pain, torture, rape. I did not understand the ambivalence of the feelings. Perpetrators seek out children who are vulnerable – they are vulnerable because they do not receive the unconditional love they deserve simply by virtue of being, regardless of what they do. They seek love desperately and perpetrators see this and manipulate it. Much sexual abuse involves a painful and confusing mixture of love and pain, need and betrayal. The child is only looking for love – the adult manipulates this to gain sexual gratification.

It is quite normal therefore for survivors to feel extremely ambivalent towards their abusers – a mixture of love and hate. Perhaps, at the time of the abuse, only the badly needed love was recognised by the child. As an adult, full of guilt and pain, he may only be able to connect with his (self-destructive) anger at himself, anger at the abuser. He may not be able to accept the other side of this reality – that he also loved the perpetrator (especially if it was a family member) – just as when he was a child, he could not have coped with the full knowledge of the betrayal and abuse taking place.

In groups, then, this repressed portion of feelings towards abusers is highly likely to re-appear. A difficult situation arose in our own group, centred on a particular member who had a conviction for a sexual offence. He made no secret of it, not out of any sense of pride but out of shame and a desire to be completely honest. He took full responsibility for what he had done and over the ensuing months it became clear that this was a more difficult issue for him than the years of abuse he had suffered, and largely come to terms with, since going to prison.

When he revealed his offence to the group, an, initially, (over-) supportive response gave way to extreme ambivalence. Feelings of unease began to be expressed simultaneously along with feelings of sexual attraction. Members of the group began to relate to him as if he were their own abuser, with the mixture of love and hate, sexual arousal and disgust, attraction and fear characteristic of abusive relationships. Such dynamics are to be expected in survivors' groups and a properly functioning group should be able to work through such issues and gain invaluable insight and healing from them. Usually, these dynamics are flowing and shifting, not becoming fixed on one particular member. But it is never easy and, after our own experiences, it is unlikely we would accept another survivor with such a conviction.

Confidentiality and secrecy

Damaging secrecy is at the core of childhood sexual abuse. The perpetrator may make threats towards the child or someone significant to the child. Or, more subtly, the adult may manipulate the situation in such a way that the child's extreme feelings of guilt are enough to maintain the child's silence. Often, both work together.

For adult survivors, secrets can be terrifying. Even innocent secrets can set alarm bells ringing for no apparent reason. And at what point does telling another person something in confidence become a damaging secret?

In our self-help group another of our ground rules stipulates that all contact between members outside of normal meeting times must be mentioned within the group meeting and that any information which one member reveals to another individual member must be considered to have been shared with the whole group. In this way we hope to prevent the development of secretive, abusive relationships between group members. We only realised the importance and significance of this ground rule (which, like the others, is taken from Lew (1993)) after such a relationship did begin to develop.

Issues such as this are, perhaps, more crucial, and more difficult, in male survivors' groups and services than in those for women. The vast majority of perpetrators are men and we have to take great care to ensure that perpetrators seeking further victims do not gain easy access to survivors contacting us for support. Total prevention is virtually impossible, therefore we need to have safeguards in place within self-help groups, within our volunteer recruitment procedures and within our practice.

The price of this safeguard within the self-help group, then, is that it also prevents one member revealing issues to another member which he is not ready to share with the whole group. This, however, as we know from our experience, is a price worth paying.

The limits of confidentiality

Issues of confidentiality can be potentially extremely difficult for those working with male survivors. I do not hold with the currently conventional idea that survivors are more likely to abuse others than non-survivors. The so-called cycle of abuse, as it is often used today, is, I believe, a misleading fallacy and one which does nothing to help us as male survivors already full of fear that we are 'doomed to repeat' the abuse we have suffered (Kelly 1996). Any grain of truth within this concept is far more subtle.

However, as well as being survivors, we are also men. And far more questionable, for me, is the nature of contemporary masculinity and male sexuality. Consequently, in working therapeutically with men – whether survivors or not – the issue of how to deal with suspected perpetrators of sexual abuse is likely to arise, and is likely to be extremely difficult. Perhaps more so for us, as I suggested above.

If, in the course of counselling, the counsellor becomes aware that his/her client is sexually abusing a child, what should be done? There is, of course, a statutory duty to report such information to the authorities. But what if it is only suspicion? At what point does suspicion become great enough to break confidentiality – that is, where are the limits of confidentiality? If the client is also a survivor, how can a counsellor explore suspicions sensitively? If they are untrue, any such suggestion is likely to confirm all the survivor's worst beliefs about himself. Survivors are often all too ready to believe themselves guilty of the most hideous crimes of abuse when, in fact, they are simply re-experiencing the guilt and shame of their victimisation.

In the course of my work this is an issue which has already arisen several times in different contexts. I have become very aware how difficult it can be for me, as a survivor myself, to have any certainty at all – if I feel uneasy working with someone, is this a genuine instinctive response to real danger or am I simply projecting my fears because raw material of my own has been 'triggered' by the client's issues?

There are no easy answers. Our first duty, whatever our role, must be to protect children from abuse. For self-help groups, safeguards can be built in, such as those mentioned. For one-to-one work, we must also ensure that we have good quality supervision to draw on and to work through dilemmas such as that outlined above. But we must also recognise that there are limits to confidentiality and that this is an area of few hard and fast rules.

Memory and doubt: the price of certainty

In recent years a backlash has begun to develop against survivors in the form of so-called 'False Memory Syndrome'. There has been much debate on this area already and I shall not pursue it further here (Etherington 1995; Campbell 1995; Grant 1996). However, I do wish to say a little about memory and doubt, which is crucial to survivors who have only remembered their abuse in adult life and has been central to my own healing process.

Since my first realisation that I had been sexually abused, I have been wracked with doubts, first about whether it could be true at all and later about who it may have been. The latter is still largely unresolved for me. At times I have known with absolute certainty, only to retreat into further doubt. But what I have realised recently is how crucial this, sometimes crippling, doubt has been for me.

Just as memories only begin to surface when the survivor is ready for them (Lew 1993), so doubt operates similarly. There is no solid, clear dividing line between repression or amnesia and conscious knowledge or truth for survivors of sexual abuse. Instead, I have found a, perhaps, transitional phase, a grey area of doubt and uncertainty. It continually amazes me how the human mind/body/spirit protects itself. A little knowledge, a little truth, seeps into consciousness at the point where the survivor is potentially able to handle it constructively. But this is a potential and circumstances change – if safety is compromised, if there is unexpected family contact or if other more immediate issues demand attention, doubt can return. It returns as a new coping mechanism, midway between amnesia and conscious knowledge. As with all coping mechanisms, it brings with it its own problems. To be in doubt is to be in a state of limbo, unsure of whether a trusted adult really did commit this unimaginable act or whether the thought is a cruel and unjust accusation. And, of course, guilt and shame, depression and anger are never far away. But this doubt is a crucial part of the process and must be respected. A counsellor may be in no doubt of the truth regarding a particular adult because of what he/she has witnessed in previous sessions, but if the client is in doubt, this is for a very good reason and the counsellor must be very careful not to destroy the client's defences by insisting on this truth too strongly. Challenging denial of whatever kind is both an essential part of the healing process and one which contains many dangers if it is done too early or too insensitively. A careful path must be trod, tending far more towards gently supporting the survivor as he works through his own doubt and questioning.

Sexuality and confusion

I have yet to meet a male survivor who has not at some time experienced great confusion over their sexuality. I am not going to explore this issue in any depth here since it is well covered elsewhere (Lew 1993). However, it is frequently an issue of central concern to male survivors. There is all too often an easy assumption from friends and families that child sexual abuse 'causes' homosexuality, that abused boys must be gay. Colleagues who work in organisations supporting gay and bisexual men have also related to me how self-defining heterosexual men have been referred to them – by 'professionals' – because they have been abused! I therefore wish to state quite clearly that there is no evidence at all that sexual abuse determines sexuality. What it does is produce immense confusion for all male survivors, whatever their sexuality. This is an important point for counsellors to bear in mind. Survivors will undoubtedly at some stage wish to explore these issues for themselves. They must be treated with sensitivity and respect and survivors must be given space and time to work through their confusion for themselves. For me, it is an ongoing issue and has been for a number of years.

Survivor-led services

Leeds Survivors' Collective is a survivor-led service, as are many such services now developing. There are important reasons for this. It may help a counsellor to understand why these type of services are so crucial to survivors. The project was founded on the principle that the best people to help male survivors are survivors themselves. Empowerment and support, choice and responsibility have remained at the core of our plans. Too often in the (recent) past, women and men survivors have been told by 'experts' and others that they are mistaken, deluded, crazy or suffering from 'False Memory Syndrome' when they have tried to speak of their experiences. Women have struggled against this societal and institutional denial for twenty years; for men, it is only more recently that progress has been made. Consequently, the simple knowledge that another male survivor exists is of incredible value in itself to the man who has just begun to realise or remember what happened to him. Breaking the painful and powerful feeling of isolation is the first stage in healing and if you know that when you dial the helpline you are going to speak to another survivor, you also know that there is a good chance you will be believed and listened to – validated, not dismissed.

This principle is being carried over into our face-to-face work. We intend to offer both face-to-face support from other survivors as well as counsellors who hold formal qualifications. This choice is crucial. Some survivors prefer to know they are speaking to another survivor who will very likely understand what they are saying. Others prefer to work with someone they know is formally qualified. This is not to say that we believe any survivor can immediately do this work – our training course was intensive and a survivor must have made sufficient progress on the path of his/her own healing before he/she will be ready to work supporting others safely. But we believe there is immense value in survivors supporting each other and, on the whole, the survivors contacting us agree.

PART TWO

There are a lot of male survivors of child sexual abuse (CSA), though it is difficult to know how many. One of the few English studies came up with an estimate of 5–8 per cent of the population (Baker 1985). Mendel (1995), drawing mainly on American studies, says that childhood victimisation of males ranges from 2.5 per cent to 33 per cent of the population (p.41). As always, these variations depend on the definition of abuse, different methodologies and changes in the population sampled.

The general consensus is that girls are more often victims than boys. Baker suggests that it is two to three times more likely that girls are abused (Baker 1985). However, Peak (1989) and Mendel (1995) both claim that there is an under-reporting of abuse of boys. Many reasons, some of which also apply to girls, are given for this: a lack of language, no permission, threats, not being asked, the experience not being identified as abusive and the fear of being identified as homosexual. Other writers suggest that society is more protective to females and that males are more reluctant to report abuse because males are socialised to be strong and to take care of themselves (Bolton, Morris and MacEachron 1989). Mendel (1995) looks at the role of masculinity in male under-reporting, such as males being expected to be powerful, active and competent rather than passive, helpless and victimised. He also says that because male survivors are more likely to act out, their behaviour is more likely to be dismissed as disruptive because it doesn't conform to the stereotype of behaviour expected of a victim. Finally, Mendel says that the presence and prevalence of female perpetrators appears to have been grossly underestimated. Etherington (1995), for example, found that of 25 men in her sample, 13 had been abused by females. In some cases, such as my own, 'male adult survivors of abuse of sexuality have worked diligently to forget these experiences…for some males it is as though they had no childhood experiences at all' (Bolton, Morris and MacEachron 1989, p.104).

My experience

I have few memories before the age of seven. My first abuse happened at the age of five or six. It happened outside the family – this supports an Edinburgh University study which concluded that girls are more likely than boys to be abused within the family whereas boys are more at risk from friends, acquaintances and strangers (Glassman 1995).

In my own case a family friend was responsible for my second childhood experience of being abused. The memory disappeared until I was in my forties. In writing about female survivors, Sheldon and Bannister (1992) say that the 'child victim becomes a survivor through the process of developing defensive strategies which endeavour to protect the inner core. These strategies or defence mechanisms of repression, denial, detachment and dissociation will often result in the adult survivor not having access to memories of her sexual abuse' (p.85).

So, for 33 years these memories of abuse were banished into some compartment of my brain. There were clues. Bannister (1992) for example, writes that 'extreme feelings of powerlessness can lead to dissociation…a useful defence mechanism which the mind employs to escape an unbearable situation' (p.10). Many situations which may seem bearable to most people are unbearable to survivors. As an example, one of my earliest sexual experiences was in a brothel – an experience which I found very threatening and, as I wrote at the time, I became 'the man on the roof, standing aloof, watching the pair, part in despair…he thought that yet, in a way, he was still pure as could be, nothing but a character in a passing odyssey for whom nothing was real'. Even though I had no conscious memory of my abuse, I had written in my thirties, as a diary note: 'There is a basic fear. I can sense it. What was it in my past which could create such distrust? Who could have shown me such a dark, bottomless pit and threatened to throw me in?'

In retrospect, I exhibited many of the symptoms or behavioural characteristics that male survivors have. Lew (1993) for example, lists: nightmares, fear that everyone is a potential attacker, shame, anger, guilt, fear of expressing anger, need to be in control, need to pretend that I am not in control, fear of being seen, running from people, fear of intimacy, pain and memories of physical pain, flashbacks, not being able to 'think straight', difficulties in communicating, self-abuse, wanting to die, sexual dysfunction, feelings of unreality, detachment, need to be completely competent at all times, self-doubt, feeling inadequate, inability to receive comfort/nurturing, low self-esteem, difficulty in expressing vulnerability, fear of authority, out of body experiences and feeling that 'if they know me, they'll reject me' (p.14).

I remember sitting in a restaurant with a girl friend and her urging me to have a joint, me refusing and her asking 'Why don't you ever let go?' The answer that I wasn't able to say then was that I know (or at least a child part of me does) what happens when you are not in control: hell breaks loose, the devil does exist, the worst can happen, the world isn't safe, men do rape and women abuse and you want me to lower my defences – you must be joking!

Many of Lew's points ring true for me. The trouble with lists like these is that while these are all experiences that CSA survivors have experienced, they can also occur for a whole variety of other reasons.

The counselling experience

In my late thirties and early forties I began to work professionally with people with mental health problems. I became aware of 'stirrings' when working around issues of abuse. Because of these stirrings and a relationship crisis, I went into therapy. My first therapist was a Reichian, into bodywork – fingers being jabbed in all over the place to flush out the tension spots when I had this memory of me as a child being abused – a flash, gone. I shared it with the therapist. He dismissively said: 'A lot of people have an experience like that at the beginning of therapy'. I felt bewildered and denied. I wondered whether it was real or was my memory false? It was painful to be disbelieved. I agree with Bannister (1992) that 'the feeling of being validated is vital to someone whose mind and body has been discounted, whose feelings have been ignored and contradicted, whose soul has been raped' (p.16). Yet, somehow, the memory felt true.

Two weeks later I was in a group selection process where we had to share something of ourselves with a partner. I, being full of my discovery, told of my new knowledge of myself as a survivor. She was not sympathetic, nor was the group when we had to feed back what we had learned about our partners. It was made quite clear that the level of sharing was inappropriate – much too intimate and needy for where the group was at.

Yet, despite these two setbacks, the fact of being a survivor made sense, it explained many failed relationships and core negative beliefs about myself. So, I found another therapist with whom I worked intensively over the next five years and whom I still see on an occasional basis. His therapeutic approach was eclectic, involving counselling, one-to-one psychodrama and Gestalt – the last two both involved working with feelings present in the moment and recapturing emotions from the past. As Bannister (1992) says: 'Adults often respond more quickly and more completely to a creative, therapeutic intervention than to more conventional methods' (p.15). The therapeutic work was usually emotionally difficult but continually valued because it clarified many life experiences. There was a lot of work on anger or on the fact that I could not express it. Lew (1993) states: 'only the abuser is permitted to express his angry feelings...anger is an emotion that is reserved for those in power. This leads the abused child to equate anger with power' (p.50). I did eventually find it and was able to write:

I am anger
I am destruction
I am desperation
I am despair
I am chaos
I am everything I do not like.

Continually, therapy meant getting in touch with my core:

When I get down like this, the abuse, it's heavy. I carry the guilt of all victims. My achievements count for nothing. I am nothing. I feel like shit. The stench invades all touch. I cannot hear the comforting words of friends and lovers. I am short-circuited, close-looped into a depressive spiral, unable to believe that anything can ever change. I do not like myself. I find it difficult to see good in anything or anyone.

I felt parts of me were out of control. In my earlier life it had been masturbation – a common response. Lew (1993) writes: as masturbation 'turns into a patterned, compulsive activity it becomes one more part of life that feels out of control' (p.186). Masturbation was always accompanied by feelings of guilt and shame, which, as Lew points out, comes from connecting sex and shame. This is not surprising given that masturbation was my first post-abuse sexual experience.

The therapy also involved two key characters from my psyche – the gatekeeper and the policeman. The gatekeeper symbolised my defence mechanisms and often appeared as the lock-keeper of my arsehole. The gatekeeper once said: 'I was created in that flash to save you'. The policeman, in contrast, was the voice telling me it was all my fault. So these characters would appear in many sessions. Usually, I would be in dialogue with them, playing both parts. Sometimes the therapist would take one of the roles. It helped me to understand how the dynamics of repression and guilt worked and to begin to change them. I discovered an adult voice which enabled me to take some control of my fears and rationalise the guilt.

The therapist followed many aspects of Chu's three stage model of working with survivors of CSA (Chu 1992). The first stage involves building relationships and setting the scene for work. It includes establishing a contract of self-care, acknowledging the trauma, building the client's sense of self-control, allowing the therapeutic expression of feelings and establishing a collaborative relationship which doesn't replicate past abusive relationships.

In my case there were clear boundaries which helped make it safe to express feelings such as the anger which had been sitting there for so long that it felt that it would be uncontainable if it escaped. I spent a lot of time beating up cushions and then crying. Also, I felt my experience was believed and I was valued as a person. Lew (1993) says: 'a major challenge of recovery for most incest survivors is rebuilding their self-esteem to the point where they begin to see in themselves what others see in them and recognise that these perceptions are accurate. As they accomplish this they move forward, liking themselves as much as others like them' (p.43).

The second stage, exploration and abreaction, should take place from a position of strength as it often leads to increased symptoms such as disturbed sleep and increased anxiety. During this stage I wrote: 'One night they broke through. I tried to pen them in by thinking about painting pictures. But I could not keep out the visions of abusive sex flashing through my head and the voices would not be drowned by the record player, however loud I turned it up'.

The next part of this stage is intense internal conflict, such as survivors having feelings of self-blame while recognising that they were not responsible for the abuse. Then comes acceptance and mourning as the full extent of past realities sinks in. For me, this was always made difficult by my doubts as to whether the abuse had taken place. Were my recalled experiences true? How does one know? I tried confronting my alleged abuser but it was inconclusive. There was circumstantial evidence but not enough to convict. I could establish that I had been to the children's home where the first abuse had taken place, but no more.

There's an explanatory power in the sense that it made a lot of my behaviour and experiences understandable, but that's hardly conclusive. If I wasn't abused, where do the memories come from and, more importantly, the depth of emotions which surfaces with them? They definitely weren't implanted by the therapist. Other support for being abused comes from sharing experiences with other survivors. These range from bedtime rituals, the degree of touching in relationships and similar physical ailments to feelings of shared experiences. Again, this is not proof but these meetings with other survivors always felt like powerful, validating experiences.

There's a psychic sense in so far as it feels true. As one therapist said to me: 'In the end does it matter? If it's true for you, it's true'. However, there's a bit of the professional me which knows the tricks memory can play. One explanation for the part of me that doubted the truth came from a further therapeutic session on confronting my second abuser, Tim, when 'I talked to him from the 80 per cent that knew he did it and from the 20 per cent that wasn't sure. If I accepted it 100 per cent, I had to accept not only the abuse but also the death threats that went with it'.

The last part of this stage is the mobilisation of strengths and the surrender of powerlessness. I experienced this particularly in a psychodrama workshop. In psychodrama, past scenes which are blocking actions in the present are re-enacted so that stuck emotions can be released and participants can be empowered to act differently in the present. The main session I remember involved revisiting the scene of my first abuse. In this re-enactment, instead of being the passive victim, the director encouraged me to use special hitting sticks to vent my anger against the key abuser onto the wall. I also used psychodrama sessions to explore options for confronting my second abuser, Tim.

The third, or final, stage consists of consolidating gains and increasing skills, in creating healthy interactions with the outside world. Chu (1992) also points out that even then people can be triggered. This is what happened over my years of therapy. At first there were a lot of triggers when things would send me back into my past. I would be aware that something was wrong but couldn't immediately extricate myself from it and would need a session with the therapist to haul me out and help me understand what had happened and develop strategies to reduce the chances of it happening again. What was useful was developing sensitivity to the moment of being triggered and being able to step back, often literally, to allow my adult awareness to stay in control.

Over time, the triggers grew more infrequent and when they appeared there was less chance of them sending me out of orbit. I also learnt to avoid them, by, for example, in groups, integrating myself quickly to minimise the risks of feeling that I was the unwanted outsider. Interestingly enough, writing this chapter acted as a trigger, bringing back to the surface feelings of negativity, of unwanted images of a time when the pain lived daily in my head. It also coincided with me developing a virulent strain of thrush. Did it carry a psychological message? Was it Tim, my abuser, warning me?

Another consequence of the abuse tackled, in part, in therapy was the sense of being an outsider in groups. As my first abuse was at the hands of a group, keeping a distance from other group members was a useful defence mechanism. The other driving force was the feeling that no one could like me if they knew what lay underneath:

> I suspect
> They suspect
> That they know something
> About me
> Which smells.
> Which is why I smile
> And exude friendliness
> To mask the smell. (Wiener 1996, p.7)

Lew (1993) puts this well:

> Along with terror came the feeling that when he had revealed enough of himself to me or to the other group members, he would certainly be rejected. We would then see how imperfect...he really is. We would be angry with him for having fooled us and would be repulsed by him. The reality was and continues to be quite the opposite...showing some vulnerability made him real and accessible. (p.115)

In order to reach this conclusion for myself, part of my therapeutic healing had to take place in groups. It involved taking risks and putting myself forward to do therapeutic work. It meant lowering defences and, on residential courses, slowly realising that people liked me. The big breakthrough came on a large Gestalt residential week of thirty people where I found myself in the centre of the room, confronting other group members until someone asked 'What's wrong with you?' and I could talk about how ugly my centre was and then I lay on the ground weeping out years of despair until people came and comforted me. It led to my being warmly accepted by most of the group and

I ended up revising my stance, shifting from 'groups are dangerous' to 'groups are okay places to take risks in'.

This didn't quite mean all groups. All male groups can often still feel quite threatening. I still find it difficult to share rooms on residential courses with strange men. Course organisers have an expectation that it's okay for men to room together – we survivors are hidden, even in the therapeutic community.

Another dominant theme near the end of the therapy was confronting one of my abusers:

> Another session with the therapist working through options. We agree that the nine-year-old me and the adult me are both going to be present at the reunion with Tim. Tim's strategy might be to go for the nine-year-old me, either via re-seduction or fear. The therapist, role playing Tim, tries out these options and my defences go up. He tries being threatening – I reply assertively – easy to do in the therapist's room which feels safe – what about Tim's room which might well be a bedsit? We talk about where I should sit: single armchair, not the sofa or the bed. Is it best to broach the subject outdoors or indoors? It depends on whether he lives alone.

We agree that what I want is validation. It happened – he did it. I'm not sure about anything after that.

Therapy was not the only pathway to surviving. It complemented and aided other changes, which included having a job in which I received a lot of positive feedback. It's not surprising that the caring services have a higher than average number of survivors. A survey of social workers found that 41 per cent suffered childhood abuse, with 22.4 per cent of women and 6.25 per cent of men reporting childhood sexual abuse (Dobson 1994).

A second factor was being in a loving relationship in which I felt cherished, despite my partner knowing all about my past.

A third factor was finding a living situation which worked for me – a house of my own that I controlled and in which I could be how I needed to be.

Fourth was a circle of friends, who became the close family I never had.

It was as if, in my middle age, I had created the conditions for a healthy childhood which I never had when I was young. My thanks, therefore, to all my therapists and to Sean, Ken and Ari in particular.

RESOURCES

There are directories which provide up-to-date information on national and local organisations. I do not, therefore, intend to reproduce this in full here.

The only national telephone Helpline for men is operated by Survivors (London), Tuesdays and Thursdays, 7–10 pm (0171 833 3737). Leeds Survivors' Collective can be contacted on 0113 262 9365. Note: the confidential Helpline operates Wednesdays 7–10 pm only and is open to men who have suffered sexual abuse at any time in their lives who live or work in the Leeds area.

Two directories we would recommend are: *The Directory and Book Services National Resource Directory*, available from Directory and Book Services, The

Sapphire Centre, 16 Beckett Road, Wheatley, Doncaster DN2 4AA, Tel/Fax 01302–768689 (DABS also provide a comprehensive mail-order service for survivors and supporters of survivors) and *The Survivors' Directory*, available from Broadcasting Support Services, Westminster House, 11 Portland Street, Manchester M1 3HU, Tel 0161–455 1212, Fax 0161–455 0066. Price: £7.00 unfunded organisation/individual, £12.00 funded organisation.

REFERENCES

Baker, A.W. (1985) 'Child sexual abuse: a study of prevalence in Great Britain.' *Child Abuse and Neglect 9*, 467–475.

Bannister, A. (1992) 'Crimes against children.' In A. Bannister (ed) *From Hearing to Healing*. London: Longmann/NSPCC.

Bolton, F., Morris, L. and MacEachron, A. (1989) *Males At Risk*. London: Sage.

Campbell, B. (1995) 'Mind games.' *The Guardian Weekend* 11 February.

Chu, J. (1992) 'The therapeutic roller coaster: dilemmas in the treatment of childhood abuse survivors.' *Journal of Psychotherapy, Practice and Research 1*, 4, 351–370.

Dobson, R. (1994) 'One in four social workers abused.' *Community Care*, 8–14 September, 3.

Glassman, D. (1995) 'Exploding the myths.' *Community Care*, 11–17 May, 13.

Etherington, K. (1995) *Adult Male Survivors of Childhood Sexual Abuse*. London: Pitman.

Grant, L. (1996) 'Beyond belief.' *The Guardian Weekend* 14 September, 22–28.

Kelly, L. (1996) 'Weasel words: "Paedophiles" and the "cycle of abuse".' *Trouble & Strife 33*, Summer.

Lew, M. (1993) *Victims No Longer*. London: Mandarin.

Mendel, M. (1995) *The Male Survivor*. California: Sage.

Peak, A. (1989) 'Under-reporting – the sexual abuse of boys.' In A. Holland and H. Armstrong (eds) *Working With Sexually Abused Boys*. London: National Children's Bureau.

Sheldon, H. and Bannister, A. (1992) 'Working with adult female survivors of childhood sexual abuse.' In A. Bannister (ed) *From Hearing to Healing*. London: Longmann/NSPCC.

Wiener, R. (1996) 'An introduction.' In C. Malone, L. Farthing and L. Mace (eds) *The Memory Bird*. London: Virago.

FURTHER READING

Bagley, C. (1990) *Child Sexual Abuse: The Search for Healing*. London: Routledge.

Coppenhall, K. (1994) 'Naming the effects of child sexual abuse.' *Health Visitor 67*, 6, 199–201.

Marlowe, H. (1988) 'The frequency of childhood sexual abuse in the UK.' *Health Trends 20*, 2–6.

CHAPTER 8

Men as Victims of Sexual Abuse, Men as Abusers

David Briggs

Lee has been abused. At age eight he was buggered by his uncle. Lee's father beat him when he disclosed the abuse. Lee went to a Detention Centre in his adolescence, having been convicted of an offence of Unlawful Sexual Intercourse. There he was physically assaulted by one of the staff. Now, some 12 years later, he has a relationship. He would like children but he has the status of a 'Schedule One Offender'. Lee has been told by the local authority social worker that if he has children he will have to undergo 'a comprehensive risk assessment'. He feels victimised again. Lee's hobbies are the martial arts.

Not an unusual story but one which highlights the ramifications of abuse and abusive systems. There are many 'Lee's', men (and women) who are victims of abuse, who struggle to survive and, often (paradoxically), who perpetrate abuse on others. The cost of this cycle of abuse, however measured, is enormous, yet somehow we struggle to intercept the cycle. The purpose of this chapter, therefore, is to consider the progression from victim to victimiser and to highlight implications for counselling. This is in the hope that those engaged in counselling victims who are also abusers will do so with an eye not only to understanding this 'victim to victimiser shift' but using such understanding to contribute to abuser rehabilitation.

The above is not to imply that abuse is best considered as a simplistic learnt behaviour or that a cycle of abuse is inevitable. Indeed, a greater challenge lies in understanding why some of those who have been abused do not go on to abuse others and why some abusers appear not to have been victimised themselves. The bigger challenge will lie in understanding the broader social and political context of relationships.

THE VICTIM'S EXPERIENCE

The experiences of men who have been sexually abused and who have gone on to abuse others are probably no different to the victim experiences of those who do not progress to abuse. Many who have been sexually abused do not recognise their experience as abusive. When asked questions such as 'Have you been abused?' or 'Were you victimised as a child?', the questions will often appear alien, the answer will often be 'no'. This is understandable when we consider the pain of abuse. It is not surprising that some victims, intentionally or unintentionally, 'blot out' that experience. Total denial of the abusive experience serves to protect and, for many clients, such denial is well rehearsed.

There are many forms of psychological self-protection. Consider dissociation, 'the defence of last resort' (Salter 1995). This is a complex psychological phenomenon to understand. It presents in many ways and serves to destroy both the experience and memory of events at the time the abuse occurs, but also serves to disrupt the retrieval of memories of the abuse at a later stage. Whilst being abused, the victim may become an 'observer', with the victim in that situation disengaging from both the abuse and abuser by 'watching' the scene as if they were a third person. Children who dissociate have been described as day-dreaming, as 'absent', as disengaged from their social surroundings. Not surprisingly, adults with histories of dissociation often show highly sophisticated and easily accessible imagery and fantasy lives. Detachment and numbing, again features of dissociation, are not uncommon signs in those who have been victimised. The challenge for those working with abusers is to understand such phenomena, to establish links between dissociation phenomena if present and those other distortions routinely seen in the abuser (e.g. distortions in intimacy, in fantasy and empathy) and to help the abuser identify and recognise their experiences of victimisation and abuse.

For those abusers who can recall being sexually abused, their description of abusive events often reflects the behaviours inherent in the targeting and grooming process. Sometimes, such men have been told why they were selected for abuse, for example because of their age, their appearance, their availability, their character, their vulnerability and so forth. Often, however, they do not understand 'why' they were selected. Sometimes they construct explanations of why, explanations which are erroneous.

Where significant grooming occurred, these men can talk of their progressive violation and the systematic escalation of their molestation. However, the manner in which events are described is often blunt and unemotive. Again, this is understandable. To perpetrate sexually abusive acts against others requires the facility to ignore the distress of the victim. For the abuser to recall or re-experience the pain of their being abused, yet at the same time not acknowledge the distress of their victim, is a difficult juxtaposition to maintain.

It is important, at this point, to note a particular characteristic of sexual abuse often neglected in the literature – the role of paraphilias in sexual abuse. Often, the sexual abuse of children is thought to be a simple manifestation of paedophilia, the sexual preference for a child. Alternatively, it might be construed as situational or transient phenomena in persons who usually are capable of age-appropriate sexual acts but, because of other needs or dysfunctions, seek sexual and emotional gratification with a child. Whatever clinical or political explanations are offered to explain sexual abuse, at a behavioural level it is common for other behaviours and fetishes (paraphilias) to accompany the sexual abuse. Hence whilst the abuse might be defined primarily by the extent of genital display and contact, it can be further described by acts which accompany it. Such acts might include the rituals and paraphernalia of sadism and masochism, the addition of pornography and 'dirty talk' to the abuse, fetishistic overtones in respect of types of clothing and materials present at the time of abuse, the involvement of bodily 'secretions' (urine, faeces, blood, saliva) in the abuse, the abuse occurring in specific places or specific times and so forth. The only limitation to these acts is the perpetrators imagination. The paraphilias are of relevance to our counselling the victims of such abuse as they can adopt a specific and independent focus of distress which can then re-emerge in phobic and avoidant behaviours. Those who progress from victim to abuser can adopt such paraphilias into their abuse repertoire.

Just as sexual abuse is often accompanied by paraphilias, it also often co-exists alongside other forms of abuse. As victims accommodate to sexual abuse, so they accommodate to physical abuse, neglect and the inevitable emotionally abusive practices which run in parallel. Those who have worked with sexual abusers who report having been physically abused are often struck by the unemotive, 'accepting', matter-of-fact tones with which physical abuse is described. It is chilling to note the repetition of the details of such physical (and, inevitably, emotional) abuse in the grooming and victim intimidation characteristics of the victim turned perpetrator.

Of relevance here, Kelly (1994) has commented on the experience of children living with violence – specifically in the context of men's domestic violence towards women. She urges consideration of the child's perceptions of the abusive situation. She questions, for example, whether the words we use to describe abuse are of significance to the child (e.g. if the abuse is labelled as 'fighting', does this contain an inappropriate presumption of mutuality within the conflict?). She questions how children make sense of violence. For example, do children respond differently to violence as a function of what they see of the behaviour of the victim, the physical signs of any abuse, the frequency of abuse and the actions which are taken following abuse, including the excuses of the abusers? Additionally, she comments that we know little about how age, gender, race, class, disability and sexuality influence children's experiences and understandings. Kelly's comments can be extended to the experience of a child subject to sexual abuse. We should explore the victim's understanding of their abuse. In the case of those who progress to perpetrating abuse against others, we should understand the influence of their earlier constructs about sexual abuse on those beliefs, attitudes, values and cognitions which might underpin their abusing in adulthood.

THE WORKER'S EXPERIENCE

Men who abuse face another challenge in telling us of their experiences of being abused. It is the challenge of the worker overcoming his or her reaction and defences to the awfulness of what the abuser has perpetrated so as to be able to listen fully to their experience. Abusers deserve the same compassion, attention and professionalism when we learn of their victimisation as do non-abusers.

If the point needs to be reinforced here, the reader is referred to the text by Freda Briggs (1995). Here child sex abusers tell their stories, of their development, of their vulnerabilities in childhood, their early sexualistion and their distorted relationships in adulthood. It is difficult when reading the stories of the men and women featured in this book not to experience contradictory emotions and not to feel the burden of the inter-generational transmission of such abuse.

Often, workers are sceptical of abusers who disclose histories of sexual victimisation, believing or fearing that such disclosures are distractions or excuses designed to deflect responsibility taking. Experience suggests, however, that it is simplistic to view disclosure of abuse as an avoidance strategy. Minimisation and avoidance of responsibility taking are ever-present dynamics within the therapeutic relationship with all sexual abusers. There may well be times when abusers choose to recall their experiences of victimisation so as to avoid other challenges given to them within therapy, but there will also be times when the abuser seeks genuine support as he attempts to ventilate and expose his trauma.

The manner in which disclosure of victim experience is received and managed by the abuse worker is crucial. A sensitive balance of support and challenge is required, yet this can so easily transmute into confrontation or disbelief. The dynamics of the 'therapeutic' relationship can adopt abuses of power and role just as debilitating as those dynamics which served to under-pin the original abuse.

Abusers who have been victimised are little different to other victims in the manner in which disclosure is made. The full detail of their victimisation might not be revealed initially. Their story might change, elements might be retracted and some details might be unknown to them. Workers trained in assumption-based approaches to sex offender work (e.g. 'all sexual offenders lie and minimise') have to be very careful in their dealing with victimisation disclosure material. Active listening is called for.

The gender of the worker, and the transferences associated with this, have an effect on the style of disclosure. Consider the abuser who reports earlier victimisation at the hands of males. Imagine that same victim/abuser disclosing the details of the abuse to a male worker, a worker who may be perceived as controlling and powerful and thereby sharing characteristics with the primary abuser. The perception within therapy of dynamics of dominance and submission, of dependency, of control and of impotency, and the counter reactions to these, will be of relevance to understanding disclosure. Kupers (1993), in commenting on the struggle for power in the consulting room, comments of men in therapy: 'because they have learned very early never to trust another man, they keep the therapist at arms length or entrap him in seemingly endless targets' (p.111).

VICTIM TO VICTIMISER

Researchers in recent times have risen to the challenge of developing models to understand the possible victim to victimiser shift.

Cathy Spatz Widom (1996) presented an analysis of the behavioural consequences of child maltreatment to the San Diego Conference on Responding to Child Maltreatment. She argued that to understand the consequences of abuse, we need to consider the characteristics of the child (bearing in mind that personality characteristics relate to subsequent behaviour), the characteristics of the parent and wider family and, importantly, the characteristics and practices of the community (with the 'community' affording both a buffer against the effects of abuse but also acting potentially as a catalyst for adverse effects). Widom suggested that childhood victimisation has the potential to affect multiple domains of functioning (neurological/medical, cognitive/intellectual, social/behavioural and psychological/emotional). She stressed that the consequences of victimisation might well be age related, with deficits and dysfunctional behaviours at one developmental period continuing to influence and lay the ground for dysfunctional behaviours at the next stage. Additionally, gender and ethnicity may affect outcome. Importantly, she points out that dysfunction is not inevitable in abuse scenarios and encourages further research to understand those who appear to have little or no symptomotology.

In a paper complementary to Widom, Martha Erickson (1996) developed notions of strategies for helping parents break inter-generational cycles of abuse. Erickson's premise is that attachment theory can be used to help understand and intervene in inter-generational abuse. For her, the key research question is that of the nature of those factors that help families survive in the face of high-risk situations. She does not argue that secure attachment is necessarily an inoculation against future difficulties but that it is a significant factor. Children with secure attachment in early childhood internalise that sense of security over time. Those who do not form secure attachment display characteristic patterns of behaviour, anxious-resistant attachment (these children do not trust comfort and so do not accept it when offered) or anxious-avoidant attachment. Whilst those working with sexual abusers are beginning to address, in broader terms, the concept of intimacy and the relevance of intimacy failure to abuse, much work has yet to be done to link such notions to underlying constructs of attachment and attachment failure.

ISSUES IN COUNSELLING

There are significant ethical issues to be addressed when counselling men who perpetrate sexual abuse and who, in turn, report being the victims of sexual abuse. Normally in counselling we have a primary client, the person who seeks our help and guidance and who expects, and has a right to, confidentiality. In orthodox counselling situations it is not the counsellor's job to dictate the direction or pace of ventilation or disclosure or to evaluate disclosed material or prescribe actions and solutions. We are faced with a dilemma in abuser counselling however, that of relating to multiple clients. Not only must we consider the abuser and his concerns as a focus of our professional activity but we also have to consider society as client also. This is especially so in the case of potential primary and secondary victims of the abuser should he relapse.

Our overriding concern must be that of public protection. This means that the needs of individual abuser clients, on occasions, will be outweighed by the needs of others. For example, when a victim of child sexual abuse discloses the identity of his abuser, we are faced with the responsibility of offering up that name for further investigation, particularly if we believe that person to have responsibility for child care. This is not open to negotiation, though, on occasions, this will alienate our abuser clients who are disclosing the details of their victimisation. It is important, however, that the client receives a clear signal as to child protection issues and a sound model of how risk is dealt with. Protecting the client's abuser from punishment, shame and social aliena-tion is not paramount; protecting others from the trauma of abuse is.

With the above in mind, it could be argued that any work with abuser as victim should dovetail into, and enhance, work with the abuser as perpetrator. There is a synthesis to be achieved between offence-focused work and victi-mology. Over recent years a consensus has developed that not only can therapy influence recidivism in sexual offenders (this being easier to demon-strate statistically with more serious offences) but certain styles of therapy, particularly those falling within the domain of cognitive-behavioural tech-niques, are most likely to prove effective. This begs the question of the style of counselling to be adopted when dealing with the abuser as victim and whether this should attempt to reflect the therapeutic style used in offence-focused therapy.

As noted above, an overriding concern in work with abusers is that of preventing the further victimisation of others. When counselling sexual abus-ers this means that, inevitably, we have to discuss the most intimate aspects of their experience in a way not usually undertaken with other clients. The currency of the abusers' sexuality, in all its aspects, is open for scrutiny. We need to learn of their contemporary sexual history and interests, their fanta-sies, their attractions and the pattern of sexual arousal at both a genital and emotional level. Even the most simple of models put forward to describe the patterning of sexual abuse call for quite demanding self-disclosure on the part of the abuser. It is not just abusers who would find such disclosure difficult, most of us would.

LEE'S CASE

When Lee was told he would have to undergo a comprehensive risk assess-ment were he to be responsible for child care, he became angry. He became angry with the social worker who advised him of this. He displaced his anger toward her and became withdrawn and verbally hostile when challenged by her. He became angry, in abstract, with the police, judiciary and those included in the criminal justice system who he believed were empowered to deal with men like his uncle. He resurrected anger towards family members who he thought had failed to protect him from the abuse. He directed anger towards a former employer who dismissed him from sessional work as a martial arts instructor, wrongly believing the employer to have discriminated against him because of his offender status. Most importantly, Lee held intense anger towards his uncle.

Lee also suffers anxiety difficulties reflecting the specifics of a post-trau-matic stress reaction. He has flashbacks to the abuse, he has nightmares of the abuse and he avoids family members and situations which remind him of his uncle. He has a secondary emotional response associated with the awareness of his anger and anxiety-based difficulties, namely that of suffering chronic depressive difficulties.

Lee remains a victim; he is not yet a survivor.

Lee also has the potential to re-abuse others. He has disclosed, several years after his conviction for USI, that he is sexually attracted to adolescent girls and, on occasions, has had sexual fantasies of pubescent girls. At 28 years old he has a 19-year-old partner whose body type and character is immature, she herself being the victim of physically, and possibly sexually-abusive parents. He has no criminal convictions since his adolescence and, to our knowledge, has not been the subject of allegations of other abusive behaviour. Nevertheless, his reported attractions and fantasy life, when placed alongside his volatility and mental health difficulties, do not allow us to rest easy about him.

Other concerns are raised. For Lee, sexual intimacy is an area fraught with confusion. It is difficult to encourage him to talk about his sexual relationship with his partner. The suggestions he makes are that he is troubled by erectile failure during lovemaking. Again, this might feed beliefs in him that he can achieve successful intimacy with immature partners but not with age-appro-priate partners, in turn, feeding the potential for him to re-abuse others.

Lee was offered choices for 'therapy' when he made his disclosure about his uncle's abuses. He was offered group counselling with other men who had been sexually victimised. He attended once. He did not return, saying that he could not tolerate the intimacy and support of the group – it was too 'overpowering'. He was offered behavioural therapy to deal with the symp-toms of post-traumatic stress. He sees his therapist monthly to six-weekly and is angry with him for not being able to provide more frequent sessions. He was offered be-friending and chaperoning when he decided to make a formal complaint to the police about his uncle. The police took his complaint seri-ously; the Crown Prosecution Service declined to pursue the matter further given the uncle's age now. The phrase 'not in the public interest' stays with Lee and fuels his resentment.

IMPLICATIONS FOR COUNSELLING

We can use Lee's case and others like it to determine guidelines for counselling abusers who have been victimised. The task of counselling should be to help alleviate the distress of the client as victim and promote healthy psychological recovery and emotional growth, but not at the cost of neglecting or ignoring the client's potential to reabuse others:

- The counsellor should ensure that whilst respecting the client's experiences of being abused, they do not support (either directly or implicitly) the notion that this prevents the client from being held responsible and accountable for his future behaviour.
- The client has choice over his future behaviour. The style of counselling should encourage the client to appreciate and make choices and, through this, learn the potential for self-control.

- Counselling should not imply 'quick-fix' solutions. The challenge for most abusers is that of long-term vigilance, an almost lifelong monitoring of their sexual urges and fantasies, and attention paid to the potential for lapse and relapse. A fine balance has to be achieved within counselling. Whilst we want clients to learn to make choices and experience self-efficacy, we do not want them to achieve over-confidence and, hence, inattention to healthy maintenance strategies. Therefore, whilst we might celebrate with our clients as they resolve the trauma of their victimisation, we should determine with them the motivation to continue to address those factors which relate to their potential to reabuse.

- Strong emotion is likely to be released as the client ventilates past experiences. Some of this might be directed at the counsellor. Additionally, the language used by the client might be abusive, might reflect values and beliefs which are dysfunctional and might serve to support sexual aggression and other power abuses. The language of this emotion should not be unchecked. Firmly and clearly, such language should be challenged, with the client given an explanation as to why.

- Often, the client will seek revenge of their abuser. Careful management of information about the abuser is needed. At the outset, and via the contracting phase of the work, the client should know that the counsellor cannot hold secrets if others are thought to be at risk from alleged perpetrators. The client himself might choose to disclose information about his abuser to the police or social workers. The client should be clear of the options for disclosure available here and the likely pros and cons of any decision taken. The counsellor should be careful not to promise a likely outcome, however. Often, decisions are taken not to prosecute or sanction alleged abusers whose abuse comes to light many years after the event. For a client who expects retribution and then sees his abuser 'going free', this can further exacerbate their feelings of powerlessness. Alternatively, this can feed revenge fantasies, which, in turn, might feed pro-abusive thoughts and actions.

- The client should be encouraged not only to review what happened to them when they were abused but to consider the similarities with how they abused others. In other words, counselling should be embedded in a framework in which the client is encouraged systematically to review his abuse of others and learn from this.

- Talking of past experiences can often trigger memories – both painful and pleasant. A health warning should be given to clients not to fantasise about material covered in sessions subsequent to the session. Particularly, the client should be made aware of the potential for disclosure of abuses to influence sexual fantasising subsequent to sessions. The client should be discouraged from such sexual fantasising, not least as in simple conditioning – the more the fantasy becomes linked with sexual arousal and ejaculation, the greater the strength the abusive interest will assume.

- Often, abusers are the subjects of authoritarian and controlling interventions designed to monitor and regulate their lifestyle. Whilst public protection is necessary, there are tactics the counsellor can use to enable the client to feel respected and supported. Open access to notes of counselling can be productive, helping the client feel a collaborator in, and owner of, the counselling process, rather than 'subject' of the process. Such openness signals honesty on the part of the counsellor; there should be nothing in the notes of counselling drawn from the client that the worker should not be able to express to the client direct.

- It is difficult for any one worker to act as both therapist for the client as victim and for the same client as abuser. Indeed, many practitioners in the area advise against this. It can be somewhat artificial to separate victim and victimiser aspects of counselling, however, and those engaged in offence-focused work often are drawn into dealing with their client's fresh disclosures of victimisation experiences. A clear contract with the client has to be drawn up following disclosure, determining the 'who', 'when', 'where' and 'how' the abusers victimisation experiences will be dealt with.

- Conversely, on occasions, abused clients find themselves drawn into a network of therapists and counsellors offering a range of complementary (sometimes potentially conflicting) interventions. For those offering counselling to support clients reconcile their victimisation experiences, close liaison and boundary setting with other workers will be necessary.

- Proper closure at the end of the sessions is vital. Many sexual abusers have a well-established pattern or chain to their abusive behaviour. Just as external events can trigger lapse or fantasies of abuse (e.g. close contact with a potential victim), so can strong internal events. Abusers report intra-personal triggers such as anger, boredom, depression, anxiety and exhilaration occurring in the build-up to their abuses. The counsellor clearly has a responsibility to ensure that the client does not leave the session in an emotional state which might trigger events leading to lapse and/or relapse.

CONCLUDING COMMENTS

This is a difficult subject for many to contemplate – the counselling and, hence, understanding, empathising and caring for men who have perpetrated some of the most abhorrent forms of abuse within our society. If those men are to learn responsibility for their future behaviour and approach emotionally healthy existences (often for the first time in their lives), their experiences of being victimised cannot be ignored. We cannot expect them to develop empathy for their victims until they are released from the past of their own victimisation. It is hoped that this chapter has raised some of the crucial issues faced by both worker and client in this special sort of counselling and that the chapter will encourage those who are called upon to help those men who abuse and who have been abused to face the challenge.

Training Exercise

For someone who has been sexually abused to then perpetrate sexual abuse on others suggests significant emotional and cognitive dysfunction. We can speculate:

(a)   that the person remains in victim mode and has not begun the journey to survivor status

(b)   that the emotion of remaining in victim mode feeds attitudes and thoughts which justify or rationalise the abuse of others

(c)   the attitudes and thoughts associated with 'victim status' are not static entities; they will react in a complex, often unpredictable, way with the client's perceptions of his environment and the manner in which he is treated by others

(d)   we cannot assume clients have the courage or capacity for healthy intimacy as a consequence of their abuse. Consequently, the client's ability to empathise might be distorted and the transferences of the counselling relationship might be skewed.

Consider those issues (a–d) and then identify for each:

- how these dynamics will manifest themselves in the counselling relationship – what behaviour, thoughts and emotions might be expressed by the client

- how the dynamics should be managed both in the short term (session by session) and in the long term (in the treatment or counselling plan).

REFERENCES

Briggs, F. (1995) *From Victim to Offender: How Child Sexual Abuse Victims Became Offenders.* St Leonards, New South Wales: Allen and Unwin.

Erickson, M. (1996) *Attachments Past and Present: Strategies for Helping Parents Break Intergenerational Cycles of Abuse.* Paper presented to the San Diego Conference on Child Maltreatment, 22–26 January.

Kelly, L. (1994) 'The interconnectedness of domestic violence and child abuse: challenges for research, policy and practice.' In A. Mullender and R. Morley (eds) *Children Living with Domestic Violence: Putting Men's Abuse of Women on the Child Care Agenda.* London: Whiting and Birch.

Kupers, T.A. (1993) *Revisioning Men's Lives: Gender Intimacy and Power.* New York: Guilford Press.

Salter, A.C. (1995) *Transforming Trauma: A Guide to Understanding and Treating Adult Survivors of Child Sexual Abuse*. Thomas and Oaks, CA: Sage.

Widom, C.S. (1996) *Behavioural Consequence of Child Maltreatment*. Paper presented to the San Diego Conference on Responding to Child Maltreatment. 22–26 January.

CHAPTER 9

Psychodynamic Counselling and Older People Who Have Been Abused

Jacki Pritchard

The aim of this chapter is to discuss how older people who have been abused can be helped by psychodynamic counselling. First, it will be necessary to explain in what ways an older person may have been abused in the past or the present. It is not my objective to go into detail about the theories of psychoanalysis or the various schools of psychodynamic counselling but rather to show how this method of counselling can help older people who are survivors of abuse. Case studies will be used extensively to illustrate how victims have been helped by this method of counselling.

OLDER PEOPLE AND COUNSELLING

The concept of older people having any sort of counselling is not a new idea but is one which has not been widely accepted. This stems from the ageism which exists in our society: 'What is the point of counselling someone who is going to die soon?'. But how do we know when a person is going to die? People are living longer. Why should someone in their 70s live with a problem without help when s/he could live for another twenty or thirty years?

We are an ageing population and as people live longer they will encounter all sorts of different problems (relationships, losses – job, health, family – bereavement, sexual issues) which could be helped by the counselling process. Being a victim of abuse is one such problem.

Since the introduction of the Community Care Act, more older people are being encouraged to remain living in the community. Assessors of need will continue to identify different needs and they will have to be imaginative about how to respond to these needs with appropriate resources. Counselling is one such resource, which, to date, is rarely written into a care plan. The need for different types of counselling will increase in future years. As social workers can rarely provide this resource now, specialist counsellors will have to be brought in.

Previously, counselling may not have been considered for older people because it was thought that older people are too rigid in their attitudes to change. Even though it has been acknowledged for many years that there is a developmental role in later life (see collected works of Jung and Erikson), many professionals believe that older people cannot change and therapeutic work which has been done with older people has not been given enough recognition.

OLDER PEOPLE AND ABUSE

So much attention has been given to child abuse in recent years that little thought has been given to the abuse an older person may have experienced in their lifetime. It is necessary to consider the fact that some older people will be victims of elder abuse, but, also, older people may have experienced abuse in their childhood or in their younger adulthood years. Therefore, it is necessary first to described the types of abuse an older person may have experienced in order to understand how counselling may help them.

Very few people think about an older person being abused, but research shows that between 5 and 10 per cent of older people suffer some form of abuse. An older person may suffer many different types of abuse in later life. This is a fairly new phenomenon, which is defined as 'elder abuse'. It is now generally accepted that there are five categories of elder abuse – physical, emotional, financial, neglect and sexual (see Pritchard 1995, 1996; SSI 1993). Table 9.1 defines these categories in greater detail.

Table 9.1: Different types of elder abuse

PHYSICAL ABUSE

Kicking, slapping, punching, hitting with hands or using implements. Causing injuries. Assaults. Force feeding. Medication abuse. Malnutrition/dehydration.

EMOTIONAL ABUSE

Humiliation. Intimidation. Ridicule. Causing fear/mental anguish/anxiety. Threats/threatening behaviour. Bullying. Verbal abuse. Harassment. Lack of acknowledgement. Isolation. Withholding social contact. Denial of basic rights. Over-protected.

FINANCIAL ABUSE

Cash/pension book is taken. Money is withheld. Money is taken to pay bills, which are not paid. Putting accounts into joint names and taking money without permission. Forced to sign over money, property, assets, valuables.

NEGLECT

Lack of basic care (not dressing/washing). Lack of food/drink/warmth/ medication. Being left sitting in urine/faeces. Absence of mobility aids. Isolation. No social contact/stimulation.

SEXUAL

Inappropriate touching, fondling, kissing. Oral contact. Genital contact. Digital penetration. Rape. Penetration with objects. Exploitation. Pornography (forced to watch or to participate in). Satanic/ritual abuse.

Sometimes, it is found that victims of elder abuse may have been abused earlier in their lives as well. Child sexual abuse is not something which only happens today. Older women and men were sexually abused as children, but because it has been a taboo subject for so long, it is very difficult for them to talk about it.

Older people may have experienced physical violence earlier in life. They may have been physically abused by parents or partners. Many older women have suffered violence from their partners all through their marriages but have never disclosed this. The older generation find it difficult to talk about such matters because they have been brought up to keep things to themselves. It was not the norm to vent your innermost feelings. Older women also took their marriage vows very seriously; it was 'till death us do part' and they were very loyal to their partners, no matter what they did.

Consequently, the counselling process can be difficult for many older people because it is so strange to them. They are used to accepting things the way they are. But counselling older people can be beneficial. The psychodynamic approach is particularly useful for older people because it helps them to go back and work through what has happened to them, to heal and get on with living the rest of their lives.

PREPARATION FOR COUNSELLING

Not everyone will be suitable for the counselling process. In elder abuse cases it is extremely difficult to get a disclosure because, often, the victim protects the abuser. However, once disclosure has taken place, the victim must be offered help. Counselling could be one of the resources offered (even if the victim does not want to move out of the abusive situation there and then) and could be included in a protection plan (see Pritchard 1996). Counselling may help a person to consider making changes in the future.

Case Example

Two women were living in similar situations. Their husbands were alcoholics and had been violent towards their wives throughout the marriages. The abuse was identified by home care staff who witnessed violent incidents and saw many injuries on the women. Both women agreed to be counselled. After two years of counselling, both women chose to leave their husbands and set up independently. When they left their husbands, one of them was 75 years old and the other was 83 years old.

Whoever is working with the victim (social worker, district nurse, community psychiatric nurse) should explain what the counselling process will involve and, if they cannot do it themselves, should refer on to an appropriate counsellor. It is very important when making a referral to consider the gender of the counsellor. Women who have been abused by a male may not wish to have counselling with a male counsellor. Conversely, a man who has been abused by a female may prefer to talk to a male. Gender issues must be discussed with the victim before referral. The victim must want help; s/he should never be forced into it or it will not be helpful to the person.

WHO CAN COUNSEL OLDER PEOPLE?

Social workers have always been proud of the fact that they counsel clients but, in recent years, the social work role has changed. Social workers are more involved with assessing need and rarely have the time to carry out long-term counselling. This is why it is likely that, in the future, counsellors will be bought in, that is purchased, to provide the service.

Abuse victims need specialist counsellors. Trained counsellors need to develop their awareness regarding elder abuse and working with older people who have suffered other types of abuse. Few older people will have experienced the counselling process and, therefore, counsellors need to be sensitive to their needs. Some counsellors may have already worked with older people, but if they have not, they need to raise their awareness of older people's needs and the different situations which will be discussed below.

WHY THE PSYCHODYNAMIC APPROACH?

Very little has been written about counselling older people and it is only now that professionals are realising that methods which are used for younger people can also be used for older people (for a fuller discussion of methods see O'Leary 1996). The psychodynamic approach can be useful because this approach helps the older person make connections with the past. Many older people do not see that the past and previous relationships can affect how they react to situations now. The counselling process may help the older person to see how the past has affected their behaviour, attitudes and current relationships. In many elder abuse cases the root cause of the present abuse often stems back to something that happened in the past.

Case Example

Whilst Mrs G was having counselling, she talked about how her mother had left her on so many occasions. During the sessions the counsellor picked up that Mrs G kept repeating the words her mother had always said to her: 'I'll be back soon. See you later'. In fact, Mrs G's mother left her daughter and other siblings for days, and sometimes weeks, to fend for themselves. Mrs G also talked about how everyone always described her as being 'headstrong', 'self sufficient' or 'never accepting of help'. Mrs G eventually saw how much her mother's actions had affected her own attitude to life. She never wanted to fully trust people in case she was let down. Mrs G came to realise just how much her mother had hurt her and how she had never admitted this to herself or anyone else.

Case Example

Katherine talked about how much she hated her father because he had never let her go to college. She had always wanted to be a teacher. She left school at 15 because 'Dad made me get a job'. She married at 18 and had a family. Her husband died when she was 30. She felt she had wasted her life and was now trapped looking after the person who had stopped her doing what she really wanted to do. Katherine had never told her father how she felt. Her frustration built up so much, she felt she had to vent it by physically hitting him. Through counselling, Katherine was able to confront her father about how she felt. The counsellor worked with Edward to review what he had done and how he felt about what his daughter felt towards him. This helped Edward come to terms with why his daughter had abused him.

Many people who are familiar with Freud may believe that the psychodynamic approach is not appropriate because Freud tended to concentrate his theories on childhood and adolescence. However, by the end of his lifetime, he had gone on to consider later adulthood. Freud changed his mind about his theory that some of his patients had been victims of child sexual abuse – later, he said that these patients had imagined or fantasised the experience. Because many people have accepted Freud's work, many victims may not have been helped because professionals have thought they have been 'fantasising'. Consequently, many older people may never have disclosed about sexual abuse for various reasons: the threats of the abuser, keeping family secrets or the fear that no one would believe them.

Many professionals find it difficult to talk about sexual matters with an older person because it makes them feel uncomfortable. Again, this relates to ageism: many people never think about older people having the same feelings as younger adults. Older people are not different to younger human beings. As Simone De Beauvoir said, 'Old people have the same desires, the same feelings, the same requirements as the young, but the world responds with disgust' (Greengross and Greengross 1989, p.34). Workers may feel uncomfortable because the client reminds them of their own parent(s) and, consequently, it feels wrong to discuss certain matters with them. But workers *must* address these issues, not pretend that they do not exist.

There are many schools of psychodynamic counselling (Freud, Jung, Klein). This is not the place to discuss them in full. A counsellor should decide which school s/he will follow and practice. I am arguing that the general theory of psychodynamic counselling can be used to work with older people who have experienced abuse. But what is psychodynamic counselling exactly? 'The word "psychodynamic" links psychotherapy and counselling with psychoanalysis…refers to the way in which the psyche (as mind/emotions/spirit/self) is seen as active, and not static' (Jacobs 1988, p.4). Psychodynamic counsellors use different methods:

- transference – the client transfers feelings onto the counsellor which enables the client to re-experience events/difficulties and obtain insight into previous relationships. The client may realise the effects of the past experiences/relationships and the causes of present problems.
- free association – the spontaneous expression of everything that comes into the client's mind. It is thought that by not controlling thoughts or feelings, the associations will reveal patterns which indicate significant underlying problems.
- dream interpretation – believed to be the way to the unconscious. Again, the past can be relived by describing the emotions and feelings which were experienced. Eventually the unconscious becomes more conscious.

One of the principal aims of psychodynamic counselling is 'to make the unconscious conscious: and in doing so, to help the person act with more conscious control and awareness than unconscious reactions permit' (Jacobs 1988, p.8). It is important to understand what is meant by 'conscious'. Freud made the distinction between 'conscious' that is mental activity which is what the client is currently thinking/feeling, and 'not conscious', that is memory of an incident, fact, emotion.

The main techniques which are involved in psychodynamic counselling are:

- listening
- observing
- responding (types of responses used are reflective, exploratory, information seeking)
- linking responses
- interpreting.

WHO CAN BENEFIT FROM PSYCHODYNAMIC COUNSELLING?

Every human being has different needs and certain counselling methods will not suit everybody. Not every older person who has been abused can be helped by a counsellor using the psychodynamic approach. The first requirement is that the older person wants to be helped and is agreeable to counselling. This should never be forced. If someone has referred on to a counsellor, the counsellor should come to meet the older person to explain what the counselling process will involve. Some older people may have weird and wonderful ideas about counselling because of what they have seen on the television: 'I thought I would be lying on a couch and he would be making notes on me'.

Usually, the counsellor makes an assessment during the first session about whether the person is suitable for psychodynamic counselling and then, if appropriate, agrees with the person how the counselling will proceed. When working with older people there may be particular problems/difficulties. Certain criteria counsellors set may not be applicable to older people. Table

9.2 shows problems an older person may have which the counsellor needs to take into consideration in the assessment process.

Table 9.2: Potential problems

SUITABLE ENVIRONMENT

If the client is still living in an abusive situation, the location of the counselling sessions needs to be 'safe'

PHYSICAL DISABILITY

The counsellor needs to be aware if the client has any particular disability, e.g. partial deafness, which might affect the counselling; the counsellor needs to sit on the side the client can hear.

ATTENTION SPAN

Some older people can only concentrate for short periods of time. If this is the case, the length of counselling sessions needs to be reduced. Some older people may have a degree of short-term memory loss; this should not exclude them from counselling but it will make the process more lengthy.

DIFFICULTY IN TALKING ABOUT THEMSELVES/
PRIVATE MATTERS

Older people may find it hard to open up about very private matters, especially the abuse they have experienced. Therefore, the beginning of the process may be quite long in order for the older person to gain confidence in the counsellor.

Some older people have special needs and this should not exclude them from psychodynamic counselling. It is not always helpful to have rigid criteria regarding who would be suitable. Some examples are:

- able to see own contribution to difficulties – this may not happen until the counselling process is well under way
- normally well functioning central ego – abuse victims often have very low self-esteem and the ego has not functioned well for years
- trusts counsellor – again, it takes time to build trust.

During the first meeting the counsellor must assess all these problems and then make an agreement with the older person about how the counselling is going to take place in the future. Agreement needs to be reached about:

- location of sessions
- length of sessions
- frequency of sessions
- recording sessions.

THE SETTING

If an older person agrees to have counselling, several decisions must be made. First, where will the counselling take place? Some older people may be immobile and housebound, so they cannot get out and the counsellor may have to come to them. An older person may choose to continue living in the abusive situation (and the abuser may be living in the same household) but want counselling. In these situations the older person may have to be seen somewhere which is considered to be 'safe'. The victim may have difficulty in leaving the house and keeping his/her movements hidden from the abuser, so the victim may wish to see the counsellor on the day s/he attends the day centre. Where there are problems and the victim could be at risk, every effort must be made to sort out the difficulties before the counselling sessions begin. Counselling should not be ruled out just because the person is still living in an abusive situation. As we have seen, the counselling process may help the victim to move on in the future.

Case Example

Jennifer had been physically abused by her husband for many years. After he had suffered several strokes, he was physically disabled but continued to abuse her emotionally. She had wanted to leave the marriage for many years but had stayed 'because of the children and I had nowhere to go'. She had been on the point of leaving when her husband suffered his first stroke. She then became the primary carer. She attended a relatives' support group once a fortnight, where she initially disclosed about the violence she had experienced. She said she would be willing to have counselling but was scared her husband would find out. A counsellor was found and she agreed to meet with Jennifer for an hour after each support group meeting. Jennifer told her husband that the group meetings were going to be extended.

Wherever the sessions are to take place, the primary requirement is privacy and the assurance that there will be no interruptions.

TIME

It is important for the counsellor and older person to agree about time and boundaries. Most counselling sessions last up to 50 or 60 minutes. As discussed, it may be difficult for the older person to find that time on a regular basis or, for some older people, that length of time may be too long for them to engage because their attention span is very short. This should be negotiated during the first session.

The frequency of sessions is also important. Most people agree to meet on a weekly basis in the early stages, but this may not always be possible (as in the case of Jennifer above, whose relatives' support group only met fortnightly). As progress is made the counsellor and older person may agree to meet less frequently.

After the first session the counsellor will make a contract with the older person. This will not be rigid as it is not normally possible to say at this stage how many sessions are going to be needed. The counsellor may agree to meet for a number of sessions in order to get to know the older person, and more about the work that needs to be done, and then renegotiate the contract.

RECORDING

The counsellor needs to record each session. This helps the counsellor to remember key things which have been said (which may be easily forgotten when a counsellor is seeing many clients). Records help the counsellor to reflect on what has been said and review the presenting problem(s) and objectives of the counselling.

Some counsellors tape each session. This needs to be agreed with the older person before the sessions take place. Some older people may initially feel that this method is offputting.

Notes can be full-length verbatim reports or shorter notes of the key points in each session. They need to be written up whilst fresh in the counsellor's mind.

WORK WHICH NEEDS TO BE DONE WITH OLDER VICTIMS OF ABUSE

Older victims of abuse may have a range of problems and feelings to work through, depending on how long it has been since the abuse has taken place. Some victims may have to go back to childhood and relive the experiences and confront their own feelings. Counsellors must have an understanding of the long-term effects of abuse in order to understand the older person and how s/he can be helped. Typical long-term effects which may have to be worked on are:

- damage to self (physical and emotional)
- physical complaints
- eating disorders
- sexual dysfunction
- anxiety problems
- mental health problems
- depression
- negative self-image
- self-injury
- suicide attempts
- feelings of guilt
- inability to trust – because of betrayal of trust

- submissiveness/lack of assertiveness
- feelings of powerlessness/helplessness
- silence – because of fear, shame, guilt.

Areas which can be worked on in psychodynamic counselling are:

- what actually happened in the past
- how the victim felt (conscious and unconscious; bringing repressed memories/feelings to the surface)
- past relationships (and their effects on behaviour and attitudes)
- distorted beliefs/perceptions
- current behaviour/current psychological functioning
- establishing trust/self-worth
- confrontation (with abuser/other people, if necessary)
- empowerment
- recovery/healing.

THE PROCESS

It is impossible to gauge how long the counselling process will take. It will depend on the pace of the client and the amount of work to be done. Objectives need to be set after the initial assessment, which is the *beginning* phase. The counsellor and older person will then build up trust, gain more knowledge about each other and become clearer about what needs to be done. The contract may be renegotiated at this stage and then they should enter the *middle* phase. The *end* will come when no more can be achieved. Case studies 1, 2, 3 and 4 illustrate the phases and work done with four different people.

Case Study 1: Mary

Background

Mary was 73 years old and had mild learning difficulties. She found it difficult to talk to her social worker but got on really well with the home care assistant. One day Mary blurted out: 'It is wrong what he does isn't it? He shouldn't do what my father did should he?' When the home care assistant asked who *he* was and what *he* did, Mary disclosed that her brother was sexually abusing her, which her father had also done.

Counselling sessions

Because Mary found it hard to talk for long periods of time, at the beginning it was agreed that the sessions would be 30 minutes long. After Mary gained confidence in the counsellor, the sessions became longer, sometimes lasting 50 minutes.

Beginning

Mary found it very difficult and insisted that her home care assistant sat in with her, which was arranged. After two sessions Mary felt she was alright on her own with the counsellor. In the early sessions Mary just wanted to talk about her brother.

Middle

The counsellor took Mary back to her childhood, which was extremely painful for Mary. Mary described herself as being 'simple' and 'the dumb one in the family'. She said no one in the family liked her because she was 'slow'. She was able to describe what her father had done to her and said she was 'very frightened' because he threatened to kill her if she did not keep the secret. She had never told anyone about the sexual abuse, which had gone on for years. Mary believed it was her fault the abuse happened because she had let the family down by being 'stupid'.

When Mary had worked through her childhood, she came straight back to her brother and the current situation. She felt extremely angry. The counsellor was able to find out why Mary was so angry (which had not come to light in the elder abuse investigation). Mary's brother was taking most of Mary's pension. She had never been to his home, so one day she went there by herself. She was so angry that he had such 'a beautiful home' and Mary said she lived 'in a mess'. Mary was being financially abused.

End

Mary was able to vent her anger and fear through the counselling process. It was helpful to her to be able to tell someone about her father and what he had done to her. She became very strong and said she did not want her brother to come to her house anymore. She needed support in doing this, so the counsellor worked with the social worker and home care staff to support Mary in being totally independent. Mary did actually confront her brother about what he had done. The sexual abuse and financial abuse stopped and Mary's standard of living improved.

Case Study 2: Agnes

Background
Agnes had been married to Jack for 40 years. While he was alive she would say very little, but was obviously a very unhappy woman. When Jack died, Agnes talked about the extreme physical violence she had experienced all through her marriage.

Counselling sessions
Agnes was a very articulate woman, who said she knew what she wanted from counselling. She met with the counsellor once a week for an hour.

Beginning
Agnes wanted to go into great detail about the violence she had experienced from her husband. She started at the beginning of their marriage and went up to the day he died.

Middle
The counsellor encouraged Agnes to talk about her feelings and thoughts through the years and her reasons for staying in the abusive situation. Agnes was adamant that her children never knew about the violence. She would then talk about her children as they are now. It became evident that she did not care very much for her middle daughter, Helen, who had been married, had two children and divorced her husband because of violence. Agnes said that Helen 'never worked at anything'. By talking about the two situations, Agnes suddenly realised that she was jealous of her daughter because she had got out of an unhappy marriage and was getting on with her life. She was able to talk to Helen about this whilst having counselling. Helen said that she and her siblings had always known about the violence and Helen had resented her mother for staying in the situation.

End
Agnes was able to talk about the violence she had experienced from Jack to her other children, who, she discovered, felt like Helen did. By using the counselling sessions she prepared herself to explain to them why she had stayed with Jack and how she felt. Because of this, their relationships with Agnes improved. Agnes felt better too and felt she could get on with a 'new life' and 'not waste any more time'.

Case Study 3: Charles

Background

Charles was financially abused by his only living relative, Matthew, who was his nephew. Matthew took charge of Charles' financial affairs and, as a result of this, Charles never had any money for himself and lived in squalid conditions. Charles was 77 years old and suffered with severe arthritis.

Counselling sessions

Charles went to his counsellor's office once a week.

Beginning

Charles had agreed to counselling because he thought it might help him think about what to do. He was very depressed and did not like the way he was living. He knew his nephew was financially abusing him but did not want anyone to intervene and he certainly did not want the police involved. He thought counselling might make him 'feel better'. Charles talked about feeling 'unhappy' and 'depressed' but found it difficult to explain his feelings. He clearly was very attached to Matthew and had no one else.

Middle

Charles believed it was a weakness to show how you feel, especially when you are upset. He had lost his sister (Matthew's mother) and her husband many years before when they were killed in a car accident. Charles had brought up Matthew as his son. Charles had never openly grieved for the family he lost. He found it hard to admit that Matthew was a failure in his eyes. Matthew had massive debts due to a gambling problem.

Charles also talked about how he had always wanted a family himself. He said there must be something wrong with him because he had never been in love or met anyone he wanted to marry. He felt inadequate emotionally. He said he found it difficult to show affection. When he talked about his own childhood, it was very similar to Matthew's. Charles' mother had also died at a young age and he had been brought up by his father and older brothers. He said there had never been any affection in the household.

End

Charles worked through his grief, both for his sister, the family he had never had and the fact that Matthew had never lived up to his expectations. Counselling was terminated when Charles had worked through his feelings and stated clearly that he wanted to remain at home. Matthew continued to abuse him.

Case Study 4: Laura

Background

Laura was 68 years old, perfectly mentally sound but physically disabled due to a severe stroke. She was raped repeatedly by her son, Thomas, who was sent to prison for four years. Laura agreed to counselling after she was admitted to residential care.

Counselling sessions

The counsellor visited Laura in the old person's home every week for one-hour sessions.

Beginning

During the first few sessions Laura was very upset. She admitted she loved her son and that she felt guilty about him being sent to prison. The counsellor explored the guilt feelings and then moved Laura back to talk about what had happened to her.

Middle

Once Laura started to disclose the details of the sexual abuse, she became very angry. This was how she had felt when she initially disclosed about the abuse to the home care assistant and said: 'I cannot take it anymore'. At this point in the counselling process she started having nightmares about the violence she had experienced whilst being raped, which the counsellor explored in sessions. The nightmares also triggered memories of her child-hood. Laura had forgotten how violent her father had been; she had totally blanked it out. She found it extremely difficult to cope with the memories.

End

Laura saw the counsellor for a year. She agreed that the counsellor could share some important information with the residential staff, so that they were aware when Laura was feeling particularly low after a difficult session. The counsellor and Laura always talked about the information which would be shared. The nightmares eventually stopped and Laura did recover. Once the counselling stopped, Laura said she felt like 'a stronger person and more open than I have ever been in my life'. She said she was capable of talking more openly about her feelings (regarding any matter) to her keyworker and other members of staff because she no longer 'bottled things up'.

Although the case studies show positive outcomes, the counselling process may not run smoothly. The older person may experience difficulties. For example:

- finds it difficult to remember what happened/to describe what happened/questions whether it really happened
- finds the re-experiencing too upsetting/cannot cope with bringing back the horrific memories/fear of remembering even more bad memories/adds to current problems
- in the early stages of counselling, cannot see the relevance of the past or make connections with the current situation
- questions the counsellor – will s/he believe what is being related?
- feelings of embarrassment, shame, guilt – worrying that the counsellor will make a judgement/lose respect for victim.

When these difficulties occur, the older person may become defensive or appear to be resisting counselling. The counsellor's role is to explore this and make it explicit:

> What perhaps distinguishes the psychodynamic approach is the recognition that there are often good reasons for a client's defences, and that the barriers that impede development towards mature relationships and attitudes frequently have to be understood and acknowledged before a person will let them down. Analysis of resistance is a major part of the psychodynamic technique, freeing the client (where it is successful) to understand more of himself, and releasing him to make the changes which he wishes. (Jacobs 1988, p.79)

Victims of abuse have developed defences as a way of coping with the abuse in the past. In psychodynamic counselling the counsellor will respect these defences because they serve a positive purpose. However, the counsellor will confront defences and resistance by trying to explore and understand them, rather than challenging them.

The end comes when the counsellor and older person agree that it is time to finish the sessions. It must be recognised that this will be another loss and that certain feelings will be evident. Even though the older person knows the work has been done, there may be feelings of panic and fear because there has been a dependency on the counsellor. Where possible, the counsellor should prepare the older person for the termination and work towards the ending. The older person should be given the opportunity to talk about how they feel about the pending loss.

CONCLUSION

I hope that in the future more older people will be referred for specialist counselling. The problem of abuse is not going to go away and as years go on we are bound to learn more about the abuse older people have experienced through their lives. At any age, a victim of abuse does need help in order to recover and heal. It should not be only younger people who are offered counselling as a resource. I believe strongly in using the past to help a person develop in the future and this is why I would promote the use of the psychodynamic approach.

REFERENCES

Greengross, W. and Greengross, S. (1989) *Living, Loving and Ageing: Sexual and Personal Relationships in Later Life*. London: Age Concern.

Jacobs, M. (1988) *Psychodynamic Counselling in Action*. London: Sage.

O'Leary, E. (1996) *Counselling Older Adults: Perspectives, Approaches and Research*. London: Chapman and Hall.

Pritchard, J. (1995) *The Abuse of Older People*. London: Jessica Kingsley Publishers.

Pritchard, J. (1996) *Working with Elder Abuse*. London: Jessica Kingsley Publishers.

Social Services Inspectorate (1993) *No Longer Afraid: The Safeguard of Older People in Domestic Settings*. London: HMSO.

CHAPTER 10

Counselling People Who Self-Injure

Lois Arnold and Gloria Babiker

INTRODUCTION

Self-injury is far more common than is generally reported or recognised. Anyone working with people who have been abused will undoubtedly come across individuals who self-injure. Yet most professional training provides little or no preparation for working with self-injury. There is often little guidance or information available for those wishing to help someone who self-injures, and there may be a lack of support for workers dealing with the difficult feelings and issues this work can raise. In this chapter we aim to provide guidance for such workers.

WHAT IS SELF-INJURY?

Self-injury is an act which involves deliberately inflicting pain and/or injury to one's own body, but without suicidal intent. The most common form of self-injury is cutting, often of the arms and hands, perhaps of the legs, and less commonly of the face, torso, breasts and genitals. Some people burn or scald themselves, others inflict blows on their bodies or bang themselves against something. Some people inflict different sorts of injury upon themselves at different times, depending upon their feelings and what is available to them.

Other ways people injure themselves include scratching, picking, biting, scraping, and occasionally inserting sharp objects under the skin or into body orifices. Less common forms of self-injury include pulling out one's hair and eyelashes and scrubbing oneself so hard as to cause abrasion (sometimes using cleansers such as bleach). Some people swallow sharp objects or harmful substances.

HOW BIG A PROBLEM IS SELF-INJURY?

Shocking though it can be to hear or read about, it is important to recognise that most self-injury is not severe. Most people who hurt themselves do so quite superficially and carefully and, although scars may often be left, no serious long-term damage is done. A small minority of people, however, do harm themselves more severely and dangerously.

To date, no studies of self-injury have been carried out in the general population, so it is not possible to be sure how many people hurt themselves in this way. Estimates have suggested that at least 1 in 600 people injure themselves sufficiently to need hospital treatment (Tantam and Whittaker 1992). This excludes those (probably many) who present their injuries as accidental. There is considerable under-reporting, with many people hiding self-injury, even from their families, and never coming to the attention of health workers. Confidential helplines receive calls from people who have injured themselves for years without telling anyone due to their shame and fear of condemnation.

It seems that self-injury is more common amongst women than amongst men. This difference is likely to reflect the different pressures and expectations placed on men and women in our society. Where men self-injure, it is usually when they have less power than is usual for men (such as in prison).

Some people do not start injuring themselves until they are adults. However, for many people, self-injury begins much younger and it may continue for many years (usually intermittently, with more self-injury at times of greater stress). Self-injury most often begins in adolescence, although for some it starts in earlier childhood when frequent scratches and bumps are disguised as 'accidents', with more systematic cutting, burning and so on developing in adolescence. It is important that professionals working with children and young people are aware of self-injury so that the problem can be picked up quickly. This is especially important given that self-injury almost always occurs in response to serious problems (such as abuse) in a young person's life.

SELF-INJURY AND OTHER SORTS OF SELF-HARM

Understandably, many people assume that when a person injures themselves they are making a suicide attempt, or at least a suicidal gesture. However, self-injury is not the same thing as a suicide attempt. In fact, it is usually something very different – a desperate attempt to cope and to stay alive in the face of great emotional pain. Most people who self-injure, if asked, are very clear that what they are doing is not a suicide attempt. They do not wish to die, only to rid themselves of unbearable feelings. Even so, sometimes an individual may feel confused about their own motivation for hurting themselves. They may need to talk through what has happened and what led up to it before they can clarify for themselves that their intention was not to die but to try to deal with their desperation.

Inflicting wounds and injuries is, of course, not the only way in which people may harm themselves. Self-injury can be seen within a much broader context of self-harm (Arnold and Magill 1996) – which includes common behaviours which are far more socially acceptable than self-injury – such as:

- abuse of alcohol, drugs, solvents; drug overdoses
- smoking
- starving, bingeing, vomiting, compulsive eating, over-exercising
- engaging in dangerous or unwanted sex

- staying in abusive or unsatisfactory relationships (n.b. there may be little choice about this)
- self-isolation
- risk-taking, putting oneself in dangerous situations
- driving too fast or when drunk
- self-neglect
- getting into fights, getting into trouble with police
- gambling, habitual over-spending
- being 'selfless', consistently putting one's own needs last
- guilt, worry, self-denigration, perfectionism
- habitual overwork, over-ambition/under-ambition
- polysurgery, 'accident proneness', factitious illness.

Although self-injury has its own very specific meanings for an individual, the problems and motivations beneath self-injury are often similar to those underlying other, more familiar sorts of self-harm. For example, in the same way that one person may use drugs or drink to escape their feelings, so another may be able to distract herself from her emotional pain by hurting her body. Many people who self-injure also, at times, engage in other forms of self-harm and there is sometimes a 'trade-off' where, for example, a person who is prevented from (or attempting to stop) self-injuring may still not be able to cope with her feelings and end up drinking or bingeing.

WHY DO PEOPLE SELF-INJURE?
Life experiences underlying self-injury

For most individuals, self-injury seems to be associated with difficult and distressing life experiences, often beginning in childhood. Research into the origins of self-injury has consistently identified certain experiences as significant. Most common amongst these are abuse or maltreatment and bereavement or loss.

Research carried out at Bristol Crisis Service for Women (Arnold 1995) surveyed 76 women with a history of self-injury. Participants commonly reported a range of childhood experiences which they believed had contributed to the distress which led them to self-injure. As Table 10.1 shows, many women reported having suffered a combination of several of these experiences, often including multiple forms of abuse and deprivation.

Table 10.1: Childhood experiences	
	Percentage of all women answering question concerning life experiences
Sexual abuse	49
Neglect	49
Emotional abuse	43
Lack of communication	27
Physical abuse	25
Loss/separation	25
Parent ill/alcoholic	17
Other	19
Source: Arnold (1995)	

The two sorts of experience most frequently reported as leading individuals to self-injure were neglect and sexual abuse. Emotional abuse was also reported by a large proportion of the women, while a quarter had experienced physical abuse. Some had frequently witnessed family violence, although not being abused themselves. Significant losses in childhood included the death of parents or siblings and prolonged or total separation from one or both parents. For a number of women, parents' illness or alcoholism led to neglect of their own needs and/or to their having to care for their parents or siblings from a young age.

A problem which many women reported as having exacerbated their situation as a child was lack of communication in the family. Some families allowed discussion of practical or intellectual matters but seemed to operate a taboo about feelings or problems to an extent which amounted to emotional neglect. This had led some women, as children, to attempt to communicate via their self-injury.

Other distress identified by some women as leading to their self-injury included being subjected to excessively high expectations within the family or school life, bullying and rejection by peers, racism and fear and shame about puberty or lesbian sexuality.

The findings of this survey in respect of childhood experiences are similar to those of other sizeable studies which have been carried out into the backgrounds of people who self-injure. Van der Kolk, Perry and Herman (1991) reported that in a study of 28 subjects, '79% gave histories of significant childhood trauma and 89% reported major disruptions in parental care...sexual abuse was most strongly related to all forms of self-destructive behaviour'. The age at which trauma occurred was significant, with the type and severity of self-destructiveness varying – the younger the child when first abused or separated from caregivers, the more cutting (as opposed to other forms of self-destructive behaviour, such as starving or binge eating or suicide attempts) and the more severe the injuries inflicted.

Arnold's survey (1995) found that where individuals related their self-injury to adult experiences, these involved similar factors to the childhood experiences reported above.

The links between life experiences and self-injury

Why should someone who has been abused or maltreated in some way, or has suffered neglect or loss, go on to repeatedly injure their own body? The links between an individual's life experiences and self-injury are complex and a range of factors may be involved (this topic is explored in depth in Babiker and Arnold 1997). Those which seem most significant include:

LEGACY OF DISTRESS

The sorts of life experiences and circumstances explored above are likely to cause individuals a range of enormously distressing feelings. Many people who self-injure report having experienced since childhood overwhelming and unbearable feelings of sadness, grief, betrayal, anger, shame, powerlessness and anxiety. The intolerable nature of their distress leads them to a desperate search for ways of alleviating and coping with their feelings.

DIFFICULTY IN IDENTIFYING, UNDERSTANDING AND VERBALISING FEELINGS

Children need to learn from their parents or caregivers how to differentiate the various kinds of distress and discomfort they experience and to express these appropriately, in words, tears and so on. Those who do not receive recognition, empathy and support for their feelings cannot learn these things. Some children growing up in abusive households may be punished for attempting to express their feelings. They may develop little ability to verbalise or even identify their experiences, feelings and needs. For such people, self-injury may become a way in which they deal with or 'speak' of their formless distress.

ABANDONMENT AND EMPTINESS

Children who have been abused or neglected are likely to suffer greatly from feelings of abandonment. They are also deprived of the opportunity to learn by example (as children who are sufficiently nurtured do) how to comfort and soothe themselves and so tolerate their feelings when distressed. As adults, they may experience overwhelming feelings of emptiness and desperation yet be unable to find ways of meeting their own emotional needs. For some, self-injury may be the expression of neediness to others, in the desperate hope of eliciting nurturance or of avoiding 'abandonment'. Some people may not even let others know of their injuries, but being injured may give them an 'excuse' or opportunity to take care of themselves in a way which they do not normally feel they deserve.

ABUSE LINKED WITH NURTURING

For children growing up in an abusive environment it is often the case that moments of suffering or terror may alternate with moments of experiencing nurture and closeness. Similarly, in adult life, in situations such as those involving domestic violence, there may be periods of calm and comfort in between passages of violence. This different experience of the abuser each time comes to signify that the abuse has ended and the 'good parent' (or 'good husband') is once again available. The person learns that they have to undergo some suffering in order to reach the 'good' in the relationship. The internalisation of this process may lead to a similar relationship to the self, which is enacted in self-injury. Self-injury is something which has to be gone through in order to be able to care for the self, to gratify feelings such as being vulnerable and needing protection.

'ACTING OUT'

Sometimes a behaviour in some way replaces a feeling or a memory associated with a traumatic experience. Hence someone may self-injure as a means of expressing both the feelings associated with trauma and the traumatic experience itself. This may happen before they are ready or able (even as an adult) to remember and to 'tell the story of' the experience.

POWERLESSNESS

Abuse and abandonment can cause children (quite appropriately) terrifying feelings of powerlessness and helplessness. These feelings do not necessarily abate as the child grows up – one of the ways in which previous trauma impacts on a person (and on their ability to cope as adults) is in the reduction of feelings of personal effectiveness or the sense that they can influence what happens to them. This sense of powerlessness may lead to self-injury as a means of attempting to gain some sense of control or autonomy.

DIFFICULTIES WITH SEPARATION/INDIVIDUATION

Abuse, neglect, loss and abandonment may all interfere with the important tasks of psychological separation from parents. In an abusive family the child's physical, as well as existential, boundaries may be repeatedly violated. She may be isolated from others outside the family and forced to maintain a high degree of identification with, and loyalty to, those who abuse her. She may be consistently expected to identify and respond to her parents' needs and feelings, suppressing her own or seeing these as synonymous with theirs. The resulting lack of differentiation and confusion between oneself and one's parents (and later, other people) may continue into adulthood. This relates to self-injury in a number of ways. On the one hand, self-injury may be carried out in a desperate attempt to identify and assert one's own self-boundaries. On the other hand, self-injury on the part of someone who has been abused may be a means of continuing the abuse on behalf of the parent. And some individuals seem to feel so closely identified with another person who has abused or hurt them that they feel that they can express their anger or desire to punish *them* on their *own* bodies.

DISSOCIATION

Many children and adults cope with traumatic experiences by numbing themselves, both physically and emotionally, or by distancing themselves from present awareness of themselves and their environment. This kind of dissociation may recur in later life, even in the absence of external threat. Although feeling distant, numb, dead or unreal may, in some situations, be protective, such feelings can also be unpleasant and frightening. Some people find that the sensation and shock of an injury to themselves can help them to regain feelings of being alive, real and present.

SELF-LOATHING

The abusive experiences which many people who self-injure have undergone often lead to a range of extremely negative feelings about the self, including shame, self-blame and guilt, low self-esteem, self-hatred and the conviction that one is 'bad', 'evil' or 'dirty'. This may be partly as a result of direct teaching, usually by the abuser, including derogatory remarks and the assertion that the reason for what is happening to the child is their own ugliness, badness and worthlessness. It may also be the child's way of attempting to understand their experience and to hold on to the belief that their parents are 'good' and would love them if only they themselves were sufficiently good and lovable. Clearly, the negative feelings induced about the self do not always lead people to self-injure but they seem to be an important pre-condition for self-injury amongst those who do choose this way of dealing with their experiences and feelings.

THE RELATIONSHIP TO THE BODY

Self-injury is an attack on the *body* first and foremost and, clearly, the feelings and perceptions the individual has about their body are highly significant in respect of self-injury. Body alienation has frequently been noted amongst children who have been sexually and/or physically abused. Sgroi (1982) reported that children who had been sexually abused viewed their bodies as contaminated and dirty, as well as alien and, perhaps, 'traitorous' to themselves. Someone who loathes and rejects their own body, perhaps blaming it for being vulnerable, hurt or abused and seeing it as alien or 'other', is far more likely to feel willing or even compelled to injure and 'punish' that body or misuse it or treat it disrespectfully.

Abuse of children frequently involves the skin, which is broken and wounded or through which pain is experienced. Some forms of abuse (such as rape) may also involve a breach of the child's physical and self-boundaries, which are delineated by the skin. The great psychological significance of the skin and the involvement of the skin in the experiences of abuse, neglect and rejection point to an important link with self-injury. Skin sensations re-establish self-boundaries, both symbolically and through immediate experience. Skin mutilation also re-creates boundary violations, which an individual may re-enact in an attempt to understand or resolve their experience. Because acts of self-injury are often followed by taking care of the skin, this may also provide soothing for which an individual longs.

SUMMARY

We have seen that people who self-injure have frequently suffered severe maltreatment, neglect or loss in childhood. Such experiences have two major effects, which may give rise to self-injury. First, they force the child to experience very complex, distressing emotions in the absence of the autonomous means of coping. Self-injury may then develop as the only alternative to feeling that one may not survive the experience. Second, such experiences often result in feelings of low self-worth, self-loathing, guilt and shame, which may lead someone to a tendency towards self-destructiveness.

The functions of self-injury for the individual

One of the most important tasks when counselling survivors of abuse who are currently self-injuring is for the counsellor and the client to establish together the functions of the self-injury, that is the ways in which it helps them to cope and the meanings it has for them. Functions which are commonly found to be important and could usefully be explored include the following:

COPING WITH UNBEARABLE DISTRESS

For many people, self-injury serves as a means of coping and carrying on with life in spite of enormous psychological distress. Some individuals have told us that their cutting, far from being similar to suicide, actually prevents them from attempting to kill themselves. Even knowing that one *can* self-injure if things become too desperate (and, perhaps, having the means to do so to hand) can help a person to get through difficult times. It is essential for counsellors to recognise the importance of self-injury as primarily a means of coping, without which a client may (at least in the short term) feel even more desperate.

The way in which self-injury can help individuals to cope is through the regulation of distress and anxiety. When things become intolerable and a person's distress exceeds their ability to cope, self-injury may reduce the extent and the intensity of the feelings and allow them to function for a while. The act of injuring the body can feel like a necessary expression or demonstration of the unbearable feelings. Where the anguish is that of loss or betrayal, it may feel as if the blood flow releases some of the grief which the person cannot alleviate through tears.

Self-injury can often express anger, as well as pain. It seems to be difficult in our society to express anger acceptably. This is particularly the case for women, who feel more unsafe in both expressing and receiving anger. If it is difficult to express anger directly, people will look for other means which carry the same powerful emotions. Many people who self-injure say that this is a means by which they deal with what feels like intolerable anger. Some people, particularly women, also speak of hurting themselves as something they do instead of hurting other people. Whether they would actually hurt someone else does not seem relevant, the fantasy that one might is sufficient to provoke self-injury.

Whilst for some people, or at some times, self-injury may be a way of *expressing* feelings, sometimes hurting oneself can also be a means of *distraction* from feelings or focusing the pain to make it manageable. The pain and injury serve to distract the person's attention away from their diffuse emotional anxiety and distress. A physical wound is far more tangible and tolerable than the emotional 'wounds' it signifies. What is notable about self-injury is its ability to serve a useful distraction or avoidance function without altering awareness, as would, for example, alcohol or substance abuse. Someone can injure themselves and then get on with work, childcare and so on. Their distress and their means of coping with it can be hidden from others for many years.

DEMONSTRATION OR EXPRESSION TO ONESELF OF ONE'S EXPERIENCE

For many people who self-injure, horrible and traumatic past experiences have been denied, minimised or ignored. An individual may feel self-injury to be a form of testimony, a way of being true to themselves and honouring their own experience and resulting feelings. Perhaps it provides evidence of their courage and endurance as well as of their suffering. This could explain why people who self-injure may feel proud (as well as ashamed) of their injuries and scars (a fact which workers may find difficult to accept). This function can be seen as akin to the importance of battle scars to some people who have served in combat.

INCREASING SENSE OF AUTONOMY AND CONTROL

Often, people in severely abusive families or in situations such as prison are reduced to self-injury as the sole means of exercising any sense of agency or feeling one has the power to make things happen. Self-injury is something over which the person has control, which they 'own' for themselves. This is one reason that attempts by workers (for example, in mental health settings) to prevent someone injuring themselves can be so ineffective and even counter-productive. The more control is taken away from the person, the more desperate they become to hurt themselves in order to assert and experience some control and power.

FEELING REAL

Sometimes people do not feel as though they are fully in the moment, living through their experiences, particularly bad experiences. This phenomenon, which, in its extremes, is referred to as dissociation or depersonalisation, may be experienced as feeling numb in the body, not quite 'there', losing time or feeling dead or as though one is in a dream and can be very distressing. Self-injury can shock the system into a sharp return to reality and end these episodes of absence from full experience – a form of 'pinching oneself awake'.

OPPORTUNITY FOR SELF-NURTURE

The period following self-injury may, for some people, provide their only opportunity to experience physical caring and comfort. Whether or not there is physical pain, the person feels they have been through something and so now 'deserve' some special caring.

SELF-PUNISHMENT

Many people, who, as children, were maltreated or abused in such a way as to make them feel bad, contaminated, guilty or evil, self-injure as a means of responding to these feelings. On the one hand, we hear reports of people who feel they rid themselves of these feelings by self-injuring – that is to say that for a while they no longer feel so bad, evil, etc. It is as if they have 'atoned' for their imagined guilt and can forgive themselves for a while. On the other hand, sometimes self-injury seems to act as a testament to someone's self-loathing. This powerful aspect may not be as amenable to the substitution of alternatives to self-injury as are some of the other functions discussed. The person's underlying conviction that they are bad, wrong and dirty will need to change before the need for the behaviour can abate, and this may take considerable time and specialist work.

CLEANSING

Individuals who feel 'dirty' or contaminated as a result of abuse may also self-injure in an attempt to bleed or cut out the 'corruption'. This function is often evidenced in very extreme forms of self-injury, such as internal cutting of the genitals, which is one of the most upsetting forms of self-injury to others. Such self-injury can be a dramatic means of trying to deal with childhood abuse and the extreme emotions engendered by it, by means of 'cutting out the abuser' or the parts of the body violated during the abuse.

AVOIDING SEXUAL AROUSAL

The physiological experience of sexual arousal may be confusing and dangerous for someone with a history of violent sexual trauma. Sexual arousal may have become associated with intolerable distress, or longing, and intense emotional pain. The direct effect of self-injury can be to deal with these feelings in an immediate physical way, which is seen as preferable to sexual release. The person may feel that they need to be punished for feeling sexual through hurting themselves.

SELF-INJURY AS A MEANS OF COMMUNICATION

The functions of self-injury we have discussed so far have, as their main characteristic, their importance *to the individual* in the internal regulation of distress. Another important function of self-injury for many individuals, however, may be the extent to which it is the only way in which they can communicate painful and complicated experiences and feelings to others. Sadly, this function is often self-defeating in that others respond in a negative way or feel manipulated and angry. Within a counselling relationship this is a very useful aspect to address. The counsellor and client need to pay attention to what is being communicated, rather than being hijacked by the means by which the message is being delivered.

GOOD PRACTICE FOR THE COUNSELLOR

The elements of good practice in counselling people who self-injure are:

The counsellor's awareness of their own feelings and reactions

In working with self-injury, as elsewhere in abuse work, perhaps the most fundamental aspect of working with integrity for the counsellor is to gain awareness of, and to deal satisfactorily with, one's own uncomfortable reactions and feelings.

Self-injury commonly arouses many uncomfortable feelings and reactions for workers and supporters, which may include:

- shock, horror and disgust
- incomprehension
- fear and anxiety
- distress and sadness
- anger and frustration
- powerlessness and inadequacy.

The counsellor monitors such feelings on a regular basis when writing up session notes and, later, in supervision. The objective of such monitoring is to remain aware of the counsellor's own progress in dealing with these difficult feelings as the client progresses through their own work.

Self-injury may also confront workers with a range of difficult issues and dilemmas, including:

- responsibility and accountability: this may conflict with their desire to allow clients privacy and autonomy
- expectations from their agency or the client's family that they will stop the self-injury
- conflicting approaches: different staff members within an agency may hold very different views as to how self-injury should be dealt with, yet there may be no provision for staff to spend time together working out their approach
- concern about the effects of self-injury on other service users.

The stress and difficulties of dealing with self-injury, and the helper's own reactions to it, can lead to ways of working which are unhelpful. This is particularly so where staff do not have sufficient support and supervision for their work. Common unhelpful responses include:

- avoidance of working with people who self-injure or of acknowledging and taking seriously the behaviour
- adopting condemnatory attitudes and simplistic explanations of self-injury
- taking authoritarian approaches to clients who self-injure
- inconsistency on the part of individual workers or within staff groups
- over-involvement and 'rescuing'.

It is natural and understandable that people working with individuals who self-injure will struggle with such difficult feelings and reactions. The paramount question then becomes how to work effectively in this context. The answer to this question rests almost solely on the necessity for counsellors to have access to appropriate supervison and support and, if necessary, personal therapy. It is assumed that counsellors who are reading this chapter and working with individuals who self-injure severely will already have an effective grasp of abuse work.

Self-injury is not an 'illness'

Counsellors (and thus their clients) should avoid a pathological view of self-injury. It is not a 'disorder' or even a symptom of disorder. It is an adaptive means of dealing with intolerable experiences and feelings. To the extent that counselling focuses on self-injury at all, the major work converges on the functional, adaptive, instrumental nature of this behaviour. The counsellor and the client need to appreciate that even the most violent forms of self-injury contain an element of self-preservation and exist for the purpose of defining, understanding and managing deep emotional pain.

The counsellor does not intervene in the self-injury

In our view, it is unhelpful to require or ask that the client stop the self-injuring behaviour. It is important to be concerned, and appropriately sympathetic, about the injury itself. Nevertheless, the main issue should be what was underlying the pain, fear or shame that the client was experiencing at the time of the injury.

This does not mean that self-injury should not be talked about. In fact, it is important to communicate that it is something which can be raised, explored and understood together and that the person will not be 'told off' or shamed because of it. It is likely that the client will fear exposing her self-injury (in the same way that she fears exposing the pain which it reflects). The counsellor who makes enquiries into areas such as self-injury should ensure that this does not come across as a violation or an intrusion into private matters. This can be helped by avoiding emotionally charged phraseology. Although we do not advocate asking about details at length, it is important for the counsellor to be able to hear, and to 'hold', the details of the self-injury. The foundation of the work consists of 'being there' for the client. The counsellor contains her need to 'do something' about the self-injury in favour of her client's need to be held.

This does not mean that the counsellor minimises or colludes with the self-injury. In fact, whilst acknowledging the self-preserving functions which self-injury has served, she also seeks, when appropriate, to help her client understand the self-loathing and self-destructive aspects of the behaviour and to explore alternative means by which the individual may cope and express themselves.

Often, therapeutic work on the issues underlying self-injury will be accompanied by a falling away of self-injury as the individual becomes more able to deal with, and integrate, her experiences. However, this may take considerable time and, in the short term, counselling or therapy may lead to an increase in self-injury as the individual faces up to buried experiences and feelings. Whilst the counsellor need not monitor the self-injury or make regular enquiries as to the frequency or extent of the behaviour, she should be open and alert to disclosure of such fluctuations. The counsellor should not see escalations of self-injury as a sign that the client is 'worsening' but rather that she is bringing into awareness previously inaccessible or unbearable feelings. The fact that the counsellor does not see increases in self-injury as a failure removes some of the shame that may be involved for the individual, who may then be able to continue to move closer to more and more of this upsetting material. However, the counsellor's awareness of escalations in the severity of self-injury may alert her to the need to adjust the pacing and focus of the work appropriately, so that the client is not overwhelmed and retraumatised but is helped to develop her own internal and external support systems so that she can tolerate the feelings which the work evokes. The counsellor and client may also need to discuss the place that self-injury has in their relationship and the extent to which it may carry 'messages' about this, as well as about past experiences in the client's life.

The work of counselling focuses upon underlying issues

In our view, self-injury is not itself a 'disorder' but a reflection of, and means of coping with, painful experiences and difficulties. It follows that the focus and bulk of the work in counselling concerns these underlying experiences and difficulties.

Counselling helps replace self-injury by providing other means to communicate strong emotions by eventually putting them into words. The ability to speak about one's experience and how it made one feel is linked directly to the acquiring of control over the effects of abuse. There is less need to self-injure, perhaps, as more potent means of communication are adopted, but there is also a deepening of respect for oneself which comes with deepened understanding and, with it, less willingness to hurt oneself. The role of the counsellor in relation to this aspect of the work is to encourage and facilitate the client in expressing their feelings and experiences in new ways. This may take considerable time and creativity and counsellors may find that means of expression such as drawing, photography, writing, etc are very helpful for people who find it hard to verbalise their experience.

The counselling relationship provides an opportunity for security and consistency and works to create a 'safe' environment where intimacy is facilitated and is helpful and positive, even when the results of this are likely to take a long time. Clearly, for the relationship to be beneficial (rather than compounding the difficulties caused by past betrayals), it must be open, safe and equal. The counsellor should always seek to facilitate the development of the client's control and power within her own life. Whilst the counsellor is flexible and offers caring and support, she does not encourage over-dependency in relation to the self-injury through, for example, setting up a 'rescuing' procedure of excessive telephone calls and emergency sessions. She encourages the client to cope, putting her in charge of her own recovery. The counsellor emphasises at every appropriate stage the client's own value systems and her need to be in control of her own life.

Self-injury can occur in the absence of immediate awareness of any difficulties in the past and the individual may construe it as a fresh coping mechanism, a response to their current situation. Indeed, it may well be the case that a client's current life circumstances themselves are extremely difficult. Counselling should pay attention to the function of the self-injuring behaviour in the present setting as well as in relation to past experience. This enables consideration of why the current situation exceeds the person's capacity to cope in their regular ways and the exploration of changes they may need to make to develop their supports and coping strategies.

REFERENCES

Arnold, L. and Magill, A. (1996) *Working with Self-injury: A Practical Guide.* Bristol: The Basement Project.

Arnold, L. (1995) *Women and Self-injury: A Survey of 76 Women.* Bristol: Bristol Crisis Service for Women.

Babiker, G. and Arnold, L. (1997) *The Language of Injury: Comprehending Self-mutilation.* London: Routledge/BPS Books (in press).

Sgroi, S.M. (1982) *Handbook of Clinical Intervention in Child Sexual Abuse.* London: Lexington Books.

Tantam, D. and Whittaker, J. (1992) 'Personality disorder and self-wounding.' *British Journal of Psychiatry 161,* 451–464.

Van der Kolk, B., Perry, C. and Herman, J. (1991) 'Childhood origins of self-destructive behaviour.' *American Journal of Psychiatry 148,* 12, 1665–1671.

CHAPTER 11

Dissociative Disorders

Liz Hall

In the past two decades there has been a growing recognition that traumatic experiences leave their mark on affected individuals. Child sexual abuse is the major trauma that has come to the attention of health and social services professionals over the last 15 years. Herman (1992) places child sexual abuse alongside other traumatic experiences that are prolonged and repeated, such as hostages, prisoners of war, torture victims in totalitarian regimes, domestic violence and paedophile or cult organised abuse. She recognises the need for a diagnostic formulation of complex post-traumatic stress disorder (PTSD) that goes beyond the simple PTSD which follows a single traumatic event, and incorporates the chronic and continuing nature of the abuse.

The central role that dissociation plays in the development of post-traumatic reactions is noted by van der Kolk and Fisler (1995). Dissociation refers to the compartmentalisation of experience so that the elements of the experience are not integrated either together or into the individual's sense of self. It is a pervasive feature of everyday life and ranges from becoming so engrossed in a task that we are unaware of our surroundings, driving familiar routes as if on 'auto-pilot' to completely forgetting all or some of a traumatic experience.

Within the trauma literature, dissociation is used to describe three distinct but related phenomena (van der Kolk, van der Hart and Marmar 1996):

- Primary dissociation – which occurs when an individual is faced with overwhelming threat and is unable to integrate what is happening into consciousness. Here, the sensory and emotional elements of the traumatic experience remain fragmented and not incorporated into the individual's memory and identity.
- Secondary or peritraumatic dissociation – where the individual dissociates at the moment of the trauma. Survivors of trauma frequently report leaving their bodies at the moment of maximum danger and observing themselves from a distance.
- Tertiary dissociation – which involves developing distinct ego-states that contain the traumatic experience, consisting of complex identities, emotional and behavioural patterns. For example, some ego-states may retain the emotional components while others retain some or all of the knowledge of the traumatic experience. This level

of dissociative fragmentation is often reported after histories of severe prolonged and chronic childhood abuse. The ultimate result of this is the development of Dissociative Identity Disorder (DID) (formerly known as Multiple Personality Disorder).

Recent research has shown that secondary dissociation at the moment of trauma is particularly associated with the development of PTSD (Bremner *et al.* 1992). It has been suggested that this narrowing of consciousness at the moment of trauma may result in amnesia for all or part of the event. The individual may be left in a state of terror which cannot be described in words and the memory of the event is, therefore, stored as a series of physical, sensory or emotional perceptions. This is confirmed by recent neuroanatomical studies where individuals show reduced activity in the brain areas dealing with speech and increased activity in areas of the brain dealing with sensory information during flashbacks (Rauch *et al.* in press; van der Kolk 1996)

Clinicians have regularly noted that survivors of child abuse describe finding ways of dissociating themselves at the moment of the abuse. Common examples include fixing a spot on the wall/ceiling, floating above the child who is being abused, hiding in the wall and counting or saying rhymes inside. This peritraumatic dissociation combined with little or no debriefing following the trauma makes survivors of child abuse highly vulnerable to the development of complex PTSD and dissociative disorders.

Evidence from studies of individuals with DID have consistently shown that up to 95 per cent have experienced child abuse which is often severe, repeated or perpetrated by multiple perpetrators. For many of these individuals, the abuse began when they were very young and was committed by their major caretakers (Kluft 1985; Putnam *et al.* 1986; Schultz, Braun and Kluft 1989).

Dissociation following and during child sexual abuse, therefore, leads to:

- the fragmentation of the experience into various components – sensory, emotional and knowledge-based information
- complete or partial amnesia for the experience
- loss of memory for normal childhood events because of the pervasiveness of the effects of the amnesia
- major effects on the developmental processes of the child. Where the abuse occurs during early childhood and continues throughout the child's formative years, the reactions to the trauma may become embedded in the developing child's personality and identity (Briere 1996)
- the development of coping strategies in the child that allow him/her to continue with some normal aspects of childhood without conscious awareness of the abuse. For example, a survivor described the necessity of dissociating from the abuse so that she could appear to be normal with the rest of the family. For many survivors, however, they are amnesic for the dissociative process and the dissociated experiences are completely unavailable to conscious awareness

- a habitual method of coping with overwhelming pain, stress and normal emotional reactions. It may be used in other normal stressful events. This results in poor development of alternative coping strategies to deal with life events and becomes an unhealthy and chronic way of pain avoidance. This in itself results in mental health problems in later life
- increasing problems in adolescence and adulthood as the long-term mental health effects of sexual abuse become more apparent but the individual is unable to make a connection between these and the abuse.

RECOGNITION OF DISSOCIATIVE DISORDERS

In the United States refining the definitions and diagnosis of dissociative disorders has become the focus of the work of many mental health workers. It has been an established diagnostic category in the Diagnostic and Statistical Manual (DSM-III and DSM-IV). The Americans have recently focused on the development of standardised assessment procedures such as the Dissociative Experiences Scale (Bernstein and Putnam 1986) and the SCID-D (Steinberg 1994). In the UK, where dissociative disorders are not part of the official diagnostic categories used in psychiatric work (International Classification of Diseases (ICD-10)), they have been recognised through work with sexual abuse survivors. The subject of dissociative disorders is still raising controversy among mental health professionals in the UK.

This section examines the signs available at interview, and through observation of the client, that may indicate the presence of a dissociative disorder. There are five core symptom or problem areas seen in clients with dissociative disorders. Individuals with Dissociative Identity Disorder (DID) will exhibit significant problems in all of these core areas. In this, distinct coherent personalities exist within one individual that may control behaviour or attitudes leading to internal struggles and confusion over issues of identity, personal history and life goals. It involves an inability to recall personal information that is too extensive to be due to normal forgetfulness.

Core symptoms

1. Amnesia

   The client reports or is observed having:

   - episodes of time that he/she cannot account for, lasting several hours or longer
   - regular brief blank spells, during which the client does not hear all or part of what was said
   - memory gap(s) for a significant period of his/her life (e.g. after the age of 5)
   - problems with consistently remembering about important people, places, aspects of his/her life
   - patchy or no memory about everyday events

- no recall of events or incidents that others tell him/her have happened
- abilities, talents and skills that he/she cannot remember learning or forgets from time to time
- knowledge of events in personal history but without memory and affect
- during therapeutic sessions, no recall of an earlier part of the session or knowledge of who the therapist is or where he/she is at that time
- confabulation to make up for the amnesia for past events in the absence of organic or psychotic problems. For example, a client thought she must have been drinking, although she could not remember doing so, and that this would explain how she had missed several hours
- times when he/she finds him/herself in a place away from home and is unaware of how he/she got there or where the place is.

2.   Depersonalisation

The client reports:

- feeling detached from him/herself
- sense of looking at or seeing him/herself as if outside his/her body
- feeling as if parts of his/her body are in some way detached or separated
- being unable to feel parts of his/her body as if they are anaesthetised
- feeling as if he/she is dead or numb
- feeling as if he/she is floating outside of his/her body. This may have occurred initially as a dissociative response to the abuse.

3.   Derealisation

The client reports:

- feeling as though familiar surroundings and people are strange and/or unfamiliar
- feeling no emotional connection with members of his/her family and with the perpetrator(s) of abuse
- feelings of unreality
- staring off into space

4.   Identity Confusion

This indicates a subjective confusion about a sense of identity. Clients often describe this as 'an internal struggle with no one knowing who is in control':

- The client reports feeling puzzled, confused or in conflict about his/her sense of identity

- The client says that it feels 'as if there are more than one of me'.

5. Identity Alteration

This represents objective behaviour indicating the assumption of different identities that are more distinct than different roles. The client:

- refers to him/herself as 'we'
- has internal dialogues with different aspects of him/herself which have unique characteristics, e.g. age, appearance. These are described as 'conversations, arguments, disagreements and discussions going on in my head'
- shows distinct changes in voice, speech, behaviour, demeanour, movement, general style of responding
- has experienced changes in identity representing distinct personalities that take control of his/her behaviour. This is often seen in changes in dress, mannerisms, interests, work habits, music likes and dislikes
- refers to him/herself by several names or others have referred to the client with different names (not nicknames or perjorative names)
- is frequently told that he/she behaves like a completely different person
- feels as though he/she has led completely different lives and is unaware of why that has occurred
- feels as though there are people inside him/her who influence his/her behaviour
- feels as if there is a child inside who takes control of his/ her behaviour and speech
- has a history of spontaneous age regressions
- shows a sudden change in presentation, often after a loud noise or because of some external changes in the environment, e.g. the client regresses, faints and then comes round as though nothing has happened
- shows evidence of handwriting changes in personal writing, including evidence of childish handwriting and spelling
- finds him/herself talking to someone who seems to know the client well but whom the client does not know
- finds articles in his/her possession that he/she does not remember buying or owning.

Background information

Additional background information about the client may be available which will assist in the recognition of a dissociative disorder.

1.   History of trauma

- history of sexual/physical/emotional abuse
- any indication that it may have begun when the client was very young
- any indication that there may have been multiple perpetrators, including women
- any indication of severe abuse, including accompanying physical and emotional abuse that may, at times, amount to severe neglect and torture of the child.

2.   Psychological difficulties

The client may show difficulties consistent with the long-term effects of sexual abuse (see Hall and Lloyd 1993 for a full description). These include anxiety and depression, relationship and sexual difficulties, sense of isolation, poor self-esteem, eating disorders and problems with touch and trust. Self-harm and suicidal attempts are particularly common in clients with dissociative disorders.

3.   Post-traumatic reactions

The client may report having intrusive memories of childhood that take the form of flashbacks, re-living experiences and nightmares. In addition, perceptual disturbances or hallucinations, particularly of the perpetrator(s) of the abuse or some aspects of the abuse itself, are extremely common in adult survivors of child abuse. These disturbances are described by Ellenson (1985, 1986) and by Hall and Lloyd (1993). They seem to be particularly associated with the threats used to silence the child and may reflect the actual abuse or the threats used by the perpetrator. Frequently, a survivor may report seeing the perpetrator in the room, laughing or behaving in a menacing way.

4.   History of psychiatric interventions

The client may have accumulated a large variety of psychiatric diagnoses suggesting widely variable presentation, rapid shifts in symptoms and levels of functioning. The client often appears to be a 'diagnostic enigma'.

5.   Physical symptoms

The client has:

- a history of severe recurrent headaches with negative neurological findings, particularly when accompanied by 'black-outs', 'lost time', seizures, regression
- unexplained pains, especially in the pelvic, rectal or abdominal regions, in the absence of physical findings. These may be physical memories.

6. Affective clues

The client reports or is observed with some of the following signs:

- flat affect
- lack of a normal range of emotional expression. The client may respond in a restricted emotional manner or appear limited in being able to express any emotion fully
- descriptions of feeling confused, distant, disconnected, floating away, dizzy, cold, numb, weird
- reporting no feelings
- reporting feelings which the client can make no sense of, as though they are detached
- showing emotion incongruent with the present situation
- rapid shutting down of emotion
- extreme terror and fear response.

7. Verbal and non-verbal clues

The following may be observed in the client:

- regular shifts in non-verbal cues such as eye contact, postural positions, mode of walking, tones of voice and ways of speaking, non-verbal gestures, breathing patterns
- flickering of eyelids as if repeatedly blinking, significant sighing or apparently losing consciousness for a few seconds prior to the changes in posture, verbal and non-verbal behaviour. This may be evidence of switching between different parts of the individual
- repeatedly answering questions with 'I don't know'
- inconsistent responses to questions about dissociative symptoms
- frequent changes in voice, tone, or accent.

WORKING WITH CLIENTS WITH DISSOCIATIVE IDENTITY DISORDER

For survivors of child sexual abuse, a point is often reached where the past experiences intrude into the present and require the individual to acknowledge and deal with the sexually abusive experiences and their consequences. This may happen because of a trigger in adult life leading to the sudden intrusion of childhood abuse memories or may relate directly to an intolerable increase in mental health problems. Survivors with dissociative disorders are no different and often enter therapy for many of the same reasons as non-dissociative survivors.

The main challenge in working with clients with DID reflects the complexity of the personality structure and the severity of the trauma that the individual may have suffered. In addition, there may be some difficulty in finding the right therapist in the UK, where considerable scepticism still exists in mental health services about the existence of DID.

The levels of adaptation and flexibility required of a therapist working with DID are complex and considerable. The therapist may have to work with:

- sexual abuse issues
- trauma memories
- individuals of different ages
- individuals of both genders
- individuals with different sexual orientations
- individuals from different racial groups
- an internal co-therapist
- an angry client
- a highly distressed client
- a mentally ill/physically ill client.

and all within one client and, perhaps, within one session.

The severity of the abuse is likely to lead to memories of abuse being recalled through flashbacks, nightmares and reliving. The client is, therefore, likely to have the memories return in sensory and emotional fragments (as they were stored at the time of the abuse) before they can be pieced together into a verbal narrative that the client can deal with.

DID clients may have remembered some of the experiences but are likely to have dissociated some into other parts of themselves (known as 'alters' in the literature). Some alters may simply act as memory holders and, once in a safe therapeutic relationship, may push the disclosure of these memories faster than the host or amnesic alters can deal with them. Continued use of dissociation through this process is highly likely and, probably, necessary, so that the impact of the return of this traumatic information is manageable.

Finding the right therapist can be a difficult task and many DID survivors have attempted to get help from a range of different agencies. Unfortunately, this may have resulted in a further stigmatisation that colours the beginning of any later therapeutic relationship.

Assessment

The recognition of DID within a client is a crucial stage in the therapeutic work. The creation of different parts of oneself is a very creative coping strategy and, as such, may be used constructively during the therapeutic process. The function of the different alters is to help and protect the core personality from the overwhelming experiences of the abuse in all its facets. However, DID clients are very hesitant and sometimes secretive about the existence of the other alters.

At this stage, gradual assessment of the dissociative process is preferable, piecing together some of the more troublesome symptoms. For example, a client spoke of her regressions occurring at work. It was necessary, therefore, to look at ways of grounding a child alter and setting limits on her emergence at work.

The aims of therapy

The aims of therapy should always be towards maintaining as high a level of functioning as is possible in the client. If the client decides to disclose the traumatic material, maintaining stability can be difficult as, for some DID clients, the memories appear almost relentlessly with little time for ordinary aspects of life. In these situations, time off work, reduction in responsibilities and, perhaps, admission to hospital may be necessary, particularly if the traumatic material is accompanied by high levels of self-harm.

For some DID clients, it may not be possible to do more than stabilise the client. Integration or resolution of the trauma may not be possible. Ross (1994) describes a range of case studies of DID clients where different aims were set depending on the needs, stability and internal resources of the client and therapist.

Building the foundation

THERAPEUTIC RELATIONSHIP

The decision to seek help from a therapist immediately involves the client in an unequal relationship. As a result, the dynamics of the abuse are likely to be brought in to the therapeutic situation. For clients with dissociative disorders for whom the abuse is likely to have been severe, started at an early age and by multiple perpetrators, these problems are maximised. The main features of these dynamics are:

- betrayal of trust
- secrecy
- abusive or intrusive touch and inappropriate physical and sexual boundaries
- gratification of the needs of the more powerful individual
- use and misuse of power
- control
- lack of empathy with the position, emotions and helplessness of the victim on the part of the perpetrator
- blaming the victim
- lack of safety.

These concerns can put an intolerable strain on the therapeutic relationship such that it prevents therapeutic work being carried out on the past. The consequence of this is that the very issue that drives much of the 'negative' behaviour of the survivor remains unaddressed.

There are a number of key issues that help in the establishment of a good therapeutic relationship with DID clients:

1. Break the traumatic rules of the past:
   - create boundaries
   - create a good, consistent and caring therapeutic relationship

- undo the secrecy
- create a climate for honesty with the therapist being willing to apologise if he/she has accidentally upset the client
- acknowledge limits.

2.   Establish a safe and well boundaried therapeutic relationship:

- safety for the client can be established by the consistent, honest and reliable behaviour of the therapist
- good quality care involving listening and hearing, interactive therapy, stepping into the 'multiple reality' (Kluft 1994) but also being able to step out. The client is unlikely to be able to tell the whole story about anything because of dissociative processes
- set clear boundaries in terms of time, place seen and for how long
- confidentiality boundaries and limits should be made explicit and, where it is necessary to inform the client's partner, GP or other supporter, permission from the client should always be sought
- boundaries should be established about touch and comfort early in the therapeutic relationship
- the therapeutic environment should be free from interruptions and intrusions, so that the client's space is valued. This is particularly important as even a telephone ringing can be enough to cause a switch to another alter and the flow of the session to be disrupted, or the client may dissociate completely, often regressing to a very frightened child alter
- rules and contracting about self-harm may need to be explored and established
- establish out-of-hours support and between-session contact, where necessary with the assistance of other agencies.

3.   Show respect for the client:

- expectations of the client clearly should be established with particular regard to:
  - daily living activities
  - medication
  - childcare where appropriate
  - household tasks
  - work
- all parts of the individual should be treated with equal respect
- the internal alters should be heard, either through the 'host' personality or for themselves
- value the ideas, skills and internal help wherever possible and safe

- all alters are part of the individual and are not separate, even though the client may experience, or wish, the alters to be separate.

MAPPING

Mapping of the personality structure is a continuous process (Ross 1989). The initial aim is to find out about the internal world of the client, with emphasis on the internal knowledge and functions of the alters. In the early stages it is likely that a child – often about 7 or 8 – will be identified, together with those alters who perform some of the routine daily tasks – such as childcare, housework, financial matters or driving. The latter are important in enabling the process of stabilising the individual in times of crisis and to complete some of the normal everyday activities.

By asking questions of the client about who inside does what and who knows who internally, a picture will gradually emerge. At the beginning of therapy the individual's system may seem straightforward but as trust develops and the traumatic material emerges the system is likely to become more complex. It is important to establish who are the self-harming and aggressive or hostile alters as they can often sabotage the therapeutic work unless they can be persuaded to help the process.

It can be useful to draw the map, delineating the names, ages and functions of the various internal alters. Some may hold the knowledge or hold an observer function. It is also possible for each alter to regress to an earlier age. The switching may occur in a defined way. The client may initially have no warning that a new alter is about to emerge, although headaches often precede the emergence. Later in therapy the client may have more control over the switching and emergence of new alters.

This encourages the development of internal co-operation and communication.

STABILISING THE CLIENT

Many DID clients seek help at times of crisis. Frequently, this crisis is a result of memories of abuse breaking through. Stabilising the client while emergency management of the breakthrough memories is undertaken is important. The DID client will need all available internal resources and, therefore, establishing good routines for basic self-care and sleep may have to be addressed.

In some situations, short-term medication can be useful. Crises in the client may also be exacerbated by the misuse of alcohol and illegal drugs and this may be the primary focus of initial work with the client.

SAFETY

Apart from therapeutic safety, there are a number of safety issues that should be addressed:

- Self-harm – self-harm is extremely common amongst individuals with DID. Understanding the function of the self-harm, and the benefits gained from it, is an essential first step. Common reasons for self-harm are release from internal pain or pressure, distraction from pain or feeling so dead inside that feeling the pain of the self-harm proves 'aliveness'. Each individual has his/her own reasons. It is important to find out which alter(s) carry out the self-harm activity, when it started and, obviously, whether there are any life-threatening risks. Contracting with the client to prevent self-harm and suicidal behaviour may become necessary, with the contract affecting all alters (Ross 1989).

- Flashback safety and grounding – when flashbacks occur, the client may switch to a very traumatised alter who may feel that the abuse is happening in the present. Helping the personality system to ground itself in the present and not in the past becomes an important safety issue. If the client lives with others, education of the carers may be necessary so that some simple grounding techniques can be taught.

- Personal safety – survivors of abuse often have issues about keeping themselves safe. This is maximised for DID clients who may have several alters with differing views about safety, including child alters who are still drawn back through fear to their abusers. Work in creating safety at home and in relation to the abuser(s) is often necessary and may result in the client reducing contact with the family of origin until he/she has sorted out the abuse related issues.

- Safety of children – for the client who has his/her own children, childcare problems may occur if the client is switching between alters and, especially, if the client regresses to the child alters. Establishing alters who may be able to maintain appropriate levels of childcare is helpful but additional support from other agencies and carers is almost always necessary.

SUPPORT NETWORK

External support networks are important in helping to stabilise the client. This might include GP, friends, family members, other professionals, church members. Contact between the therapist and this network is likely to be required (with the client's permission) without breaking confidentiality.

CRISIS MANAGEMENT TECHNIQUES

There are inevitable crises when working with a survivor of severe abuse and specific techniques for managing difficult times may have to be taught. The most frequent crises are caused by flashbacks, panic attacks, spontaneous regression or switching into an angry or hostile alter and suicidal feelings – especially around the time of disclosure. The techniques may include learning about and recognising a crisis, relaxation, visualisation, writing, phoning support person and other situation-specific methods.

The foundation work helps to build the therapeutic relationship and maximises the client's ability to use his/her own internal resources. It encourages growth of trust and self-reliance. The client's problems are likely to become worse before he/she can resolve the myriad of issues resulting from the abuse. Maintaining this work with an understanding and focus on how the abuse can lead directly to problems in adulthood keeps the client focused on the cause and consequences of the dissociative disorder.

Management of traumatic material

- The memories of trauma may appear as a combination of body memories, flashbacks, nightmares, visual and other sensory information and emotional memories.
- Some of the memories of various alters will need to be heard. The alters were created through trauma and, therefore, may need to resolve particular issues relating to a particular aspect of the abuse. For example, one alter may have been more affected by being abandoned by a parent, rather than the abuse perpetrated by the other parent.
- Emotions in the client are likely to be extreme.
- As the traumatic material increases, the client's coping strategies increase. This usually results in an increase in self-harming behaviours, including self-injury, eating disorders, workaholism and substance misuse.
- The key factors for the client may not be the worst trauma objectively. For example, one client reported that the worst part of being abused for one alter was that her abuser laughed during the abuse. Another alter held the memories of the actual sexual assault.
- Many dissociative clients come into therapy because the trauma memories are breaking through the amnesic barrier. Some work on disclosure of these memories may be necessary before any stabilisation work can begin.

Dealing with the effects of the abuse

Clients with dissociative disorders are usually survivors of child abuse. The effects of this abuse may be as fragmented as the personality system in the client. However, overall, they show the range of generalised and specific effects seen in clients without DID. The fragmentation of these problems between the alters can lead to greater difficulty in resolving them. These consequences will continuously be part of the therapeutic relationship and work but become more complex because some alters may have found a way round a particular problem that another alter is still struggling with. For example, one alter may have a sexual problem whereas another alter does not. The potential for internal healing and integration occurs, therefore, on several different levels.

ISSUES FOR THE THERAPIST

In working with DID clients there are a number of common problems faced by therapists:

- The therapist treats the client as a series of separate individuals instead of parts of one client.

- The client as a whole has to take responsibility for the actions of any alter. DID clients complain that 'it's not fair, it wasn't me' when an alter has behaved in a way that is seen to be unacceptable. By working from the start with the client as a whole, this can be minimised.
- Some alters may be easier to deal with, e.g. they are more co-operative, more trusting, not hostile. However, the therapist should respect and treat all alters equally as far as is possible.
- Sachs (1992) reported that over-involvement with the first DID client is common.
- Lack of professional support and supervision in the UK is a significant problem for many workers who work with DID clients in isolation. This can be resolved by forming therapist supervision and support networks.
- There are a range of common reactions in the therapist to working with DID clients, including fascination, preoccupation, frustration, admiration, fear, inadequacy, secondary PTSD and even burn-out. It is for this reason that education, training, support and supervision are invaluable and necessary. There are a number of books that are included at the end of the chapter to guide and assist in the education process of workers in this field.

Working with clients with dissociative disorders presents a challenge to mental health professionals, therapists and their families and supporters. It challenges many of our long-held beliefs about personality, diagnosis and mental health. However, with the right kind of help addressing the issues both associated with the traumatic experiences and the dissociative disorder, DID clients can make a good recovery and achieve their potential.

BOOKS FOR WORKING WITH SURVIVORS WITH DISSOCIATIVE IDENTITY DISORDER

Cameron, M. (1995) *Broken Child*. New York: Kensington. An autobiographical account of childhood abuse by the writer's mother and its consequences.

Casey, J.F. with Wilson, L. (1991) *The Flock*. London: Abacus. An autobiographical account of a survivor who developed multiple personalities in order to cope with child sexual abuse. Interspersed with her therapist's view of the process.

Cohen, B.M., Giller, E. and Lynn, W. (eds) (1991) *Multiple Personality Disorder from the Inside Out*. Lutherville: Sidran Press. This is a series of short articles written by individuals with MPD. Very useful in aiding the understanding of the process for clients and therapists.

Friesen, J.G. (1991) *Uncovering the Mystery of MPD*. San Bernardino: Here's Life Publishers. Extremely useful book for working with survivors with dissociative disorders and multiple personalities.

Gil, E. (1990) *United We Stand: A Book for Individuals with Multiple Personalities*. Walnut Creek: Launch Press. A useful little book for survivors at the early stages of understanding the development and use of multiple personalities.

Hocking, S.J. and Co. (1992) *Living with your Selves: A Survival Manual for People with Multiple Personalities*. Rockville: Launch Press. Useful book for clients.

Karle, H. (1993) *The Filthy Lie: Discovering and Recovering from Childhood Abuse*. Harmondsworth: Penguin Books. Account of a survivor's recovery process.

Keyes, D. (1981) *The Minds of Billy Milligan*. New York: Random House. The story of a man with multiple personalities.

Mayer, R. (1988) *Through Divided Minds: Probing the Mysteries of Multiple Personalities*. New York: Avon Books. An account of the author's work with survivors with multiple personalities and his recognition that traditional psychological models of therapy do not provide the answers.

Mollon, P. (1996) *Multiple Selves, Multiple Voices: Working with Trauma, Violation and Dissociation*. Chichester: John Wiley. This is the first British book on dissociative disorders. It uses clinical material extensively and provides a model for understanding the fragmentation of the self.

Ross, C.A. (1989) *Multiple Personality Disorder: Diagnosis, Clinical Features and Treatment*. New York: John Wiley. Looks at the development and phenomenology of multiple personality disorder in the context of a response to early and sustained trauma. Its description of the features of MPD is useful.

Ross, C.A. (1994) *The Osiris Complex: Case studies in Multiple Personality*. Toronto: University of Toronto Press. Extremely useful in describing the range of presentations and also some case studies about when not to do therapy.

Ross, C.A. (1997) *Dissociative Identity Disorder: Diagnosis, Clinical Features and Treatment of Multiple Personality*. New York: John Wiley. This is an updated and revised edition of his 1989 book. Includes sections on therapeutic neutrality and false memories.

Schreiber, F.R. (1975) *Sybil*. Harmondsworth: Penguin Books. The story of a survivor with multiple personalities.

Spiegel, D., Kluft, R.P., Loewenstein, R.J., Nemiah, J.C., Putnam, F.W. and Steinberg, M. (eds) (1993) *Dissociative Disorders: A Clinical Review*. Lutherville: Sidran Press. A book containing a series of articles by many of the prominent researchers in the field.

The Troops for Truddi Chase (1987) *When Rabbit Howls*. New York: Fontana. An autobiographical account by a woman who developed multiple personalities to survive her experience of sadistic and sexual abuse by her stepfather. Has a very useful introduction for working with survivors with multiple personalities.

REFERENCES

Bernstein, E.M. and Putnam, F.W. (1986) 'Development, reliability and validity of a dissociation scale.' *Journal of Nervous Mental Diseases 174*, 727–735.

Bremner, J.D., Southwick, S., Brett, E., Fontana, A., Rosenheck, R. and Charney, D.S. (1992) 'Dissociation and post-traumatic stress disorder in Vietnam combat veterans.' *American Journal of Psychiatry 149*, 328–332.

Briere, J. (1996) 'A self-trauma model for treating adult survivors of severe child abuse.' In J. Briere, L. Berliner, J. Bulkley, C. Jenny and T. Reid (eds) *The APSAC Handbook on Child Maltreatment*. Newbury Park: Sage.

Ellenson, G.S. (1985) 'Detecting a history of incest: a predictive syndrome.' *Social Casework 66*, 525–532.

Ellenson, G.S. (1986) 'Disturbances of perception in adult female survivors.' *Social Casework 67*, 149–159.

Hall, L. and Lloyd, S. (1993) *Surviving Child Sexual Abuse: A Handbook for Helping Women Challenge their Past.* (2nd edition). Basingstoke: Falmer Press.

Herman, J.L. (1992) *Trauma and Recovery.* New York: Basic Books.

Kluft, R.P. (1985) (ed) *Childhood Antecedents of Multiple Personality Disorder.* Washington DC: American Psychiatric Press.

Kluft, R.P. (1994) 'Countertransference in the treatment of multiple personality disorder.' In J.P. Wilson and J.D. Lindy (eds) *Countertransference in the Treatment of PTSD.* New York: Guilford Press.

Putnam, F.W., Guroff, J.J., Silberman, E.K., Barban, L. and Post, R.M. (1986) 'The clinical phenomenology of multiple personality disorder: a review of 100 recent cases.' *Journal of Clinical Psychiatry 47*, 285–93.

Rauch, S., van der Kolk, B.A., Fisler, R.E., Alpert, N.M., Orr, S.P., Savage, C.R., Fischman, A.J., Jenike, M.A. and Pitman, R.K. (1996) 'A symptom provocation study of post-traumatic stress disorder using positron emission tomography and script-driven imagery.' *Archives of General Psychiatry, 53*, 380–387.

Ross, C.A. (1989) *Multiple Personality Disorder: Diagnosis, Clinical Features and Treatment.* New York: John Wiley.

Ross, C.A. (1994) *The Osiris Complex: Case Studies in Multiple Personality.* Toronto: University of Toronto Press.

Ross, C.A. (1997) *Dissociative Identity Disorder: Diagnosis, Clinical Features and Treatment of Multiple Personality.* New York: John Wiley.

Sachs, R. (1992) *Issues for the Therapist.* Paper presented at 1st European Conference of the International Society for the Study of Dissociation held in Amsterdam.

Schultz, R., Braun, B.G. and Kluft, R.P. (1989) 'Multiple personality disorder: phenomenology of selected variables in comparison to major depression.' *Dissociation 2*, 45–51.

Steinberg, M. (1994) *Interviewer's Guide to the Structured Clinical Interview for DSM-IV Dissociative Disorders.* Revised. Washington DC: American Psychiatric Press.

van der Kolk, B.A. (1996) 'The body keeps the score: approaches to the psychobiology of Post-traumatic Stress Disorder.' In B.A. van der Kolk, A.C. McFarlane and L. Weisaeth (eds) *Traumatic Stress: The Overwhelming Experience on Mind, Body and Society.* New York: Guilford Press.

van der Kolk, B.A. and Fisler, R. (1995) 'Dissociation and the fragmentary nature of traumatic memories: overview and exploratory study.' *Journal of Traumatic Stress 8*, 505–525.

van der Kolk, B.A., van der Hart, O. and Marmar, C.R. (1996) 'Dissociation and information processing in post-traumatic stress disorder.' In B.A. van der Kolk, A.C. McFarlane and L. Weisaeth (eds) *Traumatic Stress: The Overwhelming Experience on Mind, Body and Society.* New York: Guilford Press.

CHAPTER 12

Working with Uncertainty

Zetta Bear

False Memory Syndrome
Pluck out my eyes
So I no longer cry

(Malone, Farthing and Marce 1996, p.277)

INTRODUCTION

We are living and working in the midst of a major and emotive debate about the true extent of child sexual abuse. The media is perpetuating the myth that people with so-called false memories are in the process of systematically undermining their own families in particular and the structure of family life in general.

As practitioners, we are all too aware that we are vulnerable to criticism and even legal action if we are not scrupulous in our work with clients who are recovering memories of abuse or speaking about their abuse for the first time. Discussion with colleagues leads me to believe that this environment has had a significant impact upon practice and that this is not always detrimental in that it can stimulate a review of practice to ensure that it is as ethical as possible.

Often, we work with clients whose abuse is known and undisputed, but there are occasions when people are uncertain about their history and suspect, or begin to suspect, that they have been abused. In addition, clients sometimes oscillate between certainty and doubt about their childhood experiences. Both of these situations require sensitive and skilful handling to ensure that clients are supported and assisted in their process without the interference of either excess zeal or excess caution.

In this chapter I will discuss the situations which arise in relation to uncertainty and doubt and will go on to outline basic good practice in working under these conditions.

EMERGING MATERIAL AND UNCERTAIN CLIENTS

We will sometimes find ourselves working with clients who are unsure about whether they have been abused. This can happen in a range of situations:

- the client seeks help because they suspect that they may have been abused but are uncertain about this. Perhaps a sibling has disclosed abuse or disturbing memories or feelings have begun to emerge
- in the process of working on an apparently separate presenting issue, memories of abuse begin to emerge
- the client begins to understand that events in their childhood, which they previously considered to be normal, are unusual and abusive.

These circumstances clearly demand a certain delicacy of touch. It is essential that the counsellor's approach facilitates the client's exploration of their material and does not involve any imposition on the part of the counsellor. At this stage, clients may find the notion that they have been sexually abused unbelievable. Counsellors can help by providing a space where abuse is something which can be believed without misleading, directing, or indeed terrifying, a client by interpreting their experience or diagnosing abuse on their behalf.

Many models exist to describe the symptoms a client with an undisclosed history of abuse might present. These include depression, anxiety, sexual dysfunction, problems with relating, self-destructive behaviours and somatic complaints (Drauker 1994). Counsellors may use such frameworks to make sense of the client's presenting issues but should employ caution since symptoms are not adequate evidence of abuse.

When a client discloses, research indicates that the following responses on the part of the counsellor are particularly destructive (Josephson and Fong-Beyette, 1987):

- not believing the client's story
- blaming the client for their abuse
- asking intrusive or voyeuristic questions
- minimising the impact of the abuse
- shock or disgust.

On the other hand, counsellors who can offer a calm response which conveys concern for the client provide an experience of empathy and imply that they are capable of holding the client and their material (Drauker 1994). Many counsellors now dread revelations about abuse, fearful that they may eventually result in accusations of incompetence by accused relatives or terrorised (ex-) clients. Under these circumstances, counsellors need to guard against either minimising the client's abuse or interrogating them in order to ascertain the 'truth' of their memories.

Some counsellors may not feel equipped to work safely and effectively with abuse material. In this case it is important to ensure that the client is referred to a skilled helper in a way which does not undermine them. If handled badly, referrals can leave clients feeling that they are unacceptable

Case Study 1: Michael

Michael is 26 years old. He works as a self-employed gardener and manages to get by by living rent free with his parents.

He has experienced several periods of depression and has been prescribed anti-depressants during these periods. He cannot explain why he is depressed. He describes it as 'how I am, just a part of me'.

During his late teens and early twenties he was sexually active with both men and women but has been celibate for three years since a major depression left him disinterested in sex.

He has come for counselling because his younger sister has recently accused their father of sexually abusing her throughout her childhood. Their father vigorously denies the accusation and their mother supports their father. His sister has been ostracised from the family and is appealing to Michael for support.

Michael is shocked by his sister's allegation and tells you repeatedly that he cannot believe that their father would do such a thing. However, since the incident a nightmare, recurrent in his childhood, has returned. Night after night he wakes in terror. His doctor has refused his request for sleeping pills and referred him to you instead.

Michael says repeatedly that he is sure that he cannot have been abused himself since he is certain he would remember such a thing. However, he is experiencing panic attacks and sleeplessness and is finding it harder and harder to work.

He wants you to help him to work out what to say to his sister and to his parents and to get to the bottom of his recurrent nightmare.

- How might you work with Michael?
- If you formed a hypothesis about his therapeutic needs, what might it be?
- What would your short- and medium-term plans be?

or intolerable in some way or that they are being punished for disclosing their abuse. The counsellor must ensure that the client feels heard and supported. This can be achieved by:

- discussing and negotiating with the client throughout the process
- making it clear that it is the counsellor's limitations, not the fault of the client, that a referral needs to be made
- gaining permission from the client to pass on any information

- giving the client information about the person or organisation the
  counsellor has chosen to refer them to, so that they can make an
  informed decision about whether they wish to be referred.

Finally, it is important to be alert to the possibility of disclosure with all clients. Some counsellors may overlook the possibility that older clients may recover memories or disclose for the first time (see Chapter 9). If a counsellor is not aware of this possibility, they can appear to be unreceptive and thus inhibit their client.

THE FUNCTIONS OF DOUBT

Clients doubt the possibility of abuse for many reasons:

- They may use disbelief as a defence mechanism to protect
  themselves from the extraordinary pain which usually accompanies
  the recognition of abuse.

  > The child victim prefers to believe that the abuse did not occur. In
  > the service of this wish, she tries to keep the abuse a secret from
  > herself. (Herman 1994, p.102)

- If the abuser was someone they loved or still love, or if revelations of
  abuse threaten to disrupt their family relationships, clients may
  struggle to find other explanations for their experience for some time.

  > I hate believing he raped me…I guess I wanted to hang on to some
  > feeling that he loved me, that he wouldn't do *that* to me. (Survivor
  > quoted in Fredrickson 1992, p.40)

Case Study 2: Joan

Joan is a 69-year-old woman. Her older brother, with whom she has lived for her entire adult life, died two years ago. Joan has been referred to you for counselling because she is depressed and grieving and her doctor thought she needed help to recover from her brother's death.

You have had two sessions with Joan and she has been polite but reserved. You have been working on the assumption that she is grieving for her dead brother and cannot come to terms with life without him. Suddenly, in the third session, she says that she is struggling with regrets, that she has wasted her life and that now, when she is finally free, she is too old to start living again. After this brief outburst she becomes quiet again.

- How might you respond to Joan at this point?
- How might you revise your working hypothesis?
- What do you imagine the long-term implications might be for your work together?

- People who have been abused may feel required to protect their abuser. The abuser may have threatened that the child would be punished if they disclosed the abuse. They may have been told that the abuser would be hurt, punished or imprisoned if they told. The child may have been told, or understood for themselves, that disclosure would result in considerable family disruption, for which they and others would suffer. Finkelhor (1986) points out:

    DeFrancis (1969) observed that 64% of his sample expressed guilt, although more about the problems created by disclosure than about the molestation itself. (pp.149–150)

- Abusers frequently perpetuate the myth that their victim is responsible for the abuse because of their overwhelming desirability or seductiveness. Abusers will locate responsibility for the abuse within the child rather than within themselves. The result can be that clients don't define their experience as abuse as they have been persuaded that they wanted it to happen. This dynamic exacerbates the shame usually associated with abuse and inhibits disclosure.

    Survivors feel guilty and somehow implicated and responsible for the abuse. As such they believe themselves to have encouraged it by initiating the abuse, perpetuated it by seeking out physical contact, liked it because their body responded to it, and maintained it by not doing anything to prevent it... (Sanderson 1995, p.130)

- Many abused children strive to communicate the fact that they are being abused either directly or indirectly, often many times, and will have experienced implicit or explicit disbelief on many occasions.

    Children attempting to tell their stories continue to be met with denial and disbelief. They are told that they have over-active imaginations or that they have been watching too many videos. (Bray 1994, p.X)

TRAUMATIC AMNESIA

Evidence for traumatic amnesia is extensive and, in fact, was never disputed until sexual abuse entered the arena, having appeared in scientific literature for 80 years or more. However, the extent and prevalence of sexual abuse seems to be so unpalatable that new diagnoses must be invented to discount the evidence:

    Because the findings of widespread undisclosed child sexual victimisation seem so at odds with many people's personal world views, sceptics have continued to raise the possibility that sexual abuse surveys are eliciting many fabricated or embellished reports... However, researchers have found little evidence of this kind of problem... Like researchers on other sensitive topics, they find the problem of underreporting because of embarrassment or memory loss much more apparent... (Finkelhor 1986, pp.49–50)

Research into sexual attraction to children and attitudes to assault in general male populations would indicate that sexual abuse is part of a continuum of 'normal' attitudes to sex:

> These studies clearly demonstrate that a significant percentage of the 'normal' male population believe it acceptable to carry out a sexual assault, and report the likelihood of doing so if they could be assured of not being detected or punished. A percentage also report having actually carried out forced sexual assaults against both women and children. (Morrison, Erooga and Beckett 1994, p.6)

In spite of extensive evidence of traumatic amnesia in people who have been sexually abused or traumatised in other ways, the notion is still disputed.

A review of the studies (Sanderson 1995) which have been carried out into the reliability of retrieved memories since the 1980s illustrates the availability of evidence of traumatic amnesia (Herman and Schatzow 1987; Williams and Finkelhor 1992; Briere and Conte 1993). All of these studies demonstrate that women with verifiable histories of sexual abuse in childhood were unable to recall the abuse in adulthood. Rates of traumatic amnesia in these studies varied from 38 per cent to 59 per cent and clearly demonstrate that people do forget traumatic abuse experiences. In contrast, evidence that therapists are capable of implanting extensive false memories of an abusive childhood is highly unsatisfactory and it is generally understood that the incidence of false reporting of abuse is approximately 2 per cent and certainly no more than 8 per cent (Herman 1987).

Marjorie Orr, Director of Accuracy About Abuse, states in a letter to *Community Care* magazine in March 1997: '...the indications of recent studies are that amnesia about sexual abuse affects roughly 20 per cent, and that corroboration is as easy for survivors with amnesia to find, as for those who had never forgotten their abuse.' She goes on to point out that: 'My experience is that abuse survivors themselves are usually highly uncertain of their recovered 'memories' and wish to find corroboration for their own certainty'.

This reflects my own experience that clients struggle not to believe the possibility of their own abuse, sometimes in the light of considerable evidence to the contrary. They exercise extreme caution as they negotiate their way through a territory which has become a mine field for all concerned.

As Orr points out: 'Forgetting is an adaptive response to the horrors of life'.

MEMORY AND TRAUMA

It can be difficult for us to understand how a major event, such as being sexually or physically abused, could possibly be forgotten. Common sense notions about memory can render us incredulous about amnesia.

However, even a brief overview of the factors which help us to store and retrieve memories illustrates why certain kinds of experience are almost impossible to recall in an ordinary way. In his humane and thorough book, *Memory and Abuse*, Charles Whitfield (1995) outlines a range of factors which promote the memory of an experience. The trauma of abuse actively inhibits recall by undermining these factors. An extensive description of the technical details of remembering is beyond the remit of this chapter and the reader is advised to refer to Whitfield's work.

Memory is influenced by the extent to which an experience is meaningful and the degree of opportunity present for processing the experience afterwards. The greater the level of meaning and processing, the more likely we are to be able to recall an event clearly. Sexual activity which is inappropriate to the child's stage of development will be confusing and, probably, frightening. The child will not have a frame of reference in which to place the experience and will have difficulty making sense of it for themselves. This will particularly apply to abuse which occurs at a very early age. In addition, the characteristic secrecy and denial associated with abuse will mitigate against any form of useful processing.

It is easier to recall an experience which we *share* with others, particularly near to the time of the event. Under usual circumstances we might tell, discuss or write about what is happening to us. However, abuse of all kinds usually requires secrecy. Moreover, attempts at sharing are often discouraged or even punished. Under such circumstances, abusive experiences are more difficult to retrieve.

Linked to this, the degree to which it is *safe* to remember an experience will have a bearing on how possible it is to recall it. Children who are abused are frequently subjected to threats of various sorts, which increase the extent to which memories are inhibited. This also diminishes the *usefulness* of remembering. Recalling abuse is often unhelpful to functioning and survival, particularly when someone continues to be dependent upon their abuser.

A general developmental need is *validation*. Children require validation in order to develop a sense of self. Validation also assists memory. Abusive experiences are invalidating, often involving shaming, confusion and lying. Under these circumstances, a child's experience and their memory is seriously undermined.

Our ability to remember is also influenced by our *conscious awareness* during an experience. People who are abused frequently resort to altered states of consciousness to survive (see Chapter 7) and such dissociative states can inhibit recall.

Moreover, in our culture, visual, chronological memories are regarded as valid. Other forms of memory, especially those which are fragmented or relate to other senses, are usually doubted or may not be recognised as memories at all. Memories of abuse, however, may often be encoded in dreams (Cushway and Sewell 1994), physical sensations (Caldwell 1996; Kepner 1993) or fragments (Fredrickson 1992) and can, therefore, be undermined more readily.

This is only a brief overview of the information related to remembering and forgetting but it serves to illustrate how and why an abused individual may struggle to recall events.

RECANTING AND DEFENCE

Defence mechanisms demand respect. We all employ defence mechanisms to enable us to function in a difficult world. They can assist us to retain our separateness, sense of self and integrity when under pressure. It is normal to defend oneself. '…some, perhaps all, of the defences play a part in normal development…' (Rycroft 1995, p.32).

People who have been consistently subjected to abuse have needed to employ their defence mechanisms more frequently and more vigorously than those people who have not been abused. Their defence mechanisms may well have meant the difference between living and dying at some point in their lives. As time passes, these defences may become less relevant and increasingly rigid. They may be activated by situations which are not, in themselves, extreme enough to warrant their use but which are reminiscent of past experiences which were dangerous to the individual. In other words, they may stop being useful and begin to inhibit or hamper the person to such an extent that they seek our help.

Defence Mechanisms are familiar to us all, experientially if not theoretically. They include:

Splitting

This often manifests as an inability to experience others in their complexity. People, including the counsellor, are regarded as either all good or all bad. The client finds it intolerable to hold a model of both/and, and resorts to either/or. A child who is being abused by an adult upon whom they rely for survival and long-term well-being may require this mechanism in order to cope with the impossible dilemma of having to depend upon someone whose actions are experienced as potentially annihilating. People who have been abused can also experience an internal split. It can be difficult to sustain a sense of self which includes both the damaged, abused self and the functioning, effective self. Many adults who have been abused report that they alternate between an image of themselves as damaged and an image of themselves as healthy. Belief in their abuse can be experienced as incompatible with a healthy self-image.

Projection

This mechanism involves projecting intolerable aspects of oneself onto and into others. These aspects are often regarded as 'negative' (for instance aggression) but may also be 'positive'. It is important not to overlook the fact that we can all find our assets intolerable.

Usually, people who have been abused have been permitted only a narrow range of emotions and qualities during their childhood. Sorrow may have been condemned as melodrama, anger as disobedience and so on. In addition, qualities which are reminiscent of the abuser, for instance assertion or aggression, may be abhorrent to the abused person even though they will, inevitably, possess these traits.

Clients may, for example, project their rage onto the counsellor and imagine that the counsellor is angry with or judging them. Under these circumstances it is important to check that you are not, in fact, angry with your client before you begin to explore the possibility that this is a projection.

Denial

This defence mechanism is core to working with issues of abuse with both perpetrators and victims. The term refers to the process of denying a painful experience. People who have been abused may deny that they have been abused in an attempt to avoid the pain associated with the abuse or the impact that acknowledgment of the abuse might have on family relationships. Denial can manifest in many ways. You may watch for moments when your client fails to hear or instantly forgets an intervention on your part or a statement of their own or appears to be reluctant to define an abusive experience as such in spite of evidence to the contrary. This mechanism is fundamentally useful when a person is required to endure otherwise intolerable experiences. It can also become an ongoing defence in that the client may need to deny any abusive experiences in adulthood to sustain the illusion that terrible things do not, and never have, happened to them. In this way it can damage the client's ability to take care of themselves and avoid dangerous situations. Denial differs from repression, which refers to internal states, in that it relates to external realities which are too painful or dangerous to acknowledge.

Repression and suppression

Repression is the process by which a notion or impulse which is unacceptable to us is consigned to the unconscious. In other words, we have no conscious awareness of it. The process of repression is itself unconscious. Suppression results in a similar outcome but is a conscious act of will designed to preserve life and functioning.

Clients will, therefore, be unaware of repressed material, although counsellors may begin to suspect that it is 'leaking' and effecting the client's functioning, whereas suppressed material may be more accessible. For instance, a client may avoid certain places or activities which remind them of their abuse without being aware that they are doing so.

Counsellors may also need to be alert to the use of intellectualising, minimising and humour when working with people who have been abused. These strategies are all employed to diminish the impact of a history of abuse and to control pain. This may be important to the individual who is struggling to continue to function but if a counsellor does not address such behaviour, they may inadvertently collude with it or leave someone with a sense of not being heard. My experience is that when I feedback to a client that they have described an event which I imagine may be painful to them as if it is insignificant, this has provided an important opportunity for the person to release long-repressed emotions and has enhanced the therapeutic relationship.

People who have been abused often experience periods of doubt as their defence mechanisms intervene in their process. This can result in a sense of uncertainty or outright recantation. Recourse to such defences can be triggered by a range of situations, such as:

- the emergence of previously unknown material
- the death of an abuser or significant person

- contact with the family, either directly or indirectly
- a new relationship, job or the birth of a child.

In such situations, defence mechanisms serve to protect the person from fully acknowledging their abuse and this protection allows them to function under circumstances where they might otherwise falter. In other words, under difficult circumstances, people who have been abused may resort to tried and tested coping mechanisms and these frequently involve minimising or denying the abuse in some way. As a child in an abusive situation, such denial will have been required by the family and by a society which still denies the widespread existence of abuse.

The counsellor's role under such circumstances is to allow the client to experience their doubt or denial whilst holding onto the truth of their experience of abuse on their behalf until they are capable of containing it themselves. It is essential that the counsellor maintains at least a neutral position during this process since, in my experience, clients are often either seeking affirmation of their experience or testing the trustworthiness of the counsellor. If the counsellor agrees too readily with their client that they have fabricated

Case Study 3: Francesca

Francesca is a 45-year-old woman with whom you have been working for 18 months. During the last few sessions she has been working intensively on her feelings toward her uncle, who sexually abused her for many years. This work has included a process of mourning as she counted the losses resulting from the abuse, including her inability to sustain a relationship and the consequent absence of children in her life.

During this work she experienced many flashbacks, which disrupted her life considerably, and she has taken some sick leave from her job.

She recently spoke to her mother about the abuse by her uncle, who is her mother's brother. Although initially sympathetic, her mother has now accused Francesca of being melodramatic and advised her to stop dwelling on the past. Her mother has told her that she was also abused by her brother and has simply 'got on with life'.

Francesca arrives at the next session announcing that she doesn't think that what her uncle did caused her any real harm and might not have been sexual abuse as such anyway. She has returned to work and taken on several new projects and says she has decided not to feel upset any more.

- How might you understand what is happening for Francesca at this point in her process?
- How would you respond to her immediately within the session?
- How might what she is experiencing effect your work with her in the immediate future?

or misjudged their past, they may recapitulate earlier, damaging experiences of disbelief.

THE MEANING OF RESISTANCE

This oscillation between acknowledgment and denial can be unnerving for a counsellor. Often a period of depth work will be followed instantly by a period of denial as the client struggles to remain intact and functioning in the face of the grief, rage and terror characteristic of work in such territory. Sometimes, this recourse to old protective strategies is described as resistance. This implies that the client is being unco-operative and that they should be challenged. Whilst I accept that it might be helpful to work gently with clients to make such patterns explicit and conscious, to frame them as resistance seems disrespectful or, at least, to miss the point – which is that there is only so much a person can take. The pace dictated by the client is usually the right pace for them. Under these circumstances, some or all of the following might be helpful:

- Review your work and downscale the intensity if appropriate. You may need to work further on other areas before returning to this area.
- Plan to concentrate on your client's internal and external support structures before proceeding further, to increase their ability to tolerate painful emotions. You may need to review their coping mechanisms and sources of internal strength as well as their friendship networks and contact with other helpers, including self-help groups or emergency phone lines.
- Review the therapeutic relationship to check that there is a sufficiently strong alliance between the two of you to sustain your work on these issues. It may be that you have not yet earned your client's trust and you may need to attend to this issue before work can proceed. This is an opportunity to affirm your client's right to take care of themselves and to ensure that they are safe. You may be able to use this work as a means to establish how the client discriminates between safe and unsafe situations and helpful and unhelpful relationships.

In all cases, remember that the person before you has probably survived life experiences which can and do result in death. They have done so by employing the very defences which now appear to be hampering your work together. Therefore, there is almost certainly a survival charge attached to the work you are doing and your client should be valued and respected for the extraordinary resourcefulness which has enabled them to stay alive to date. Resistance is a part of the process, not an interruption to it, and presents you with opportunities to deepen and extend your work in the service of your client.

PRINCIPLES OF GOOD PRACTICE

The false memory debate has stimulated discussion about what constitutes good practice in working with abuse. I would contend that good practice in this context is not different to good practice in general. If we are diligent in observing these principles with all clients, we will be in a position to assist them.

Abuse engenders isolation and powerlessness. Your job as a counsellor is, therefore, to provide your client with an experience of being met, valued and respected. It is my firmly held belief that techniques and theoretical frameworks have less impact upon a client than the quality of the counsellor's presence and the extent to which the client experiences the counsellor as validating, authentic and capable of holding their material.

If you create a relationship between yourself and your client where you meet together in an atmosphere of respect and compassion, you will serve your client well. It is your task to extend yourself in order to appreciate your clients' experience of themselves and the world.

There are a few simple measures which will support you in working in this way with clients:

- Be sure and clear with your boundaries, including time and money. In this way you can model clean, non-exploitative ways of relating to your client.
- Resist the temptation to rescue. It diminishes your client and reinforces their experience of helplessness as a child. This is easier said than done when witnessing the acute pain caused by abuse. However, rescuing is often motivated by a desire to make ourselves feel better. A fundamental requirement of any counsellor working with someone who has been abused is the ability to tolerate their pain.
- Always check that anything you do or say is done or said in the service of your client, to meet their needs and to support their process. Any other reason is inappropriate and could be abusive.
- Do not interpret. If you do, keep interpretations to a minimum. You are in the business of exploring your client's experience of themselves and the world.
- Hold your theories and models lightly and be ready to abandon them if they do not match your client's experience.
- Remain open minded and curious. Do not make assumptions. If you do make assumptions, be aware of the assumptions you are making and be prepared to drop them if they prove to be inaccurate.
- Attend to your own needs through supervision and support. Working with clients who have been abused can have a substantial impact upon you and you are entitled to care from yourself and others. It is also your responsibility to be fit and capable when working with your clients.

In order to adhere to good practice it is imperative that you accompany your clients on their journey and create an environment in which they feel safe enough to allow you access to their experience of themselves. As Emmy van Deurzen-Smith (1997) points out:

> The therapist who imposes a worldview, or an interpretation, is in all cases abusive and in the wrong. The therapist who forces the client to retreat into an inner world, rather than drawing the client out into the safety of the shared field, is missing the point of the encounter. (p.226)

Training Exercise: Facilitating Disclosure

1. On your own, think of a piece of information about yourself which you do not share. *NB You will not be asked to share this information with anyone else.* It may be something which your family knows but your colleagues do not, or that your friends know but your family does not. It may be something no one else knows.

2. Consider why you do not share this information with others. Is it that you are afraid that you will be judged or misunderstood? Do you worry that you would be perceived as less professionally competent or less trustworthy personally? Try to be honest and thorough in your assessment.

3. In pairs/small groups, share your understanding of what prevents you from disclosing information. You do not need to disclose the information itself in order to do this.

4. On the basis of your own experience, explore what would help you to feel able to disclose the information you keep hidden. Perhaps you need certain assurances or the security of particular policies or procedures. Perhaps you need to see evidence of particular attitudes or beliefs on the part of others before you would reveal this information.

5. Use this information to draw up good practice guidelines for staff for creating an environment which would facilitate the disclosure of intimate or difficult information.

6. Be prepared to present your guidelines to the rest of the group.

CONCLUSION

Bearing witness to the extent of childhood sexual abuse and its repercussions in the lives of adults can expose us to criticism. Credible therapists who have done valuable work on behalf of survivors have become targets for litigation, most notably Ellen Bass and Laura Davies in the United States. We are vulnerable to the accusation that we have been a destructive influence in the

lives of our clients. When we address abuse issues, family and other relationships may be disrupted as the work progresses. As the client adjusts their
relationship with an abuser, the repercussions upon other people in the client's
life are likely to be extensive and can be beneficial. This is part of the process.

I am not an advocate of confrontation unless there are current child
protection issues to address. I do not believe that confrontation is a necessary
component of recovery. In my experience, all the work which needs to be done
can occur within the counselling room. The legitimate remit of the counselling
relationship is the inner world of the client – their sense of self, inner freedom
of movement and choice and their access to emotional and spiritual resources.

Following the process of the client respectfully and with a conscious
lightness of touch is, in my opinion, the right approach, particularly in
situations where abuse is a possibility but not a certainty.

However, we must not be intimidated by the False Memory lobby into
betraying our clients or letting them down out of a fear of being criticised later
on. Our primary responsibilities are towards our clients and our own sense
of integrity and these often require us to abandon the safe path.

REFERENCES

Bray, M. (1994) *Poppies on the Rubbish Heap: Sexual Abuse, the Child's Voice.*
Edinburgh: Canongate.

Briere, J. and Conte, J. (1993) 'Self-reported amnesia for abuse in adults molested
as children.' *Journal of Traumatic Stress 6,* 1, 21–31.

Drauker, C.B. (1994) *Counselling Survivors of Childhood Sexual Abuse.* London: Sage.

Caldwell, C. (1996) *Getting Our Bodies Back: Recovery, Healing and Transformation
through Body-Centered Psychotherapy.* Boston: Shambhala.

Cushway, D. and Sewell, R. (1994) *Counselling with Dreams and Nightmares.*
London: Sage.

Finkelhor, D. (1986) *A Sourcebook on Child Sexual Abuse.* London: Sage.

Fredrickson, R. (1992) *Repressed Memories.* New York: Fireside/Parkside.

Herman, J.L. (1994) *Trauma and Recovery.* London: Pandora.

Herman, J.L. and Schatzow, E. (1987) 'Recovery and verification of memories of
childhood sexual trauma.' *Psychoanalytic Psychology 4,* 1, 1–14.

Josephson, G.S. and Fong-Beyette, M.L. (1987) 'Factors assisting female clients'
disclosure during counselling.' *Journal of Counselling and Development, 65,*
478-480.

Kepner, J.I. (1993) *Body Process: Working with the Body in Psychotherapy.* San
Francisco: Jossey-Bass.

Malone, C., Farthing, L. and Marce, L. (1996) *The Memory Bird.* London: Virago.

Morrison, T., Erooga, M. and Beckett, C. (1994) *Sexual Offending Against Children:
Assessment and Treatment of Male Abusers.* London: Routledge.

Orr, M. (1997) 'Traumatic Amnesia doesn't suit those who claim False Memory.'
Community Care Magazine, 27th February–5th March, p.14.

Rycroft, C. (1995) *A Critical Dictionary of Psychoanalysis.* London: Penguin.

Sanderson, C. (1995) *Counselling Adult Survivors of Child Sexual Abuse.* London:
Jessica Kingsley Publishers.

van Deurzen-Smith, E. (1997) *Everyday Mysteries: Existential Dimensions of Psychotherapy.* London: Routledge.

Whitfield, C.L. (1995) *Memory and Abuse: Remembering and Healing the Effects of Trauma.* Florida: Health Communications Inc.

Williams, L.M. and Finkelhor, D. (1992) 'Adult memories of childhood abuse: Preliminary findings from a longitudinal study.' *The APSAC Advisor*, Summer 1992, 19–20.

CHAPTER 13

The Impact on Professional Workers

Kate Kirk

INTRODUCTION

In this chapter I intend to define and describe the nature of the stresses the professional may experience when they work with victims and survivors of sexual abuse, the what of these stresses and how they impact on the individual worker and helping relationship. I will focus on strategies for the management and reduction of the stresses within this work, with some consideration of preventative measures. The material for this chapter has been gleaned from personal, professional and research experiences, both mine and others.[1]

THE NATURE OF STRESSES IN THE WORK

The word 'burnout' has been defined by Ayala Pines (1982):

> burnout is best defined as a state of physical, emotional and mental exhaustion. It is marked by physical depletion and chronic fatigue, by feelings of hopelessness, and by the development of negative self-concept and negative attitudes toward work, life and other people. The negative self-concept is expressed in feelings of guilt, inadequacy, incompetence and failure. (p.455)

It is important to acknowledge that this is an extreme of helpers' experiences of stress. The process of burnout is insidious and, if unrecognised, can represent tremendous loss to the individual worker, the organisation and their clients. In describing the process and progress towards burnout, Edelwich and Brodsky (1980, pp.28–29) identify a series of stages of disillusionment in the worker, which can be recognised by the person themselves and their fellow workers and supervisor. They can be summarised as follows:

- Enthusiasm: the 'initial period of high hopes, high energy and unrealistic expectations when one does not know what the job is all about'. Major hazards at this stage are 'over-identification with the clients and excessive and inefficient expenditure of one's own energy'.

---

1 Case material drawn from my research will appear in *italics*.

- Stagnation: the stage where the job no longer holds the thrills; 'one is still doing the job' but reality has crept in, 'issues of money, working hours and career development are important'.

- Frustration: in this stage the workers question their effectiveness in the job and it's value. Here the 'limitations of the job situation are now viewed as not simply detracting from one's personal satisfaction and status, but as threatening to defeat the purpose of what one is doing'.

- Apathy: described as 'the typical and natural defence mechanism against frustration', occurs when the person needs the job to survive yet is chronically frustrated by it; apathy is the attitude that 'a job is a job is a job'.

- Intervention: the final stage, is the stage which breaks the cycle and, on a hopeful note, the cycle can be 'interrupted by a decisive intervention at any point'.

The stages of disillusionment are where a helper's initial enthusiasm changes to stagnation, which, in turn, leads to frustration, apathy and, in some cases, withdrawal from work. What is it within helping relationships which leads to stress and ultimately to burnout? Pines (1982, p.455) is clear that 'burnout is always caused by emotional stresses' and is a consequence of working in emotionally demanding situations over long periods of time. In short, the intense emotional involvement with clients generated as part of professional helping relationships.

However, the emotional dimension is not the sole contributing factor. Grosch and Olsen (1994) explore the complex interplay between the helper's internal world pathology and that of the organisation. Whilst they acknow-ledge that there are some working environments which are 'so stressful and burdensome that they would exhaust the resources of almost anyone', they believe that the occurrence of burnout depends upon 'the internal state of the person experiencing the lived events and the way in which the person expresses herself in the system. In the interactional approach we assume that neither the individual characteristics nor aspects of the environment solely determine burnout' (p.84).

Kafry and Pines' (1980) trilogy of studies into tedium recognised the interaction between the these two factors, the individual's sense of themselves and in relation to their work. Important internal features in the individual were found to be connected to their sense of meaningfulness and achievement. This was judged by feedback from those around them and their feelings of significance and success in their work. Other aspects of internal features included an individual's perceptions of their role in relation to autonomy, variety and complexity. The negative internal features were those of over-ex-tension and over-commitment. External features were those connected to the organisation, for example organisational effectiveness, opportunities for time off and work sharing. The social environment of work was considered with the 'quality of work relations, degree of support and social feedback' (p.482), all seen to play a part in keeping the individual either stimulated or switched off in their work.

WORKING WITH CLIENTS WHO HAVE BEEN TRAUMATISED

Having considered the general nature of stress within helping relationships, let us focus on specific stresses arising from the broad experience of working with clients who have been traumatised. There is an increasing body of work considering the notion of secondary traumatic stress (STS) or vicarious trauma in the professional worker. Hopkins (1992) alludes to it in his use of the term 'secondary abuse'. Figley and Kleber (1995) define STS as:

> the knowledge of a traumatising event experienced by a significant other. For people who are in some way close to a victim, the exposure to this knowledge may also be a confrontation with powerlessness and disruption. *Secondary traumatic stress* refers to the behaviours and emotions resulting from this knowledge. It is the stress resulting from hearing about the event and/or from helping or attempting to help a traumatised or suffering person. (p.78)

Figley and Kleber, having focused on the impact of trauma on family members, turn their attention to 'helping professionals: psychotherapists' (p.91). They acknowledge that this is not a role that is perceived as being high risk, in comparison to, say, emergency service workers. However, they do believe that psychotherapists are 'especially vulnerable to secondary traumatic stress' – the nature of the work is such that they are brought into contact with the 'extraordinary experiences of traumatised people'. It is hardly surprising that the professional helper experiences the influence of traumatic stress.

Figley and Kleber describe some of the after-effects of the work reported by mental health workers: 'shock, confusion and sadness', that there were behavioural changes in 'eating, smoking and drinking patterns' with an increased need for support. A more full representation of the effects of STS is found in Yassen (1995) where she describes the effects both from a personal and a professional perspective – for these details see Table 13.1, on the personal impact of secondary traumatic stress, and Table 13.2 on the impact of secondary traumatic stress of professional functioning.

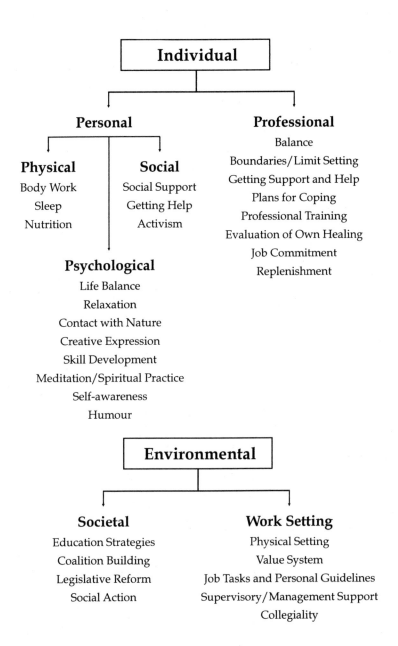

Figure 13.1: Ecological model for the prevention of STSD
Source: Yassen (1995, p.205)

Table 13.1: The personal impact of Secondary Traumatic Stress

Cognitive	Emotional	Behavioural	Spiritual	Interpersonal	Physical
• confusion	• powerlessness	• clingy	• loss of purpose	• withdrawn	• shock
• diminished concentration	• emotional rollercoaster	• self-harm behaviour	• questioning the meaning of life	• decreased interest in intimacy or sex	• sweating
• spaciness	• guilt	• irritable	• anger at God	• mistrust	• rapid heartbeat
• loss of meaning	• anger/rage	• impatient	• ennui	• intolerance	• somatic reactions
• decreased self-esteem	• survivor guilt	• use of negative coping (smoking, drinking, etc.)	• questioning prior religious beliefs	• impact on parental role (concern and overprotectiveness)	• breathing difficulties
• preoccupation with trauma	• shut-down	• regression	• lack of self-satisfaction	• projection of anger or blame	• aches and pains
• thoughts of harm to self and others	• numbness	• sleep disturbances	• pervasive hopelessness	• isolation from friends	• impaired immune system
• apathy	• fear	• appetite changes		• loneliness	• dizziness
• rigidity	• helplessness	• nightmares			
• disorientation	• sadness	• hypervigilance			
• whirling thoughts	• depression	• accident proneness			
• self-doubt	• hypersensitivity	• losing things			
• perfectionism	• overwhelmed	• moody			
• minimisation	• depleted	• substance misuse			
• trauma imagery	• anxiety	• withdrawn			

Source: Yassen (1995, p.184)

WORKING WITH CLIENTS WHO HAVE BEEN SEXUALLY ABUSED

To complete the picture of the impact and the stresses which arise from the work with clients who have been sexually abused there is a model which enables the worker to make sense of the processes involved. Finkelhor (1988) developed the Four Traumagenic Dynamics Model (4TDM) in an attempt to take into account the wide variety of symptoms and the diversity of experiences within child sexual abuse. This model was produced in lieu of the post-traumatic stress disorder (PTSD) model, which Finkelhor believed failed to address adequately experiences in sexual abuse. He stated that 'the PTSD concept was formulated exclusively in application to adults, particularly around the trauma of war' (p.63). He stated in an earlier paper that:

> one virtue of the 4TDM is that it allows sexual abuse to be conceptualised as a situation or a process rather than simply an event. In discussing PTSD, it was mentioned that one characteristic of CSA that distinguished it from PTSD was the fact that it was often an extended process of traumatisation. (Finkelhor 1987, p.362)

The debate continues today as to the appropriateness of PTSD formulation when treating survivors of sexual abuse.

McCann and Pearlman (1990) found that when counsellors worked with clients who had been traumatised, their inner world experience paralleled that of the trauma survivor. It is here that the pertinence of Finkelhor's model to this piece of work becomes apparent; the dynamics within it have also been experienced by those who work with victims and survivors of sexual abuse. They therefore act as broad descriptors for such experiences. Hopkins (1992, p.149), in exploring 'the interrelationship between the experiences of the worker and those of the child', calls the effects of this work upon child protection workers, 'secondary abuse'. Given that the four dynamics are described as causing trauma by distorting the child's self-concept, world view and affective capacities, it is worth bearing in mind the potential impact on the helper.

APPLYING FINKELHOR'S MODEL (1987)

Traumatic sexualisation

This is where the 'child's sexuality is shaped in developmentally inappropriate and interpersonally dysfunctional ways'. Finkelhor describes five distinct processes that contribute to this dynamic:

- the rewards by the perpetrator for sexual behaviour inappropriate to their development
- the children subsequently learn to use sexualised behaviour to manipulate others
- distortion in meaning and importance of parts of the child's anatomy
- confusion and misconceptions, in the child, about sexual behaviour and morality

- the child's sexuality is traumatised when sexual activities are linked with fearful and unpleasant memories.

Despite being adult, the helper is also in danger of being traumatically sexualised. Listening to a catalogue of sexual abuse stories and descriptions of sexually abusive experiences suffered by clients at the hands of perpetrators can lead the worker to have *'confusion and misconceptions'* about sex, as well as placing considerable stress upon the worker's sexuality generally and, more specifically, the sexual expression within their own intimate adult consenting relationships. Appropriate acts of normal sexual behaviour become contaminated by the client's story. Counsellors taking part in my research project talked about the impact on their sex lives and sexuality, for example as *'not wanting to do certain things within a sexual relationship because of the connections with the client's story'*. The *'unpleasant memories'* of the abuse can leave the worker with flashbacks to their client's vividly recalled story. Simply put, another counsellor stated that *'the experiences of working with sexual abuse can damage your sexual health'*.

Betrayal

The child has discovered that 'someone on whom they were vitally dependant has caused them or wishes to cause them harm'. The timing of experiencing betrayal varies from the first to subsequent abusive experiences, when the realisation arises that they have been duped by the perpetrator through his or her lies. The degree of betrayal is not necessarily concomitant to the closeness of the relationship with the perpetrator – an important element being 'how taken in the child feels by the offender regardless of who the offender is'. An additional dynamic is the sense of betrayal the child feels when other members of their family are unwilling to believe them or unable to protect them, for example the mother.

Betrayal, for the worker, is mostly experienced when the organisation lets them down, fails to support them in this work, does not recognise the vulnerability of the worker to stresses or leaves the worker with vague and uncertain roles or multiple responsibilities. Maslach (1976) considers role ambiguity (where there is a lack of clarity about the work role) and role conflict (when the worker is caught between competing demands or faced with demands to do things he or she does not want to do). These role-related stresses are more likely to be present within voluntary organisations and self-help groups. Society also continues, in some way, to betray the worker through its denial of the reality of both the survivor's and the worker's experience and the abuse.

It is important to note that the client's sense of betrayal may be acted out within the therapeutic relationship. The feelings of betrayal attached to the non-protecting parent are transferred to the counsellor. The boundaries of the relationship will be tested, time limits pushed, increased telephone contact, etc. Sometimes, simple clinical interventions will be responded to by the client 'as-if' they have been abused; the counsellor's sense of therapeutic integrity is betrayed. In offering a safe space to explore the abuse, they feel as though they have become the 'abuser'. There are times when the roles are reversed and the worker feels abused by the client (for a greater exploration of this process it is worth reading Bessel A. van der Kolk's (1989) article).

Stigmatisation

This dynamic refers to the internalisation of negative messages the child has received – those that have an impact upon the child's self-esteem, -concept and -worth. They may be verbalised as 'I am bad, evil, worthless', 'I am a deviant', 'I am unclean'. There are also gender differences in this dynamic, for example 'males may be more stigmatised by the homosexual connotations of their abuse while girls suffer from the "spoiled goods" attribution'.

There is stigma attached to this work; after all, what motivates decent people into the sordid world of sexual abuse? A declaration of interest in this work invites a variety of responses: titillating fascination, change of subject or simply stunned silence. Statistical evidence indicates the predominance of men as abusers and male counsellors responding to my questionnaire revealed that they feared being perceived as abusers. Their experience of stigmatisation lay in the assumptions attached to their gender. Their female colleagues were also in danger of promoting this feeling further by believing, for example, that only women should do the work. This led one male counsellor to become overcautious, stating that 'the fear of being inadvertently abusive constrains and disempowers me'. Another male counsellor was left with feelings of 'guilt for being a man' and even 'denied being a man' in the process.

Powerlessness

The two components to this dynamic are when 'a child's will, wishes and sense of efficacy are repeatedly overruled and frustrated' and when 'a child experiences the threat of injury or annihilation'. The first most basic form of powerlessness is 'the experience of having one's body space repeatedly invaded'. The second is the experience of powerlessness connected not only to the violence and/or coercion of the abuse but also to the chaos that arises in the aftermath of the discovery of the abuse – 'when they find themselves unable to control the decisions of the adult world that may visit upon them many unwanted events'.

> You talked of boundaries
> Gulliver came to my mind
> Thinking about the size
> The size of the problem
> The size of the person
> I am a Lilliputian
> Gulliver the abuse
> He was strapped down, but
> Pulls the strings off
> Yes and then
> He rises up

These words come from a counsellor who was part of my research group. They belong to an ongoing metaphor in which the impact of the work was explored. It communicates a powerful image connected to this final dynamic of powerlessness, which might also be called helplessness. The nature of this work is likely to give rise to strong feelings in workers of inadequacy and failure. A fundamental helplessness within this work lies in our inability to redeem the client's childhood and our failure to rescue the child, within the adult, from abuse. Workers are also unable to rescue the clients from their most destructive and dysfunctional behaviours, having to sit back helplessly and watch the client's self-harm, drug and alcohol abuse or their slow self-destruction through anorexia. There is the powerlessness in the face of the reality of sexual abuse, its devastation and consequences. This may be summed up and heard in the final admission of one counsellor who recognised '*that some clients are beyond my skills*'.

In an overview of three papers, Chu (1988), Walker (1993) and McBride and Markos (1994) all look at the difficulties inherent in the work for the counsellor. There are many similar themes that emerge, though, perhaps, under slightly different headings. Chu (1988) considers the experience of working with this client group, noting their 'intense neediness and dependency which make them superb testers of the abilities of their therapists' (p.24). He highlights ten common treatment traps which may be presented to the counsellor in this work. They are: trust, distance, boundaries, limits, responsibility, control, denial, projection, idealisation and motivation. These are not the only areas of difficulty in the counselling process but they serve to focus on the complex experience of the work.

Walker (1993) explores the effects of counselling on both the protagonists. She identifies factors relating to the counsellor's internal and external world. Internal world processes include the effect on the counsellor's boundaries and the need to avoid getting over-involved and coping with difficult feelings that emerge, such as inadequacy, hopelessness and despair (p.43). Walker's external world perspective concentrates on the interpersonal world of the counsellor, particularly their relationships with their partners and their own children. In focusing on other relationships, she relates the following experience:

> We went out to dinner in the evening with friends. They are quite interested in my job, but you can hardly say, 'I spent this afternoon with a woman who was multiply abused. And what you're talking about seems utterly unimportant'. I started feeling I was on a different planet; and very angry – quite unreasonably. I remember thinking that if anyone mentions mortgages again, I'll scream... It changes you. And it's lonely. (p.42)

There is something terribly poignant about the last statement 'And it's lonely'. It reflects the awful reality that this work transforms the worker. Janoff-Bulman and Frieze (1983) identify three assumptions that change as a result of victimisation: '1) the belief in personal invulnerability; 2) the perception of the world as meaningful; and 3) the view of the self as positive.' (p.1). The reality of this was described by counsellors in my sample. They noted loss of trust in day-to-day encounters – both this and their loss in the belief of the world as a safe place they attributed to contamination from their work. This was described as follows:

> 'loss of trust in relationships and people's motives, especially those who work with children and disabilities.'
> 'hyper-awareness – observing people very carefully, listening for particular attitudes and responses.'
> 'overprotection of my own children, not wanting my young son to go into men's loos.'

McBride and Markos (1994) take a wide perspective in considering the sources of difficulty in counselling CSA survivors and victims. Their view is based on acknowledging what counsellors bring into the work, 'emotional baggage, knowledge and skills deficits', and how these factors contribute to difficulties 'in hearing, acknowledging, and being with a client who is dealing with sexual abuse' (p.89). The counsellor's lack of information and understanding about sexual abuse and related issues plays an important part in promoting difficulties in counselling. There is a truth that almost no amount of training is enough to deal with the impact of the work. Counsellors, in my research, described the feeling of not really 'knowing enough' being compounded by their being invested with specialist skills, 'being viewed as the local expert', and feeling pressurised by the organisation to be a 'valuable internal local resource to train and supervise others'. They were invested with an authority they did not feel.

McBride and Markos (1994) describe counsellor inexperience as being a factor which makes the therapeutic process difficult. Other issues covered are counsellor denial and disbelief and, again, the issue of personal boundaries. They state that 'personal boundary issues in the counsellor are problematic because many abuse victims come from families whose members have either distorted boundaries or lack them altogether' (p.91). The chaos of the abusive family is replayed within the therapeutic arena.

Given the preponderance of women in counselling, as demonstrated in the British Association for Counselling (BAC) membership statistics showing that 69 per cent of members are women (BAC Membership survey 1993), there is also the statistical majority of women as victims. In a national survey of 500 clinical and counselling psychologists, Pope and Feldman-Summers (1992) note the distinct gender difference in that 'over two thirds (69.3%) of the women and one third (32.85%) of the men had experienced some form of physical and sexual abuse' (p.353). The specifics of that experience were that women reported more frequently than men childhood or adolescent sexual abuse by a relative and that 'the average number of abuse categories checked by women (50) was significantly greater than the average number checked by men (29)' (p.354). Elliot and Guy (1993) compared abuse experiences amongst women from different professional groups. Their conclusions showed female therapists experienced higher rates of childhood trauma, with sexual abuse reported by 43.3 per cent as opposed to 31 per cent in other professional women (p.85).

Within my own research, a female counsellor suggested that women in this work may be reminded of times within their own socialisation process when they thought themselves 'to be abnormal for not wanting nor liking unsolicited touching'. This aspect in their history gave rise to memories of difficult situations where they have had to extricate themselves, even with minimal damage, from sexually threatening situations, the memory leaving a nasty taste in the mouth and the thought 'there but for the Grace of God go us all'.

There has been no mention of the pleasures and the rewards in this work. True, they may be few and far between, or even so minuscule as to be missed, but they do exist. They can play an important role in coping, as is described in the next section.

MANAGING, REDUCING OR PREVENTING THE IMPACT OF THE WORK

In recognition of the interplay between the external and internal factors which promote the stresses and impact of the work, we return to Yassen (1994) for a model of strategies to deal with the pressures. The ecological model for the prevention of STSD (see Figure 13.1) is a multi-dimensional response to the wide variety of stresses. Using the model, Yassen suggests an eight-stage programme to assist in the development of a prevention plan. This plan is used to formulate strategies to reduce stress and promote health in the individual, with some potential for use in the organisation as a whole. She believes that:

> In general, the successful implementation of a prevention plan involves an understanding of the personal characteristics of the individual, the social and cultural context in which s/he was raised and the contemporary work and social context in which s/he currently lives. Personal and environmental obstacles need to be assessed in order to develop a realistic prevention plan. (p.204)

Table 13.2: Impact of Secondary Traumatic Stress on professional functioning

Performance of Job Tasks	Morale	Interpersonal	Behavioural
• decrease in quality	• decrease in confidence	• withdrawal from colleagues	• absenteeism
• decrease in quantity	• loss of interest	• impatience	• exhaustion
• low motivation	• dissatisfaction	• decrease in quality of relationships	• faulty judgement
• avoidance of job tasks	• negative attitude	• poor communication	• irritability
• increase in mistakes	• apathy	• subsume your own needs	• tardiness
• setting perfectionist standards	• demoralisation	• staff conflicts	• overwork
• obsession about details	• lack of appreciation		• frequent job changes
	• detachment		
	• feelings of incompleteness		

Source: Yassen (1995, p.191)

EIGHT STEPS TO PREVENTION

1. Review and assess present coping and self-care strategies.

2. Select one goal from each category, individual and environmental.

3. Assess the helpful and hindering forces present to achieve these goals.

4. With a supporter set SMART[2] action plans to implement goals, set reward dates.

5. Activate plan

6. Engage the supporter in the timed evaluations (weekly, monthly, yearly).

7. Notice and appreciate the changes, remember built-in rewards.

8. Return to the first step.

Rather than taking each facet of the model separately, I will give an overview of those coping strategies which were reported by the counsellors involved in my research project. For ease of description I have divided them into personal and professional types.

PROFESSIONAL COPING STRATEGIES

One of the most important professional factors in coping, identified by 75 per cent of counsellors within my research, was 'frequent, adequate supervision'. Models of supervision and other creative working practices were suggested to improve the work arena; supervision could be through peer, individual or group supervision. It was clear that counsellors preferred two complementary forms of supervision giving them a firm sustaining foundation to the therapeutic relationship. Individual supervision allowed specific time for the individual to experience support and the opportunity to explore case material. Peer or group supervision reduced the counsellors' sense of isolation, they were able to give and receive support from each other, promoting unity and a sense of belonging. In today's climate of economic pressures, such groups would prove to be the cost effective; though, there was some concern and suspicion that the organisation introducing a group would lead, at most, to the loss of one-to-one supervision or at least be instrumental in reducing its frequency.

The supervisor should be experienced in their work as a supervisor, given the chaos of the work and the powerful processes the supervisee will be subjected to. The supervisor should also be knowledgeable about the issues related to working with clients who have been sexually abused. Perhaps one of the main tasks of supervision is the monitoring of the counsellor's stress levels. Edelwich and Brodsky (1980) believe that the supervisor is most useful in enabling improved coping, by helping 'staff members experience the four

---

2   SMART is an acronym used in the setting of goals. S = Specific, M = Measurable, A = Achievable, R = Realistic, T = Timed. Within the process, rewards are set at timed intervals and potential sabotage points are explored. If done properly with a caring and challenging supporter, the results are more successful than *ad hoc* goal setting.

stages (of burnout) with greater awareness and thus be less subject to violent swings of emotion'. They offer an objective view where the counsellors are more subjective in assessing their own emotional states.

An important organisational and professional strategy is the active management of case work. One counsellor did this by specifically *'limiting the amount of child sexual abuse work'*. Thus she was liberated to explore alternatives in the work. The organisation did not always back up counsellors in their case management. Consequently, they had to be clear about *'not bowing to waiting-list pressures by taking on more clients'* and *'cutting other stressful work out'*.

The organisational aspects for prevention may require structural changes to be made, for example in work hours, distribution of responsibilities, patterns of authority and communication and lowering the ratio of clients per staff member. Adequate training, more information and updating of skills and negotiating periods of time out from the work were viewed by the counsellors involved in my research project as paramount.

PERSONAL COPING STRATEGIES

Time for reflection, whether through meditation or visualisation, was one of the common coping strategies; positive images were used by one counsellor *'to cast out intrusive images'* and as an antidote to the flashbacks engendered by the work. To counteract the despair in the work, some of the counsellors made conscious efforts to focus on the rewards. They summed these up as follows:

> *'The pleasure of seeing healing after horrific abuse; the client leaving abusive relationships.'*
> *'If the therapist can survive – it is gratifying to see the clients making improvements.'*
> *'No matter how small the step the client takes, noting it for them and me is important, otherwise I would give up.'*

Given the impact on the counsellors' inter-personal world (see Table 13.1), partners and families played an important part in the coping. In their intimate relationships, the impact of this work upon their sexual relationships had to be acknowledged. One counsellor suggested that it was important to *'just keep talking healthy normal sex'*. Another counsellor suggested that *'a supportive partner and a reasonably stress-free home life'* was an absolute necessity. It was important to be explicit with partners about the general impact of the work upon the counsellor by letting their partners know just how they could give support.

Another inter-personal aspect was the role played in keeping healthy social relationships and the invaluable support which could come from friends. One counsellor would negotiate with her friends by *'contracting people to look out for me'* and for the counsellor to allow herself to receive *'love, warmth and support from others and their validation'*. There was something to be said for *'having friends not connected with the work to have "normal" conversations'*. This served to develop and maintain outside interests unconnected with work *'to promote a balanced life style'*.

CONCLUSION

> Effective and improved coping strategies are those which enable the person to renew his or her sense of original purpose of helping people; at the same time learning to deal with the stresses, that are intrinsic to this work, in ways which are healthy to the counsellor, his or her family, the client, organisation and society, so she or he may continue in the work for as long as she or he chooses and the work is there.

(Coppenhall 1995, p.42)

The importance of this work cannot be denied, as the number of victims and survivors of sexual abuse coming forward increases. There is, as a consequence, a demand for more practitioners who are not only informed in this work but also professionally credible. Given the furore caused by the debate about False Memory Syndrome, professionals must be seen to be working in ways that will brook no criticism. However, most important of all is the health and well-being of the practitioners involved in this work. Their support needs must be seen neither as expendable nor, when financially expedient, solely rewarded on merit. Support structures should be more than adequate and responsive to the needs of the individual worker. They should also be untouchable and out of the reach of cavalier managers.

It is in healthy and functioning workers that the future lies, and so too lies the healing of the thousands of known and unknown clients.

I would like to finish with the words from one of the counsellors who gave up her time to be part of my research group. They come from her metaphor generated within the research process and are the final part of her reflection on what it was like to have been part of the research group:

> *I used to cower at*
> *the bottom of the mountain*
> *as the therapy went on, I...*
> *up the mountain and*
> *threw myself off*
> *Where I am now,*
> *is on a ledge on the mountain,*
> *Feeling safe.*

REFERENCES

B.A.C. Membership Survey (1993) *Individual Members and Organisations: A Short Summary of the Results.* Rugby: Mountain and Associates.

Chu, J.A. (1988) 'Ten traps for therapists in the treatment of trauma survivors.' In *Dissociation* 1, 4, 24–32.

Coppenhall, K. (1995) 'The stresses of working with clients who have been sexually abused.' In W. Dryden (ed) *The Stresses of Counselling in Action.* Sage: London.

Edelwich, J. and Brodsky, A. (1980) *Burnout: Stages of Disillusionment in the Helping Professions.* New York: Human Sciences Press.

Elliot, D.M. and Guy, J.D. (1993) 'Mental health professionals versus non-mental-health professionals: childhood trauma and adult functioning.' *Professional Psychology: Research and Practice 24,* 1, 83–90.

Figley, C.R. and Kleber, R.J. (1995) 'Beyond the "victim": secondary traumatic stress.' In R.J. Kleber, C.R. Figley and B.P.R. Gersons (eds) *Beyond Trauma: Cultural and Societal Dynamics.* New York: Plenum Press.

Finkelhor, D. (1987) 'The trauma of child sexual abuse.' *The Journal of Interpersonal Violence 2,* 4, 348–366.

Finkelhor, D. (1988) 'The trauma of child sexual abuse: two models.' In G.E. Wyatt and G.J. Powell (eds) *Lasting Effects of Child Sexual Abuse.* Sage: California.

Grosch, W.N. and Olsen, D.C. (1994) *When Helping Starts to Hurt: A New Look at Burnout Among Psychotherapists.* New York: W.W. Norton & Company.

Hopkins, J. (1992) 'Secondary abuse.' In A. Bannister (ed) *From Hearing to Healing: Working with the Aftermath of Childhood Sexual Abuse.* London: Longman/ NSPCC.

Janoff-Bulman, R. and Frieze, I.H. (1983) 'A theoretical perspective for understanding reactions to victimisation.' *Journal of Social Issues 39,* 2, 1–17.

Kafry, D. and Pines, A. (1980) 'The experience of tedium in life and work.' *Human Relations 33,* 7, 477–503.

Kleber, R.J., Figley, C.R. and Gerson, B.P.R. (eds) (1995) *Beyond Trauma: Cultural and Societal Dynamics.* New York: Plenum Press.

Maslach, C. (1976) 'Burned-out.' *Human Behavior,* September, 16–22.

McBride, M.C. and Markos, P.A. (1994) 'Sources of difficulty in counselling sexual abuse victims and survivors.' *Canadian Journal of Counselling 28,* 1, 83–99.

McCann, I.L. and Pearlman, L.A. (1990) 'Vicarious traumatisation: a contextual model for understanding the effects of trauma on helpers.' *Journal of Traumatic Stress 3,* 131–149.

Pines, A. (1982) 'Helpers' motivation and the burnout syndrome.' In T. Wills (ed) *Basic Processes in Helping Relationships.* New York: Academic Press.

Pope, K.S. and Feldman-Summers, S. (1992) 'National survey of psychologists' sexual and physical abuse history and their evaluation of training and competence in these areas.' *Professional Psychology: Research and Practice 23,* 5, 353–361.

Schauben, L.J. and Frazier, P.A. (1995) 'Vicarious Trauma: The effects on female counsellors of working with sexual volence.' *Psychology of Women Quarterly, Vol.19,* 49–64.

van der Kolk, B. (1989) 'The compulsion to repeat the trauma: re-enactment, revictimisation and masochism.' *Psychiatric Clinics of North America 12,* 2, June, 389–411.

Walker, M. (1993) 'The aftermath of abuse: the effects of counselling on the client and the counsellor.' *Counselling,* February, 40–44.

Yassen, J. (1995) 'Prevention traumatic stress disorder.' In C. Figley (ed) *Compassion Fatigue: Coping with Secondary Traumatic Stress Disorder.* New York: Brunner/Mazel.

The Contributors

Lois Arnold is a trainer, researcher and group facilitator at The Basement project in Bristol (telephone 0117 922 3801). The project works with survivors of abuse and women who self-injure and provides training and literature on good practice. She has carried out research into self-injury and the service needs of abuse survivors. She is co-author, with Gloria Babiker, of *The Language of Injury*.

Gloria Babiker is a consultant clinical psychologist working in Bristol in the area of maltreatment trauma with adults. She is also Assistant Course Director of the Doctoral Programme in Clinical Psychology at Exeter University. She is co-author, with Lois Arnold, of *The Language of Injury*.

Zetta Bear works as a Psychosynthesis Guide in private practice in West Yorkshire and as a Training Manager for NACRO (The National Association for the Care and Resettlement of Offenders). She has worked for many years in the voluntary sector, mainly with young people who are homeless due to family violence. She provides training and consultancy to voluntary and statutory organisations working with adults who have been sexually abused and related issues. She specialises in work with people who self-injure.

Madge Bray, together with her colleague, Mary Walsh, co-founded the Sexual Abuse Child Consultancy Service (SACCS) and, later, Leaps and Bounds, a specialist residential provision integrating care and therapy for severely abused young children. She trains and lectures nationally and internationally and her therapeutic skills with abused children have won her an international reputation. Her second book, *Sexual Abuse: The Childs Voice* is available from Jessica Kingsley Publishers.

David Briggs is a chartered clinical and forensic psychologist working in independent practice. He has extensive experience in working with the perpetrators of sexual abuse in a variety of settings. A founder member of NOTA (the National Sexual Offender Treatment Association), he consults and trains nationally.

Pete Brown is 28 years old and lives in Leeds. He is a survivor himself and the founder and current co-ordinator of Leeds Survivors' Collective. He also co-parents his four-year-old daughter and participates in environmental and non-violent direct action.

Ronno Griffiths, CQSW, BA, is an independent consultant. She provides training in relation to Substances and Sexual Abuse, HIV, Sexuality, Groupwork, Supervision and Management Skills. Her consultancy includes supervision to counsellors, project workers and managers in mental health, counselling, social work, health promotion and drugs agencies, along with research and strategic, policy and practice development evaluation.

Liz Hall works in Lincoln as an independent clinical psychologist. She worked in Scotland in the mental health services of the NHS for over twenty years, developing an interest in adults who have experienced sexual abuse. She co-authored *Surviving Child Sexual Abuse: A Handbook for Helping Women Challenge Their Past,* published in 1989 and revised in 1993 by Falmer Press. She conducts training courses on working with sexual abuse survivors throughout the UK.

Janet Hughes worked for 20 years as a social worker, mainly in the field of mental health and learning disability. She has been developing her independent work as a trainer and as a counsellor with individuals, couples, families and groups since 1993 and is in training as an Integrative Psychotherapist.

Nerys Hughes combines working as a psychiatric social worker in child and adolescent mental health with freelance specialist social work and consultancy. Her freelance work includes therapeutic work with people with learning disabilities and with their carers in residential settings. Nerys is in training as a psychoanalytic psychotherapist.

Kate Kirk works as a psychodramatist, supervisor and trainer for the public, private and voluntary sectors. She is a founder and trustee of a local charity in Cheshire called SURVIVE. Their work is with clients who have been sexually abused and their families and partners. She is currently completing her PhD at Keele University. The focus for her research is the impact upon the worker when they work with clients who have been sexually abused.

Siobhan Lloyd is a Lecturer in Sociology/Women's Studies at the University of Aberdeen, where she is also Head of the Counselling Service. Among her publications are *Surviving Child Sexual Abuse* (Falmer Press, 1993), with co-author Liz Hall, and *Women and Access in Rural Areas* (Avebury, 1996), with co-editor Pollyanna Chapman. She is currently working on a book on sexuality and therapy.

Marjorie Orr, MA (Hons) in English Literature and Philosophy, Glasgow University. An ex-BBC documentary TV producer and newspaper journalist, she trained in Jungian psychotherapy and founded Accuracy About Abuse (Telephone 0171 431 5339) in 1994, with the help of MIND, an information network to raise awareness about sexual abuse and trauma, to improve health care for adult survivors and promote humane treatment of abused children in the legal system.

Jacki Pritchard, CQSW, MA, is currently working as an independent trainer, consultant and researcher. She has 13 years experience working as a practitioner and manager in social services. Her main interest is the concept of 'abuse' and she is currently working on The Vulnerable Adults Project for Wakefield Community and Social Services Department and undertaking postgraduate research into the life experiences of older survivors of abuse at Nottingham University.

Sara Scott has recently completed three years research with adult survivors of ritual abuse at the University of Manchester. Prior to this return to academe she worked in social action broadcasting. She was a counsellor and trainer at Manchester Rape Crisis for 13 years, and currently holds the Sociological Review Fellowship at the University of Keele.

Ron Wiener is the chairperson of the Advisory Committee of the Leeds Survivors Collective. He is a community psychologist, sociodramatist, training facilitator and staff group consultant. He works with, among others, teams involved with child protection. He is also an Associate Consultant at the School of Continuing Education at Leeds University.

Runa Wolf, following her early career as a mental patient, gained a first-class degree and did research work and teaching. She has published various autobiographical pieces, articles and poems about sexual abuse and mental illness most recently in the Virago anthology *The Memory Bird*. She is now training as a Gestalt Psychotherapist and has a private practice in West Yorkshire. She is seeking ways to combine her professional status with her commitment to writing and speaking about her personal experiences of abuse.

Subject Index

Author Index